Touching Encounters

Touching
Encounters

*Sex, Work, & Male-for-Male
Internet Escorting*

Kevin Walby

THE UNIVERSITY OF CHICAGO PRESS | CHICAGO AND LONDON

Kevin Walby is assistant professor of sociology at University of Victoria. He is coeditor of *Emotions Matter: A Relational Approach to Emotions* and *Brokering Access: Power, Politics, and Freedom of Information Process in Canada.*

The University of Chicago Press, Chicago 60637
The University of Chicago Press, Ltd., London
© 2012 by The University of Chicago
All rights reserved. Published 2012.
Printed in the United States of America

21 20 19 18 17 16 15 14 13 12   1 2 3 4 5

ISBN-13: 978-0-226-87005-2   (cloth)
ISBN-13: 978-0-226-87006-9   (paper)
ISBN-13: 978-0-226-87007-6   (e-book)
ISBN-10: 0-226-87005-7   (cloth)
ISBN-10: 0-226-87006-5   (paper)
ISBN-10: 0-226-87007-3   (e-book)

Library of Congress Cataloging-in-Publication Data

Walby, Kevin, 1981–
    Touching encounters : sex, work, & male-for-male internet escorting / Kevin Walby.
        pages ; cm
    Includes bibliographical references and index.
    ISBN 978-0-226-87005-2 (cloth : alkaline paper) — ISBN 0-226-87005-7 (cloth : alkaline paper) — ISBN 978-0-226-87006-9 (paperback : alkaline paper) — ISBN 0-226-87006-5 (paperback : alkaline paper) — ISBN 978-0-226-87007-6 (e-book) — ISBN 0-226-87007-3 (e-book)   1. Prostitute-client relationships.   2. Male prostitutes.   3. Prostitutes' customers.   4. Male prostitution—Psychological aspects.   5. Escort services.   6. Queer theory.   I. Title.
    HQ119.W35 2012
    306.740811—dc23

                                                                    2012005114

This paper meets the requirements of ANSI/NISO Z39.48-1992 (Permanence of Paper).

*The thought of sexual difference within homosexuality
has yet to be theorized in its complexity.*

JUDITH BUTLER, *Bodies That Matter*

Contents

Acknowledgments

Thanks to all of the men who spoke with me about their work. If this book can do a little to show why what they do deserves respect and understanding, it will have been worth the effort.

Aaron Doyle. Thanks for always pushing me to become a better sociologist. Andrea Doucet and Chris Bruckert. Thanks for always supporting me and for being kind and generous.

Mary Elizabeth Leighton. Thank you for being a great person and for helping me in so many ways over the years. This book has benefited from your insights, acumen, and mastery of languages. Thanks also to Jean Eckenfels for going over everything with great discernment and being exceptionally wonderful to correspond with.

Thank you to the reviewers, who pushed me to go further.

Thanks to Mariana Valverde and others (especially Matt Light and Sandra Bucerius) at the Centre of Criminology, University of Toronto. I was able to work on this text while visiting there as a post-doctoral fellow. Many thanks to the Social Sciences and Humanities Research Council of Canada for funding my work at the doctoral and post-doctoral levels. Without SSHRC, we sociologists would not do much work in Canada.

Thanks are also due to Mike Haan—a very fine social theorist trapped in the body of a statistician. He helped me get where I needed to go.

Tim McGovern. Thanks for helping me stickhandle all of the ins and outs of contracts and paperwork—and dealing with my neuroticism and paranoia. I now see how much work goes on behind the scenes to get some words to the printed page. I have a deep respect for the pros of the publishing world, especially Tim and others at University of Chicago Press.

Douglas Mitchell. I have benefited from your guidance. I have enjoyed our correspondence. It is always satisfying to find that a note has arrived from you. With your careful words, you have spurred me to write more creatively and freely. You are a true wordsmith. Your list at the University of Chicago Press is one of the finest in all the world of publishing. You have helped to form the sociology of sexuality in North America and abroad— no small task. And the beat goes on.

Dale, Chris, Salena, Jeff, Benjamin, Justin, Jamie, and Mike. Thanks for your many, many insights. Thanks for all our collaborations and days and nights together. I have benefited from your talents and encouragement. Parts of this book have benefited from your comments and consideration.

Sean and Nicolas. Thanks for always encouraging me and inspiring me to think analytically. I greatly appreciate all of your sharpness and backing and guidance over the years. I wouldn't be too far along without your support and intellectual zeal.

Mom, Dad, Mike. Thanks for raising me up and keeping me going. There is a lot happening outside Saskatchewan, but those country roads we used to travel all summer are never too far from my mind.

SA. You are the most wonderful human. You are so very thoughtful, delightful, understanding, and generous. How fortunate I am, for you. kw

Chapter 1 | **Introduction**

I remember meeting a very shy and awkward 30-ish guy for a date
over Christmas a few years ago.
He was a soldier in the army
and had recently returned from Afghanistan.
This guy clearly needed to be as far away from that conflict as possible.
He wanted some fun in the big city for the weekend
before going back up north to see family.
We met at his hotel. He was quiet and reserved.
In these situations, I let them take the lead.
I was somewhat uneasy with him at first.
After a few beers, we both relaxed and ended up just talking and
cuddling for hours watching TV with the sound off.
At some point he asked me about my fee.
We were going on three hours, but I told him one hour was fine.
I was enjoying our time together.
He asked me to stay over, which I did. I wouldn't normally do that,
but I was drawn to him. He wanted me there by his side.
I don't usually fall for geeky army-types!!
In the morning, he was distant again but looked me in the eye and
shook my hand to thank me.
I felt a strange connection to this stoic
young man who lived such a different life than mine.
I wanted to return the money, but I needed it for the holidays.
On my way out, he said to me (I'm paraphrasing): "isn't it strange
that our government pays me to kill people and our society accepts it.
But if I pay you to make me feel better after I get home from that war,

like you did last night, we could both get arrested?"
Good point, I thought and smiled before leaving.

This is Conrad's narrative about an encounter with a client. Conrad is 42 years old, but he advertises that he is closer to 30 on the website where his escort profile is posted. Conrad is one of 30 male-for-male Internet escorts whom I've spoken with about this work. Male-for-male Internet escorts arrange commercial sexual encounters with other men using email communications and websites rather than going through an agency or soliciting on the street, as has typically been the case in male sex work.

I asked these men to tell me about their work, their clients, and their lives. One trend emerged with these conversations: among the male-for-male Internet escorts I spoke with, their interactions with clients are often touching encounters. I use the term *touching encounters* because it suggests two meanings, both physical and affective. First, the interaction materializes through two or more bodies coming together, pressed up against one another in cuddling or pressed into one another in sex. Conrad's narrative is suggestive in this regard. Conrad never explains why he smiled before leaving. Given the details, it seems that this encounter does not remain strictly economic. Conrad could be smiling because he enjoyed the sex as much as the soldier did. But we cannot tell if the encounter ever turned to sex. All we know is that the bodies of Conrad and the soldier were touching. As Conrad's narrative suggests, however, the term touching encounters implies a second meaning—that is, a joint action in which people care and support one another through their bodies coming together. Certainly the soldier feels that Conrad brightened his mood. Conrad also describes being drawn in, feeling a bond. Conrad could have walked out the door with a smile because making the soldier "feel better" proved pleasing. Touching denotes bodies coming together, but it also connotes compassion— even if this compassion is curtailed by the commercial parameters of this encounter.[1]

More common than Conrad's touching narrative are depictions of men who have sex with men as deviants. Male-with-male sex is often represented according to the classifications conjured up by scientists of sex, such as sexologists and psychoanalysts. As Debra Boyer (1989:176) explains, "the image of the homosexual is one of distorted and exaggerated sexuality, of promiscuity and deviance. This image has unfortunately been reinforced with public discussion of homosexual lifestyles resulting from the AIDS epidemic." If male-with-male sex is construed as dangerous and deviant, then men who sell sex to men are doubly castigated. As Aidan Wilcox and Kris Christmann (2008:119) remark, "the stereotypical image of a male sex worker remains one of a coerced psychopathological misfit who has been sexually abused as a child and is desperate for money." This depiction of desperate men who sell sex to men is widespread in both social and health sciences.[2] Such depictions lead to misunderstandings of men who sell sex to men as risking violence, drug addiction, homelessness, and as lacking access to health care. Most academics I speak with about my research assume that I approach the topic from a criminological perspective, presupposing that sex work is best thought of as criminal. And when the public finds out about escorting, it is usually through sensational stories about sex and drugs, such as the high-profile case in the United States involving Mike Jones and the Reverend Ted Haggard.

The men I interviewed do not fit this deviant image. They are not desperate or on drugs. Over three quarters had attained or were in the process of attaining a college or university degree. Their average age was just under 35 years, with an average starting age of 28 and an average length of "career" at just over six years. I spoke with men in Montréal, Ottawa, and Toronto, in Houston and New York City, as well as in London. One man moved from Mexico to the Greater Toronto Area to work in the automotive industry before being laid off during the recession beginning in 2008, another moved to New York in the early 1990s after growing up in Brazil, and several lived elsewhere before heading to New York or London to find work. One lived with his parents outside Toronto and worked as a porn star on the side, whereas several others were putting themselves through post-secondary education or working as escorts to supplement their incomes.

In order to move beyond deviance studies and instead explore issues related to sex and work, I emphasize neither the identities of client or escort nor the financial aspects of exchange, but rather the relational and corporeal elements of clients and escorts coming together. My analysis of the creative or otherwise unintended elements of these encounters breaks from sexological and psychoanalytical accounts of gender inversion and prostitution. In this book, I suggest that a focus on touch can help reorient the literature referred to as "queer theory" away from abstract starting points toward a greater understanding of how discourses of sexuality are made sense of through processes involving concrete interactions and gestures.

Male-for-Male Internet Escorts and the Sociology of Sex Work

To provide a context for gaining insights into the sex and work of these men, I begin by surveying what kind of space has been provided for them in sociological understandings of sex work. How do scholars think of sex work? And how did this idea of "sex work" emerge?

Commercial sex is a divisive issue in social science, not least amongst feminist scholars. At least three discrete feminist arguments have emerged, which all shape the sociology of sex work. The first argument concerns sex workers' rights, contending that men and women who sell sex should enjoy the protections that all other workers do. From this perspective, people selling sex are thought to be conducting work and providing a service.[3] A second argument conceptualizes sex work as violence against women, an argument that I refer to as "prohibitionist." Scholars such as Andrea Dworkin (1987) insist that performing sex for compensation exemplifies women's commodification and sexual exploitation. The "prohibitionist" camp claims that commercial sex is gendered and predicated on exploitative violence.[4] The third argument is sex radical, framing sex work as only one element of a broader movement of sexual politics. Many scholars and activists who have contributed to this sex radical argument are sex workers. For instance, Carol Leigh (1997), also known as Scarlot Harlot, coined the term "sex work" in conjunction with pro–sex work advocacy groups. This sex radical element of feminism contests the criminalization of commercial sex and the censorship of sexual expression.[5] Carol Queen (1997) observes, however, that sex radicalism and feminism are not always in bed together; many feminists hold gender oppression to be the overriding issue, whereas sex radicals argue that sexual oppression is a form of domination not reducible to gender oppression.

Both sex workers' rights feminists and sex radical feminists have initiated legal battles and constitutional challenges against laws that criminalize sex work. Sex workers' rights feminists and sex radical feminists agree that sex work can be voluntary, although some sex workers' rights feminists devote energy to organizing "exit" programs, a strategy that aligns with prohibitionist goals. These arguments, colloquially referred to as part of the "sex wars" (the 1980s "sex wars" included more debate on pornography and obscenity), are not new; rather, they emanate from debates about the so-called white slave trade in the late nineteenth century (see Walkowitz 1992).

In the United States, Canada, and the United Kingdom, the sociology of sex work has developed in unique ways. In the United States, Ronald Weitzer has long argued that state-based laws against commercial sex are applied differently to various commercial sex sectors, targeting female street-based prostitution.[6] In Canada, contributions by Fran Shaver (1996) and Deborah Brock (1998) created space for scholars to apply sociological theories and methods and to understand how commercial sex becomes subject to moral regulation. Sex work in Canada is not illegal, but it is not decriminalized either. Though the sex act itself is not illegal, a number of associated activities remain criminal under the *Criminal Code of Canada,* including living off the avails of prostitution (s. 212) and communicating in public for the purpose of prostitution (s. 213). Mary Whowell (2010) points out that a legal limbo exists in the United Kingdom, too.

This book is not about the legal regulation of sex work, but rather on the touching elements of commercial sex between men. Most debates regarding commercial sex have focused on women, passing over the diversity of sexualities and masculinities represented in male sex work. Few researchers have focused on male-for-male Internet escorts, and those who have draw from criminology or public health rather than the sociology of sexuality and interactionist sociology. There is thus a need for empirical studies of various forms of male sex work, as well as a need to theorize the queer male sexualities and masculinities involved.

Historical research on male commercial sex provides an important starting point for making sense of male-for-male Internet escorting today. What is more, historical research on male commercial sex provides an account that is absent from feminist debates. John Scott (2003) suggests that, unlike female prostitution, "male prostitution was not regarded as a significant social problem throughout the nineteenth century, despite its close association with gender deviation and social disorder" (p. 179). Sexology discovered male prostitution around the same time it discovered homosexuality, in the nineteenth century. Young working-class men were involved in prostitution across North America and Europe, choosing sex work over the industrial factory's dangerous labor conditions. Middle-class men's fetishization of working-class bodies, led to the creation of specialized brothels; such late nineteenth-century London brothels (called "peg houses"), which offered young working-class men, were closed down as a result of moral hygiene campaigns.

After World War II, views on male sex work changed: "It became possible to speak not only of 'male prostitutes,' but also of specific 'types' of male prostitute" (Scott 2003:187). Sexologists and psychoanalysts started attributing psychopathologies to male hustlers. Sociologists of deviance portrayed "hustlers" as engaged in deviant careers. Novelists associated with the emergent gay rights movement painted similar scenes of young men selling sex on-street, as in John Rechy's *City of Night* (1963). *New York Hustlers,* by Barry Reay (2010), and *Strapped for Cash,* by Mack Friedman (2003), capture this gritty world of hustling and muscling. Gay identity, however, was not yet fixed in the early twentieth century. It was not until the mid-century struggles for gay rights that the idea that there is one immutable identity we can refer to as gay was firmed up: "if the ideology of homosexuality brought difficult personal challenges for some hustlers, for others, the rise of gay liberation led toward an increasing acceptance of gay or bisexual self-identity" (Kaye 2003:32–33).[7] While a preference for so-called "straight trade" dominated the hustling scene up to the 1960s, different services emerged in a celebration of gay identity: "the gay liberation era marked the first time that the majority of gay men began to buy sex from other gay men, rather than from straight outsiders who lived the bulk of their lives outside the gay world" (p. 34). Male commercial sex started to move off-street and "the new social meanings which were applied to male prostitution in the 1960s and 1970s derived from the progressive integration of prostitution into the gay cultural orbit" (p. 34). New sexual practices emerged out of this ascendance of gay identity.

Depictions of male sex workers changed again in the 1980s with HIV/ AIDS. Scott (2003:193) holds that "prior to the appearance of HIV/AIDS, male prostitution was primarily understood as a criminal or welfare issue," but in the late 1980s male prostitutes became objects of epidemiology and were said to be "reservoirs of disease and transmitters of infection from the gay population" (p. 194). The idea of sex workers as "risky" persists in public health agencies.[8]

The most recent development concerning male sex work has been the use of the Internet as part of the labor process. Internet escorts, like independent sex workers, are in some ways better able than on-street workers to determine cost of labor, select clientele, and consent to work activities. Escorts' clients post reviews online and rate the sexual encounter, helping to determine the escort's position in the hierarchy of commercial sex profiles and the escort's ability to solicit future clients. Male Internet escorts do not work for agencies and are unlikely to hustle on-street or in bars. Whereas magazines and newspaper classifieds were once the key venues for advertisements, most advertising today occurs through profiles on specialty websites. Some sites charge escorts a fee for posting, while others are free (e.g., Men4rentnow.com internationally, Canadianmale.com in Canada). Many escorts' bodies are advertised as physically fit. For instance, Victor Minichiello and colleagues (2008) claim that "the stereotypical image of an effeminate gay persona is challenged by the number of escorts . . . who display the body image of the hyper masculine body builder" (p. 166). I do not want to place too much emphasis on this image of muscling men, since my primary goal is to explode the "young, hung, dumb, and full of cum" stereotype used to demean these men and their work. The central issue is, rather, how to advance a complex understanding of male-for-male Internet escorting, one that does not reproduce existing stereotypes.

The recent influence of labor studies has been key as sex work scholars build on the sex workers' rights movement to chart new directions in their research. Chris Bruckert and Colette Parent (2006:97) argue that focus on the labor side of sex work allows scholars "to step outside of the traditional criminological analysis of deviance to examine these jobs as jobs." The point of such scholarship is to examine commercial sex as a form of nonstandard work.[9] The trick here is not to go too far by suggesting that male escorting is like other kinds of service industry jobs. Some scholars such as Teela Sanders (2005) and Jan Browne and Minichiello (1995) suggest that selling sex requires the surface acting of emotional labor (that is, "putting on" a face to engineer a feeling for a customer), similar to what any customer service agent might do. However, Leslie Jeffrey and Gayle MacDonald (2006) question the conflation of service and sex work labor processes. *Touching Encounters* likewise tries to move beyond the limits of thinking about sex work in terms of surface acting or service provision. If commercial sex offers a way of earning income without participating in the minimum-wage service sector, then escorting may provide some sex workers with a way of maximizing control over their work.

There is theoretical and methodological room to maneuver in the sociology of sex work, as labor process analysis remains limited to the consideration of work tasks and client relations, not sexualities, masculinities, or bodies per se. In this book, I want to think outside the boundaries of how work and sex are conventionally conceived. Livy Visano (1987:24) defines commercial sex as "a semi-skilled occupation in which an actor sells or is hired to provide sexual services for financial gain." While sex workers generally share this starting point, the labor process of sex work is diverse across the industry; some sex workers share little in common in terms of their labor processes (e.g., on-street work versus webcam work). Indeed, there remain many nuances to be explored concerning the labor processes—including the body, intimacy, and diverse sexualities—among men who have sex with men and sell sex to men.

Making Sense of Sex and Sexuality

In order to explore these nuances, I focus on the materiality and activity of sex. This focus involves connecting the sociology of sex work to the sociology of sexuality, fields which, for all they have to offer each other, have not communicated as much as one might expect.

At the heart of sociological understandings of sexuality lies the idea that social change shapes sexual identity and conduct. Anthony Giddens (1992) explores this idea in his comments on what he calls decentered sexuality: forms of intimacy not bound by tradition, family, gender roles, or custom. Zygmunt Bauman (2003, 1998b) similarly suggests that postmodern uses of sex are self-sufficiently erotic, with sexual pleasures being sought for their own sake at one's convenience. Partly as a result of these transformations, more middle-class people than previously now engage in sex work. Elizabeth Bernstein (2007a) contends that sex is currently "available for sale and purchase as readily as any other form of commercially packaged leisure activity" (p. 7). This shift of the middle class toward selling sex is part of a move "to a recreational model of sexual intimacy" (p. 141). Bernstein uses the idea of "bounded authenticity" to conceptualize how broad economic shifts translate into relations between sex workers and their clients. She argues that sex work can be touching and meaningful, that it is not universally oriented toward quick service transactions.

In order to determine how social and cultural changes are shaping the sex and work of male Internet escorting, I have looked closely at the sex and the work of male escorts. I do not contest the political usefulness of sex work as an idea, but I do step back from its focus on labor rights and decriminalization to consider instead how escorts make sense of their sex and work. I also want to see how these meanings can inform the way sociologists theorize connections between sex and work. My goal is not to discredit the stories that other sex workers tell about violence. But stories about violence and exploitation are not what male-for-male Internet escorts have shared with me. Many of these stories ended up being less about commercial transactions and more about the specificity and the diversity of sexualities amongst men who sell sex to men.

Yet male-with-male sex is not without its own forms of power. Power operates in these encounters, especially as it relates to age, aging, and body types. Mutuality is often considered a core characteristic of male-with-male sex, and there exists an ample literature on care in male-with-male sex.[10] To touch is sometimes to be tender. But it would be essentializing to suggest that all male-with-male sex revolves around care. Touching can facilitate care; however, it can likewise usurp someone else's agency. I suggest that sociologists need a way to think through these two tendencies in male-with-male commercial sex: the tendency toward a quick cash transaction and reliance on sexual stereotypes, on one hand, and the tendency toward friendship and mutuality, on the other.

The work of Michel Foucault can help us explore these two tendencies in male-with-male encounters. Foucault's contributions are often associated with a vague notion of discourse, but readers who know his work agree that it is not uniform; indeed, he amended his arguments again and again throughout his writings. His *Histoire de la Sexualité* (1978a) is central to my project. Showing how the sexual self came to be discovered and governed with the arrival of secularization, *Histoire de la Sexualité* tells a story about the way sexuality and power have been and should be conceptualized. Foucault maintains that the connection between sexuality and power is not bound by repression.

Most scholars who use Foucault's work are concerned with the subjectification that occurs in relation to medicine and government—that is, how we come to understand ourselves as types of human subjects. I use Foucault to do something else: to provide "an understanding of how the forms of discourse become part of the lives of ordinary people" (Hacking 2004:278). My project is to make power and discourse visible in corporeal and commercial sex relations between men. My use of Foucault, then, attempts to understand how subjects are discursively constituted when they interact in dyadic, bodily encounters. This is one way to put Foucault to work, to look at how discourses and stereotypes shape our encounters. Yet Foucault can be useful in other ways as well. His later interviews take up erotic relationality as a means of breaking down the categorization regime imposed by discourses of sexuality. This erotic relationality lands us on the terrain of what Foucault calls friendship—affective relations not governed by ruses of sexuality. Foucault's later interviews regarding friendship are crucial for understanding the encounters described by male escorts.

Foucault's work is valuable, but there remain some limits. Two criticisms of Foucault cannot be ignored, one that he anticipates and one he does not. The first criticism, leveled by Gary Dowsett (2000, 1996) and Leo Bersani (1995), is that Foucault fails to acknowledge the creativity of sexual encounters. In *Histoire de la Sexualité*, Foucault seems only to imagine an administered sex. I believe that Foucault anticipates this critique when discussing erotic relationality and friendship in his interviews, though he does not take these ideas too far. The second critique is that Foucault provides only an empty frame of sexuality in which the body awaits inscription. Those scholars, such as Judith Butler, who have tried to extend Foucault's analysis into queer theory have likewise been accused of neglecting the materiality of sex. By the materiality of sex, I refer to the "facts of our bodies" (Crossley 2007:85). Of course there are no bare facts of the body—the body is always interpreted—but what I am getting at is that our bodies sometimes do what they do without our command. For example, if a man has not defecated recently and another man is invited to have anal sex with him, the first man might involuntarily make a mess all over both bodies. It is a simple fact of the body that if you try to bottom without cleaning up, this can happen. In the words of Harvey, a 36-year-old escort from Montréal, "most people know that if they are a bottom and they want to get fucked they should douche first," but not all men do, especially not closeted men like some of the clients of male Internet escorts. Escorts must work on their bodies to make sure that messy facts of the body do not hinder their encounter with clients. The facts of bodies also transform over time through aging; these men must make diverse uses of their bodies as they age. And these men must manage the appearance of their bodies and their age on the Internet, where they advertise. Indeed, male-for-male escorting involves a lot of body work.

Because "to think and talk about sexuality is first of all to think and talk about bodies" (Valverde 1985:29), corporeality and touch must enter the story if sociologists want to advance beyond treating the body as a discursive effect. We acquire habits of touching, a tendency toward repeating touches in particular places, as a way of communicating about how to orchestrate sexual conduct. But this habitual tendency, this orientation, can be altered over time and even through the course of one encounter. In this way, bodies coming together are not simply constituted by discourses of sexuality. I want to get away from the idea that sex as a practice is more or less determined by scripts or discourse. Sexual encounters themselves are creative and productive of meanings attached to bodies. Sociologists of sexuality must start with bodies coming together, their parts and fluids, the interactions between bodies and the meanings produced therein. In order to conceptualize sexual encounters as creative and productive of meanings,

I flip Foucault's framework to put the corporeal encounter at the core of sexuality's productive power.

Making Sense of Bodies and Interaction

Discourses of sexuality provide a grid of intelligibility that categorizes our relations with one another. How, then, can Foucault's writings on discourse be brought to bear on bodies and interactions? Investigating the ways that discourse operates in the sexual encounter requires a different level of analysis, a level provided by interactionist sociology. In this book, I bring together Foucault and interactionist sociology by placing touch and gesture at the center of Foucault's comments about productive power and sexuality. Discourse bears on our touching encounters with others by structuring our confessional moments and providing certain repeatable tropes that shape our gestures and habits of touching. Male-for-male Internet escorting is an apt example in bridging these levels of analysis because discourses about sexuality proliferate in it, as do interactions between escort and client.

Interactionist writings, such as the works of G. H. Mead, developed out of pragmatist philosophy and, from the earliest contributions, have been concerned with the minutiae of human conduct. In the mid-twentieth century, these pragmatist writings were consolidated into interactionism by Erving Goffman and Herbert Blumer. Ian Hacking (2004) suggests that Foucault's writings should be connected with those of Goffman. Yet Goffman represents only one trajectory of interactionism, a fact that seems to have been forgotten in sociology today. Goffman (1959) represents the trajectory of interactionist thought focusing on roles, rituals, and social reproduction at the level of face-to-face interaction. The second trajectory of interactionist thought, however, focuses on swerves, the unanticipated, new meanings and practices produced out of interaction, as theorized by Blumer (1969). We must remember that there are two tendencies in interactionist sociology, both of which need to be put in touch with Foucault. This book makes ample use of Foucault, Goffman, and Blumer as they provide useful conceptual tools for theorizing encounters.

Integrating these theoretical positions is not easy, since interactionist sociology itself needs to be supplemented in numerous ways. Some notable proponents of interactionism, especially Charles Cooley, did not place bodies in encounters as much as is necessary for the study of sexuality. Some of interactionism's foremost thinkers are accused of being mentalist, of stressing the mind too much. Indeed, interactionist sociology suffers from spontaneism when it fails to account for how meaning-making occurs in material and discursive contexts. And interactionist sociology slips toward subjectivism and qualitative realism when it fails to account for interpretation, elaboration, and embellishment in the way people speak and listen to one another during interaction.[11]

Although interactionist sociology has always formed an undercurrent in gender and sexuality studies, it has not been placed in relation to Foucault's writings. More surprising, perhaps, is the failure to integrate an interactionist approach to sexual encounters with queer theory. Queer theory trains its focus on the transgression of categories concerning sexuality and gender. Whereas gender studies scholars hold that material inequality between the sexes overrides issues of sexual diversity, gender was evacuated as a category by queer theory and critiqued as heteronormative. Queer theory also questions the extent to which a gay identity or community is possible. *Touching Encounters* makes a contribution to queer theory insofar as it displaces identity as a starting point for analysis. Yet queer theory has trouble moving away from the starting point of identity, instead positing "queer" as a general identity. In practice, "queer" is used to represent some identity groups, such as gay men, more than others. Queer theory is thus unclear about what "queer" means and suggests that the disruption of identity categories is radical per se.[12]

Whereas some queer theory has theorized abstractly above sexually engaged bodies, interactionist sociology grounds analysis back in the encounter. Stevi Jackson and Sue Scott (2010, 2007) argue that interactionist sociology helps make sense of the abstract twists within queer theory. Interactionism also brings the body back into sociology by emphasizing that bodies do not make sense in and of themselves. The lens that interactionist sociology provides is partial—it starts with small-scale interactions—but fundamental: all that is organizational starts with the encounter.

Foremost amongst interactionist theories of sex and sexuality are two approaches that emerged in the late 1970s: John Gagnon and William Simon (1974), with their discussion of sexual scripts, and Ken Plummer (1995, 1982, 1975), with his work on sexual stories. Representing the sexual scripting perspective, Gagnon and Simon suggest that the script acts as a metaphor for the way sexuality is reproduced. Representing the sexual stories perspective, Plummer (1995:34) argues, "no longer do people simply 'tell' their sexual stories to reveal the 'truth' of their sexual lives; instead, they turn themselves into socially organized biographical objects."

Stories and scripts, however, constitute very different concepts. Emphasizing the dramaturgical element of sex, the metaphor of sexual scripts fosters analyses that highlight the regularity of results as opposed to more fluid outcomes and meaning shifts produced by the encounter itself.

According to Adam Green (2008:602), scripting theory depicts actors who are less agents actively composing sexual lives and more "wooden puppets who mechanically follow the puppet master—i.e., cultural 'instructions.'" This is an overstatement, as Gagnon and Simon have accounted for how scripts change. However, in order to ground queer theory and return scripting theory to its interactionist roots, I focus on how the materiality of bodies pulls the encounter away from the set sexual script. Meanings of sex change according to cultural trends but also shift in the corporeal present. Sexual scripting theory must be supplemented to emphasize the unanticipated and touching aspects of encounters, and I use examples of male commercial sexual encounters to explore this idea.

More than a grounded empirical analysis of escort narratives concerning sex and the work, this book is about the sexual stories men tell after coming together and their talk about touch. I have conducted interviews with male-for-male Internet escorts. I have also invited them to share their stories with me in prose (the narrative at the beginning of this chapter is one example). Interview-based data collection is not a clear-cut process, and neither is narrative analysis as a way of working with interview transcripts. The sociological tradition of qualitative research emphasizes that narrative and interpretation are integral to the way people elaborate their encounters with others. The narratives we share about our lives are formed through elaboration. Elaboration is the process through which past encounters come back to life. Part of this project involves reconciling Foucault's writing on power and sexuality with research methods that are more interaction-oriented. It is exactly Foucault's concern with power and sexuality that needs to be materialized by methodological strategies that have been divorced from his work for too long.

Overview

To get away from the problems of categorizing and pathologizing sexual relations, as sexology, psychoanalysis, and public health research are prone to do, I have tried to produce a book that swerves as much as sexual encounters between men do (there is an excursus between most chapters). Yet attention to instances of touch should not obscure reflection on generic social processes. This story does not lose sense of how sexual encounters are socially ordered.

Sexologists and psychoanalysts have a long history of pathologizing men who have sex with men and men who sell sex to men. My project entails casting off the sexological and psychoanalytic frameworks that still constrain our thinking about same-sex relations. After providing a short history of the sexological science of gender inversion, I deal with the recent contributions of queer theory and sexual scripting theory in chapter 2.

To supplement queer theory and sexual scripting theory, in chapter 3 I take up the relationship between Foucault and interactionist sociology to provide a theorization of encounters. There are two tendencies in Foucault's writings, one closed and one open. The closed tendency is toward deployment of and adherence to discourses of sexuality in the way we touch and the way we narrativize our relations. The open tendency is toward unanticipated relations as well as friendship (an openness to others). There are also two tendencies in an encounter according to interactionist sociology: one closing and one opening. Goffman (1959) accounts for this closing tendency in his comments on roles and rituals, while Blumer (1969) accounts for openings in his theorization of interactionism. Drawing on the work of Tim Dean (2009) and John Paul Ricco (2002) on itinerant and anonymous sexual relations, I suggest that male escort encounters combine these closed and open tendencies. Men engaging in encounters do not necessarily need to be known by one another in any official or formal way but are, nevertheless, together, touching, at once closed and open.

In chapter 4, I discuss methodological issues. At the end of the book, I include a postscript on methodology where I comment on my approach to interviewing and data analysis. In the postscript, I also discuss issues regarding narrative and biography to justify how I have made sense of male-for-male Internet escort narratives. Some readers might want to advance directly to the postscript before reading the earlier theoretical and empirical material.

In chapter 5 I put my theorization of encounters into practice through an analysis of my own interactions with escorts during interviews. Goffman and Blumer figure prominently as I theorize the interactions between researcher and respondent. Few qualitative sociologists have considered that men who have sex with men hold diverse understandings of sexuality and how these matter in research encounters, especially regarding sensitive interview topics such as intimacy, intercourse, and men's bodies. Drawing from transcripts and field notes concerning interviews, I analyze moments when respondents sexualized me, often posing a first question at the beginning of interviews: " Are you gay?" The question not only seeks out a singular identity declaration but also overturns established researcher-respondent roles, indicating that the reflexivity of the respondent is as important as the reflexivity of the researcher in shaping the conversation to come. My analysis demonstrates why it is important to consider the impact of researchers' bodies and speech acts during interviews. I reflect on how my responses to escorts' propositions and sexualization shaped and modified the meanings produced through the research encounter.

As much as this book emphasizes the relational aspects of escorting, male-for-male Internet escorting is still about work and money. I focus in chapter 6 on the work of male-for-male escorts, including entry into the trade, labor process, advertising, payment, and retirement. Specifically, I consider the work of the entrepreneurial self-employed through a discussion of how crucial the sexualization of men's bodies has become to some nonstandard work. The labor process of male-for-male Internet escorting is individuated, which stifles notions of collective labor from emerging but meshes with the sexual entrepreneurialism required to attract clientele. Because of Internet-based client booking, little communication occurs between escorts and there arises little sense of collective labor or solidarity among them as workers. Part of the reason why male Internet escorts do not always identify with the idea of sex work is that using the Internet to book clients has fractured and compartmentalized their labor process.[13] I reflect on how diversity in the commercial sex industry and the individuated labor process of male-for-male Internet escorting point to challenges for sex work organizers in generating solidarity among workers.

In chapter 7 I consider the argument of some scholars that sex workers feign intimacy with clients in relation to Foucault's writings concerning sexuality.[14] The men I interviewed situate escorting as integral to their biography, which includes their sexual biography. The sex of their work as escorts is often the sex of their life. Some male sex workers find their work pleasurable, but the presence of pleasure does not mean that power is absent from the encounter. Drawing from Foucault to understand how forms of discourse become part of peoples' everyday lives, I suggest that there are two tendencies in male-for-male Internet escorts' encounters with clients: the first is a tendency toward strategic deployment of sexuality and the use of ready-made tropes (e.g., the "daddy," the "twink"); the second is an open tendency toward friendship—which runs contrary to feigned intimacy. Where this open tendency characterizes the encounter, the line between escort and client is replaced by friendship. These two tendencies are immanent to the encounter, not scripted in advance; although the intimacy between escort and client may be performative, escorts may, nevertheless, experience difficulty erecting barriers between their "work" selves and their "private" selves.

I explore the sexual stories that these men share about aging and the life course in chapter 8. Indeed, the work narratives of male-for-male Internet escorts suggest that aging is important for both escorts and clients. Talk about aging is talk about one's changing position in the life course, but it is also talk about what the body can and cannot do. Escorts' aging bodies prompt these men to remarket themselves and face how aging bodies limit the extent to which sexual encounters can center around the alleged sign of virility: an erect penis. I explore these issues about aging in relation to the scholarly literature on age-graded sexualities.

In chapter 9 I consider the centrality of the body and body work in escorting, reflecting on what escorts say about the use of their bodies and the bodies of clients, as well as about HIV/AIDS and health issues. Sociologists are not accustomed to talking about the centrality of body fluids, such as semen, to sociological work. Yet semen holds significance for understandings of masculinity (Moore 2007) and, in escort-client sexual encounters, the smell and touch of this substance are integral. Male-for-male Internet escorting is a form of body work that requires what are known in sociology as body reflexive practices (Crossley 2005) generated by touching other men's bodies, but body reflexive practices lead to various kinds of self-surveillance and composing of the body toward certain ends. As part of this chapter's emphasis on body work, I discuss how racialized bodies are valorized in this economy of pleasures and touching. I also argue that male-for-male Internet escorts negotiate health risks as part of their work through touching or "feeling it out," even with men who have HIV/AIDS or sexually transmitted infections.

Finally I consider how the concept of the encounter invites social scientists to reassess how sex and work are interwoven. *Touching Encounters* is meant to seduce, but also to persuade. The pleasure of a text for the reader is not guaranteed, and so it must "cruise" in slow circles. As Tim Dean (2009:xii) expresses it, the "principal virtue of cruising is to initiate contact with strangers." I am not sharing these stories to undermine the idea of sex work or to undermine the efforts of sex workers and their allies who have struggled for safer work places. Rather, I supplement understandings of how one kind of sex work happens, exploring its continuities and discontinuities with other forms of work as well as with other kinds of sex. I hope thereby to diversify the kinds of stories that one can tell through the coupling of "sex" and "work" and to dismantle the "young, hung, dumb, and full of cum" stereotype that too often limits our understandings of these men and their working lives.

Chapter 2 | **Visions of Sexuality and Sex Work**

This chapter offers an overview of how sexuality and sex work have been conceptualized from sexology through queer theory. Sexuality studies were once limited to sexological and psychoanalytic frameworks, so I begin by examining the sexological works of Richard von Krafft-Ebing and Have-lock Ellis, before considering Sigmund Freud's partial break from sexol-ogy. In sexological and psychoanalytic writings, sexuality is assumed to be congenital, instinctual, or propelled by innate drives (in Freud, the case is slightly different). My critiques focus on Krafft-Ebing, Ellis, and Freud since their works buttress many essentializing claims about same-sex acts.[1]

The mid-twentieth century was an era of social change concerning the recognition of same-sex relations. The *Criminal Code of Canada* was amended to decriminalize private "homosexuality" in 1969; similar de-criminalization had happened in the United Kingdom in 1967. The June 1969 Stonewall riots in Manhattan galvanized the growing gay and lesbian rights movement. In this period, scholarly perspectives on sexuality and sex work changed, too. Moreover, nascent theoretical positions moved be-yond sexological and psychoanalytic frameworks. Throughout the 1970s, the field of gay and lesbian studies legitimized sexual orientation and iden-tity as social science topics. Yet gay and lesbian studies generally assumed a normalizing notion of sexual identity that sometimes reduced gender to anatomical sex.[2] This same criticism has been leveled at queer theorists' early gay and lesbian studies. For instance, many scholars criticized John Boswell's *Christianity, Social Tolerance, and Homosexuality* (1980) for pro-moting a fixed, transhistorical sense of identity. As this example suggests, even the sociology of sexuality and sex work has sometimes assumed fixed notions of sexual identity and the idea of a unitary subject.

Partly to address this limitation, queer theory emerged in social science during the mid-1990s (though it started earlier in literature and film studies). Queer theory differs from gay and lesbian studies in its insistence that identities are contingent and that power permeates all social relations; queer theory interrogates how desire is ordered instead of assuming that gay or lesbian identity is natural.[3] Yet queer theory has not been fully accepted in the discipline of sociology. Gamson and Moon (2004) argue that sociology is "resistant to what had initially been a humanities-based intellectual enterprise; complaints abounded about queer theory's tendency to understate the role of institutions in sexual regulation" (p. 48). And despite its subversive potential, queer theory has not escaped the tendency to reify identity.[4]

One productive way to supplement queer theory is to focus on the interactions in sexual encounters. I argue at the end of this chapter that the interactionist writings of Gagnon and Simon (1974) on sexual scripts anticipate the arguments of queer theorists, but they emphasize the habitual rather than creative elements of sexual conduct. In this way, the repositioning of scripting theory can offer a starting point for theorizing touching encounters and reorienting queer theory.

Theorizing Sexuality and Sex Work: Looking Back

Sexology's chief invention—the category of "homosexuality"—still frames the way male sex work and sexual practices deviating from monogamous, heterosexual, and procreative sex are understood today.[5] It is important to retrace sexological writings on gender inversion since this idea is still a powerful imaginary that shapes public views of same-sex relations.

Sexology did not appear out of thin air. Prior to the rise of sexology in nineteenth-century Europe, sperm was valued as a magic fluid. In this spermatic, excretory economy, people believed that sperm should not be squandered (Thompson 2007) and that men should "judiciously conserve" their sperm if they were to compete in the marketplace (p. 113). Sex panics about masturbation and prostitution were driven by this anxiety to preserve. The copulating, excreting body was treated as excessive—and certainly not aligned with the masculine, controlled body of the stereotypical industrial laborer.

Projects to regulate masturbation were grounded in a spermatic economy and the management of excretion (Barker-Benfield 1972). Too great an expenditure of sperm, too large and too constant a flow of semen: these excesses were thought to lead to mental derangement that jeopardized people's financial prospects. "Sturdy manhood" was thought to be lost through too much ejaculation, and sperm had to remain "souped up to a particular level of richness" for a man to deliver on his familial obligations (p. 50). Sexology entered the stage against the backdrop of this spermatic economy. How would sexologists characterize men who "wasted" their semen with other men? The answer: as inverts and bearers of other sexual pathologies.

Krafft-Ebing's *Psychopathia Sexualis* (1886) became a key reference point in sexology, informing both expert and lay understandings of sex and gender and providing the commanding metaphor of inversion to frame how sexuality and gender are imagined.[6] Of inversion, which he believed to be prompted, like other sexual pathologies, by auto-eroticism, Krafft-Ebing writes:

> the essential feature of this strange manifestation of the sexual life is the want of sexual sensibility for the opposite sex, even to the extent of horror, while sexual inclination and impulse toward the same sex are present. . . . this abnormal mode of feeling may not infrequently be recognized in the manner, dress and calling of the individual, who may go so far as to yield to an impulse to put on the distinctive clothing corresponding with the sexual role in which they feel themselves to be. (p. 221)

This sexological understanding of inversion assumes that gender roles are natural and that mimicking them through forms of talk, dress, or sexual practice goes against nature. One must be vigilant against inversion since "there is always the danger that homosexual feelings, in that they are the most powerful, may become permanent, and lead to enduring and exclusive antipathic sexual instinct" (p. 232). Krafft-Ebing thus conceptualizes inversion as a contravention of sex and gender rules, describing the invert as alien. He deems "prevention of onanism" as well as "mental treatment, in the sense of combating homosexual, and encouraging heterosexual, feelings and impulses" (p. 299) the only techniques useful in correcting inversion, since "castration is out of the question . . . [and] to confine such people in an insane asylum is a monstrous idea" (p. 306).

Havelock Ellis (1897) extended Krafft-Ebing's account of inversion. For Ellis, "the sexual invert may be roughly compared to the congenital idiot, to the instinctive criminal, to the man of genius, who are all not strictly concordant with the usual biological variation" (p. 134). He flags the segregated school system as a primary cause of inversion, identifying seduction of young men by older homosexuals as a second cause that produces "a taste for homosexuality" (p. 139) and disappointment in "normal" love as a third cause. For Ellis, the invert leans toward abnormal sexuality because of homosociality, homoerotism, or the failure of heterosexual subjectification. Of male commercial sex, Ellis (1910) writes, "the prevalence of homosexuality has led to the existence of male prostitutes. . . . the definition must be put in a form irrespective of sex, and we may, therefore, say that a prostitute is a person who makes it a profession to gratify the lust of various persons of the opposite sex or the same sex" (pp. 225–26). According to Ellis, prostitution arises in every society that disapproves of intercourse outside marriage. From Ellis, the English-speaking world has inherited sexology's definition of the prostitute and the designation of sexual pathologies.

Early sexology's clinical language prevents an understanding of how sex and sexuality are constantly changing. Gagnon (2004a) purports that even "progressive" sexology, like Alfred Kinsey's work, constitutes a taxonomy. Kinsey's importance lay in shifting the conceptualization of sexuality away from claims about singular innate drives. Deeply influenced by the natural sciences, however, Kinsey believed that sexuality reflected nature's diversity, which his six-level scale aims to represent. In such sexological analyses, touch gets reduced to a series of behaviors and indicators. Dowsett (1996) argues that sexological research has "continued to attempt to reduce homosexuality to a set of characteristics of deviancy and manifestations of psychic and biological damage to be somehow repaired and rendered inoperable and noncontagious" (p. 32). Sexology's quest to classify and contain the so-called invert/pervert therefore manifests low sociological relevance.

Freud's *Three Essays on the Theory of Sexuality* (1962/1905) represents an account that does not reduce gender and sexuality to biology. Freud remained skeptical about attributions of degeneracy in inverts since "inversion is found in people who exhibit no other serious deviations from the normal. . . . it is similarly found in people whose efficiency is unimpaired, and who are indeed distinguished by specially high intellectual development and ethical culture" (p. 25). He also critiqued sexology's understanding of sexuality as hard-wired and doubted "the very existence of such a thing as innate inversion" (p. 27). Instead, Freud provides a different definition of inversion, one that rejects congenital explanation and the idea of the spermatic economy. Freud challenges the idea that gender roles are fixed by sex:

a large proportion of male inverts retain the mental quality of masculinity. . . . they possess relatively few of the secondary characters of the opposite sex and . . . what they look for in their sexual object are in fact feminine mental traits. If this were not true, how would it be possible to explain the fact that all prostitutes who offer themselves to inverts—today just as they did in ancient times—imitate women in all the externals of their clothing and behavior? (p. 32)

What makes Freud important is his effort to understand sexuality as relational instead of congenital: masculinity and femininity can be detached from men and women because gender (in this case, for the "inverted" or male-for-male prostitutes) is a matter of imitation. Because of this potential for imitation, Freud contends that all human beings are capable of making a homosexual object-choice. Freud thus expands definitions of sexuality in relation to the masculine and feminine, since drives are not conceived of as governed by body fluid levels or evolution.[7]

Although Freud makes a partial break from sexology as the "first pluralizer of homosexuality," according to Leo Bersani (1995:104), his claim about gender and sexuality nevertheless comes with conceptual baggage—namely, the phallus. Freud asserts "the masculine genital zone of the glans penis" (Freud 1962/1905:122) as the leading erotogenic zone in men, building around this assertion his theory of character, family, and symbolism. For Lacan, the phallus becomes a model for desire. After sexology's deconstruction, however, it makes little sense to pin a whole theory of sexuality back onto the symbolic relevance of one single body zone. Yet the problem remains that a psychoanalytic framework most often relegates sexuality to the realm of fantasy and symbolic relations, overlooking the realm of corporeality and touching.

Foucault (1972a) views psychoanalysis as an offshoot of nineteenth-century psychiatry insofar as "Freud's role in psycho-analytical knowledge" (p. 233) has created a whole new range of sexual pathologies. This interpretation is controversial. Tim Dean (2000) compellingly argues that "Foucault's critique ends up reobscuring distinctions between psychoanalysis and psychology, as well as between psychoanalysis and psychiatry" (p. 3). While my characterization of the phallus would perhaps be described by Dean as "Foucault-inspired antipsychoanalytic orthodoxy" (p. 4), in Dean's own attempt to show how psychoanalysis sheds light on the normalization of sexual conduct he suggests that "it is purely conventional and therefore . . . arbitrary that the phallus should hold any indisputable priority" in the symbolic realm (p. 50). For him, "the phallus as Lacan's model for the causal principle of desire may be bracketed" (p. 50). Dean's purpose is to understand what role the unconscious plays in normalization, so he replaces the symbolic relevance of the phallus with Lacan's other key concept, the object. Because one of my purposes is to understand what role touching plays in the production of discourses concerning sexuality, however, I require a more materialist and interactionist framework.

I also hesitate to claim that Freud marks a total break from sexology. Teresa de Lauretis (1993) suggests that Freud reposits a notion of normal sexuality in his vocabulary of tensions and drives, one that renders inversion as a fixed, abnormal form. Gagnon and Simon (1974) also begin by abandoning the focus on drives in Freud. Ultimately, Freud's account of male-with-male sex is based on heteronormative logic and a case study method that pathologizes and categorizes confessions. If biomedical sexology and Freudian psychoanalysis offer problematic versions that cast same sex relations as pathological, then we need another theoretical basis for understanding sex, sexuality, and sex work. What I suggest below is that queer theory and interactionist sociology can help to conceptualize the confessions and ongoing conversation of gestures that make up sexual encounters.

Theorizing Sexuality and Sex Work: Looking Forward

Sexology and psychoanalysis were once the only scholarly formats for telling stories about men having sex with and selling sex to other men. Mary McIntosh's (1968) work on the homosexual role was one of the first scholarly works to situate sexuality in a field of social relations rather than taking it to be a natural ingredient of the individual. The work of scholars such as Kinsey and McIntosh helped form gay and lesbian studies. To be sure, gay and lesbian studies, as well as queer theory in the 1990s, posed a challenge to sexology and psychoanalysis. But there is a trend in some gay and lesbian studies to treat sexuality as a permutation of gender: if two men are together, then those men are gay; if two women are together, then they are lesbians. Queer theorists contend that sexuality and gender are not reducible to one another and that sexuality should not be assimilated to gender in analysis. For Butler (2004a:16), "sexuality does not follow from gender in the sense that what gender you 'are' determines what kind of sexuality you will 'have.'" Next I review what I consider to be some of queer theory's pivotal contributions, examining these writings for generative themes that will assist in my theorizing of encounters. Queer theorists tend to dwell on discursive effects. To go beyond this tactic in queer theory, I contend that sexuality is shaped by touching and that the encounter can undo discourses of gender and sexuality through corporeal contact.

Much Ado about the Phallus

One debate that has been central to queer theory and feminist debates pertains to the phallus, which symbolically represents the universality of male dominance. Elizabeth Stephens (2007) claims that a key strategy of some feminist scholars is to focus on the phallus, effectively privileging the symbolic over the material. But this construction of the male body, envisaged as clean, lean, and linked to authority, effaces the actual penis. Ironically, in such analysis, "the ubiquity of the penis is maintained by its cultural invisibility" (p. 86).[8] Emphasizing the importance of the symbolic phallus can create an essentialist category of "male," which fails to provide a basis for investigating how power operates between men. Focusing on the actual penis (and other body parts) destabilizes traditional notions of masculinity—or at least emphasizes that power operates within sexual communities of difference, as well as between them. Yet a more complex understanding of male-with-male sexuality is required to deconstruct the privileged masculine subject and to show how conventional categories of "men," as gendered and sexual beings, are essentializing.

Deleuze and Guattari (1983:351) likewise advance the idea of the phallus as a "despotic signifier" that no one possesses. Obsession with the phallus is itself a product of heteronormative understandings of sex and gender relations, which privilege the symbolic and neglect the material. Preoccupation with the phallus's symbolic power also sidelines how power operates in corporeal and commercial sex relations between men. When the material penis gains precedence over the symbolic phallus, and when the material body is conceptualized as fallible, the common cultural depiction of men's bodies as impermeable and all-powerful may be questioned. When the materiality of the penis comes into view, sociologists can theorize the male body as permeable and fallible and undo the universal male subject that has for so long been at the center of sociology.

Sociologists have long separated sex and touch from sexuality, but numerous scholars now emphasize the need to account for what bodies do together.[9] As I explore in later chapters, even among men who self-identify as gay, inequalities emerge—most significantly, along the dividing lines of age and body type. Age-graded sexualities among men who have sex with men (and between escorts and clients) create divisions between young and old. Stephens's (2007) point is that bodies need to be central in sociological claims about sexual encounters and that thinking about the aging body is informative for understanding how sexualities change over time.

Sex-Positive?

If sociologists accept the materiality of bodies as a topic of inquiry, does this mean that they should celebrate sex? This question has already received considerable attention in queer theory, which has a different agenda from gay and lesbian studies and focuses on the transgression of norms. For instance, Queen (1997:134) declares it is time for sex workers to "become ambassadors for sex and gratification." Pro-sex discourses, however, are not all destabilizing. Elisa Glick (2000), for one, challenges the sex-positive focus on transgression in feminist and queer discourses. Glick is not for or against sex or particular sexual styles but advises that scholarly analyses should not limit themselves to celebrating "the politics of genderfuck" (p. 20). Glick argues that pro-sex scholars engage in a "project of personal sexual liberation" (p. 22) but suggests that a problem emerges insofar as "pro-sex theory has set up transgressive sexual practices as utopian political strategies and, in the process, has inadvertently endorsed the emancipatory sexual politics that its Foucauldian supporters meant to overthrow" (p. 24). Foucault criticized identity politics and even the gay and lesbian rights movement precisely because these movements reified identity. One difficulty of the pro-sex position is that it revalues stable sexual identities as a basis for making claims about liberation. A second difficulty is that sex radicalism posits a kind of free-floating sense of desire that is easily aligned with consumer capitalism, thus collapsing politics into personal style.[10] A third difficulty is the "defensive refusal" (Martin 1997:109) by some sex radical queer scholars to consider how discourses of sexuality are related to the gender order.

Like Glick, Sally O'Driscoll (1996) remains hesitant to embrace pro-sex discourse and tentative about the notion of "queer." Queer is used to reference a subversive identity, but it can also be used as an anti-identity critique. One reason queer theory has not cohered into a stable literature is this ambiguity. Queer theory's questioning of identity may also undermine the visibility and political space of representation that gay and lesbian studies tried to open up. As O'Driscoll (1996:35) notes, "confusion arises between sexual transgression and sexual identity partly because gender and sexuality . . . are so closely linked as to be almost inseparable." O'Driscoll holds that the idea of "queer theory" should be relegated to the domain of gay and lesbian studies, of "gay theory" and "lesbian theory," since "queer" cannot be teased out from identity.[11]

Pro-sex discourses, then, tend to offer an identity-affirmative conceptualization of sex acts and to gloss over issues of touch and power. I want to explore these very issues, analyzing how our touching encounters with others can undo our sense of self, thereby reorienting senses of sexuality as well as gender, and how this reorientation happens in commercial sexual encounters between men.

The Performativity Paradigm

Judith Butler has written extensively on power and bodies, elaborating her influential accounts of gender and performativity in *Gender Trouble* (1990) as well as in *Bodies That Matter* (1993). In *Gender Trouble*, Butler (p. 6) writes that gender does not stem neatly from supposed sex categories: "presumption of a binary gender system implicitly retains the belief in a mimetic relation of gender to sex whereby gender mirrors sex or is otherwise restricted by it." A male versus female binary compels subjects toward recognizing themselves as being one or the other gender. Internal coherence of either pole "requires both a stable and oppositional heterosexuality" (p. 22).

A "performative" is a practice of improvisation within a field of power. When Butler comes to the section of *Gender Trouble* where she focuses sustained attention on the idea of performativity, she draws from Foucault's *Discipline and Punish*. Foucault (1977:149–56) demonstrates how mechanisms of domination were supplanted by new forms of regulatory knowledge or, in Butler's (1990:134) words, how prisoners were made "to compel their bodies to signify the prohibitive law as their very essence, style, and necessity." These corporeal signs interest Butler because, when it comes to gender, it is these performative gestures that "create the illusion of an interior and organizing gender core, an illusion maintained for the purpose of the regulation of sexuality within the obligatory frame of reproductive heterosexuality" (1990:136). Gender is performative rather than expressive; it possesses no essence to be expressed.[12]

Butler provides scholars with tools for debunking biological determinism, but her work has been critiqued based on its implications for agency, the subject, and the body. Some critics accuse Butler of obliterating the sexed body, while others argue that she exaggerates the uniformity of gender norms. Furthermore, she does not develop the possibility of subjects intervening in their own constitution and she glosses over the forces that compel us toward performatives.[13] Kathi Weeks (1998:128) argues that Butler does not "adequately account for the forces that induce our practices" and that her focus on discourse ignores the contexts in which people interact. These criticisms of Butler's work echo feminist debates in which materialist feminists accuse cultural feminists of reducing the body to discourse. They also suggest ways that Butler's concept of performativity might be supplemented by considering the context in which corporeal interaction takes place: the encounter.

In addition, the notion of performativity is not designed for analyzing the many subject positions assumed by men who have sex with men. Rob Cover (2003) notes the partial collapse of compulsory heterosexuality that has given rise to signifying economies not necessarily governed by what Butler calls the heterosexual matrix. The performativity paradigm, then, fails to acknowledge the multiplicity of sexuality (by reducing it to the heterosexual matrix, in which heterosexuality and homosexuality remain the only options) as well as the materiality of sex in touching encounters. While the idea of performativity does make use of Foucault to conceptualize how power operates on our sense of self in a gendered way, it is not explicitly intended to theorize sexual encounters. Yet sexual performativity must be treated as a joint encounter requiring touching and interaction.

The relationship between sexuality and stereotypes is key to understanding performativity. Gays and lesbians are assumed to comprise a number of stereotypical kinds of bodies that correspond with gay and lesbian masculinity and femininity.[14] Gay and lesbian performatives thus produce the illusion of a fixed subject, with discourse relaying the stereotype that is materialized through performatives. In this sense, Dowsett (1996:267) claims that "gay communities are constantly manufacturing gayness." The transformation of gay and lesbian movements into markets, into the so-called pink economy, has shaped gay and lesbian relations by fostering sexual stereotypes.[15] Gamson and Moon (2004:57) further claim that "understandings of and attitudes about sexuality are both affected by and reflect global political-economic phenomena such as commercialization." More research is required to understand how the stereotypes and discourses of the so-called pink economy become part of the touching encounters and sexual performatives of men who have sex with men.

A key issue that remains to be explored is how existing research has failed to investigate the way sexual performatives are tied to labor process. To be a coherent worker, one must offer coherent gender identities and sexualities. Male-for-male Internet escorting is an apt case study for exploring how bodies are compelled toward coherence in work contexts because of the body's centrality in escorting work. In this way, queer theory can be aligned with a materialist lens to focus on the performativity of recognizable sexual stereotypes as a necessity of coherent work practices.[16]

Let me summarize the foregoing arguments. The performativity paradigm eschews sexuality's materiality in favor of analyzing discursive instantiations of gender. Queer sexuality is performative but occurs in the context of labor and consumption. Scholars should have some trepidation about the notion of "queer" since it can reproduce an emphasis on identity. And research should focus on the materiality of bodies but not simply in a way that celebrates sex. These important claims provide a basis for moving beyond sexology and psychoanalysis. But can theory get us any closer to the encounters between escorts and clients?

Sexual Scripts

Many authors note that queer theory is best understood as an extension of interactionist approaches to sexuality, to which I turn next.[17] Gagnon and Simon's *Sexual Conduct* (1974) was one of the first sustained considerations of sexuality to draw from interactionist sociology. Gagnon and Simon anticipated much of what queer theory has recently attempted: scripting theory does not treat identity as fixed, but as something precarious that must be constantly achieved, and it focuses on the location and context in which sexual interaction takes place. In an interactionist approach to sex and sexuality, the specificity of the body and its gestures becomes the focus.

The idea of sexual scripts became influential in the sociology of sexuality starting in the mid-1970s. These scripts, Gagnon and Simon (1974) suggest, are organized in two ways. First, actors bring with them conventions that govern sexual conduct. These conventions are culture-bound, and they order comportment. Second, the script must be accepted to produce arousal. If the script is rejected, the interaction may fail. Gagnon and Simon argue that what sexologists assumed for so long to be biological behavior is really a social process of meaning-making. The idea of sexual scripts detaches sex from biology and emphasizes instead its social character. For Simon and Gagnon (1986), the significance of practices (sexual or not) is constantly achieved through interaction. Jackson and Scott (2010) also point out that Gagnon and Simon became more nuanced over time, accounting for cultural, interactional, and intrapsychic scripts.

Scripting theory originally opposed biological determinism but has ironically come to stand for a kind of cultural determinism. Some authors regard sexual scripts as "blueprints" for sexual behavior, detailing with whom one will have sex and how (Markle 2008). Edward Laumann and John Gagnon (1995:190) claim sexual scripts are culturally specific "instructions" for sexual conduct, including the "who, what, and when" of sexual conduct. For Michael Wiederman (2005:496), "social scripting theory rests on the assumption that people follow internalized scripts when constructing meaning out of behavior" and that "scripts provide meaning and direction for responding to sexual cues and for behaving sexually." B. J. Rye and G. J. Meaney (2007) suggest that if scholars could change the script, societies would achieve sexual equality. Matt Mutchler (2000) argues that all forms of sex between men can be conceived of as sexual scripts: commercial sex follows a script; unsafe sex follows a script; sexual violence follows a script. All of these authors assume that people internalize sexual scripts, as if people simply take on roles that are waiting for them. Moreover, the notion of sexual scripts has deeply influenced the sociology of sex work, and this fact has implications for how scholars understand the sex of sex work.

Analysis of sexual scripts has moved away from the interactionist analysis with which it began toward a sexological concern for cataloguing behavior. Gagnon (2004a:275) thus laments, "I think we lost control of it [scripting theory]." The consequence is that meaning-making has been deemphasized and the importance of bodies to encounters downplayed. Scripting theory now assumes relatively stable patterns of sexual interaction. Similarly, Gagnon's and Simon's notion of the script only accounts for recognizable types of sexuality based on stereotypes and conventional settings of sex. The script is said to be enacted (that is, it exists prior to the encounter), rather than transmuted through the act of touching. Jackson and Scott (2010, 2001) claim interactionist sociology as a useful way of grounding the claims made by queer theorists, but my claim is that scripting theory does not adequately explain the link between discourse, scripts, and interaction.

Though not as unpredictable as park cruising, itinerant sex between client and escort often has the aim of evading the patterned interaction in favor of an unscripted encounter with strangers. I want to supplement sexual scripting theory by emphasizing the open tendency in encounters. What is produced out of the encounter is as important as the script going in.

One of the first interactionist scholars of sex, Ken Plummer (1982) argued that to place all emphasis on scripts is to ignore open meaning-making tendencies in sexual encounters. The sexual script is not provided in advance by culture; rather, this script, if it comes to be followed, must be produced by participants learning what they can do together with their bodies. Discourse and scripts provide tropes and stereotypes, but touching, gestures, and interaction mediate these discourses and scripts in ways that alter accepted meanings. Sociologists need not point to an abstract notion of culture to decipher sexual scripts. Instead of assuming that an encounter's script is written in advance, I explore how touching during an encounter can itself produce sexual meanings. The notion of sexual scripts is useful as a challenge to biologically reductionist accounts of sex, but I emphasize the unanticipated elements of sexual encounters, how scripts mutate through gestures and touch.

By alluding to unanticipated elements of the encounter, I do not mean the idea of being "swept off one's feet" as in Western ideas of romantic love. What I suggest instead is that the escort and client sometimes form a relation that moves in directions neither of them anticipated prior to their encounter. Simon and Gagnon (1986) recognize this unanticipated element insofar as they argue that sex occurs on a continuum between improvisation or "the excitement of uncertainty" and a more closed tendency toward a predictable "sexuality of reassurance" (p. 118). While notions of romantic love and monogamous partnership have emerged alongside same-sex marriage as elements of younger communities of men who have sex with men (Warner 1999), there remain forms of sexual practice between men that are oriented toward encounters that stray from set scripts.

The relations of many men who have sex with men are not tied to the script of monogamy. The idea that men who have sex with men have "problems" developing long-term relationships suggests that a "till death do us part" script is at the center of how many social scientists conceive of intimacy, sex, and the self.[18] Does scripting theory resonate with short sequences of surprising interactions between two strangers who come together, offer their bodies, and then part ways as if they will never meet again? I suggest that it must be revised to do so.

Discussion

The following is a summary of the central claims made in this chapter.
- Sexology and psychoanalysis are problematic because notions of fixed identity and innate drives are at the root of their claims.
- Queer theorists contend that scholarly analysis cannot start with the question of identity.

- Bodies need to become central in sociological claims about sexual encounters.
- Gender performatives involve and are conditioned by sexual performatives, which often occur and are made sense of in local contexts of work and consumption.
- Sexual scripts exist, but there is a specific logic to sex work encounters between men based on anonymous sociality and itinerant spatiality. Sociologists must expand their theorization of sexuality and sex work to make sense of itinerant and anonymous encounters.

There is no a contradiction between the last two propositions: that gender and sexual performatives are compelled toward coherence by work and consumption at the same time that the encounter always involves an unpredictable element. These are the two tendencies in an encounter, one that is closing and one that is opening, one that leans toward repetition and one that moves toward difference. If sociological analysis starts not from identity but from the assumption that interaction can generate new meanings and ways of bodies coming together, the sociology of sexuality can get away from abstract starting points and move with the contingency of corporeal encounters.

The Faciality of Male Internet Escorting
.................A.n....E.x.c.u.r.s.u.s..

Faciality is a layered term. Deleuze and Guattari (2003/1980) use it to refer to surfaces that obscure a complex movement. Dan O'Connor (2004) uses it to refer to
close-up mechanisms and singularizing portrayals in moving images. While faciality
evokes a surface that conceals a deeper texture, this distinction suggests that the
surface stays the same and that authenticity lingers below it. Depths and surfaces exist in a tumultuous relationship. And while faciality evokes a face in place of a body,
this is also a false division because the surface that is singularly depicted can portray
more than a face; that is, all other parts of the body can stand in as a synecdoche.
In this excursus I touch on what I call the faciality of male-for-male Internet escorting in two ways. First, I explore the sensational and overcoded dream world of male
escorting: the Hustlaball. Second, I assess a piece of scholarship that takes representations of male-for-male Internet escorting at face value; I critique this positivist
rendering for what it captures and where it fails.

Faciality: Hustlaball
Hustlaball features leading names in male-for-male pornography and escorting—live,
on stage, screening their wares. Enthusiasts in the crowd watch on, hoping to arrange a date or to get some hands-on relief after the tempting display. Hustlaball
is organized by a company that operates one of the largest male-for-male Internet
escort advertising websites. Indeed, some of the Hustlaball men humping and pumping across the stage with such vigor are escorts who are there to be had. Hustlaball
typically takes place in a global city (New York, London, Berlin), so it requires money
to get there. For the clients of many male Internet escorts, that poses no hurdle.
This clientele might have scheduled a business trip for the same weekend to attend,
see the sights, and make an offer. Yet Hustlaball performers represent a minority of

male-for-male Internet escorts. They are the best circus performers, who become part of the traveling show under the big tent; the rest of the bazaar sticks closer to home and is nowhere near as bodacious or buff. And not all clients are loaded with cash, ready to blow.

Hustlaball Internet promotions present a shiny, sexy surface, touting the newest, most physically stunning male-for-male Internet escorts in the world. The Hustlaball monthly newsletter is full of hunky bodies, and there is no beating around the bush with the possibilities on offer. Catchy banner phrases, enhanced photos, and direct links to the profiles of some escorts round out the page. Like Hustlaball itself, these Internet promotions give the viewer a sense that male escorting is all flare and fuck for big profit. But this faciality is masklike. It obscures the relations, the emotions, and the tensions of male-for-male Internet escort work.

Faciality: Positivism

Trevon Logan's (2010) article on male Internet escorts is a welcome addition to what is a small body of literature. For his study, Logan quantified all characteristics of male escorts as listed on the most popular of these websites in the United States. Matt Pruitt (2005) has also reviewed the websites of male-for-male Internet escorts in America but does not focus on the questions that Logan raises about geographic location and race. Using these data, Logan (2010) makes several arguments about commercial sex, sexuality, and, notably, hegemonic masculinity.

Several strengths mark Logan's (2010) analysis. First, his focus on power relations in male-with-male sexual communities is important because it has not been fully examined in sociological research on sexualities or masculinities. As Logan puts it, he focuses on the "differences *within* gender" (p. 682), an admirable academic pursuit precisely because sociological literature on sexualities and on masculinities tend to speak past one another. Second, Logan focuses on race and how escort pricing is correlated with racial stereotypes. He thus provides refreshing insights while tackling a taboo topic that sociologists have shied away from.

My concern with Logan's work is his operationalization of the concept of "hegemonic masculinity." This concept is notorious in the sociology of gender, where scholars have debated what it means. R. W. Connell (1987) coined the term as a way of making sense of how different categories of gender are valued in various cultures. Like all concepts, this one has earned detractors, who formulate at least three criticisms. First, sociologists have critiqued the underlying concept of masculinity for being too realist and for positing a fixed gender meaning. This critique decries the idea of masculinity for essentializing men's characters (see Collier 1998; MacInnes 1998). Second, psychoanalytic critics (see Jefferson 2002) fault the idea of masculinity for failing to consider the unconscious and subconscious aspects of gender. Third, geographers posit that highly valued forms of masculinity differ from region to region and that the issue of place has been glossed over.

Responding to these critiques, R. W. Connell and James Messerschmidt (2005) have attempted to revise the concept of masculinity. First, they insist that any use of the concept of hegemonic masculinity must analyze more than representations of masculinity. Second, they argue that any use of this concept must concentrate on the practices through which masculinities are embodied and enacted. As Connell (2002) notes, men make great efforts in producing conventional and unconventional masculinities. Third, Connell and Messerschmidt argue that the practices and interactions through which masculinities are embodied and enacted cannot be treated as expressing a unitary or fixed sense of masculinity. In their view, masculinity cannot be reduced to psychological or physical traits.

Logan (2010) not only glosses over these debates about hegemonic masculinity but also does not borrow insights from these discussions in designing his study. Logan defines hegemonic masculinity as a physical ideal that "is typified by a muscular physique and other markers . . . such as height, body hair, whiteness, youth, and middle-class socioeconomic status" (p. 684). He takes this to mean a rejection of "feminizing features" (p. 684), assuming that escorts who present "masculine traits and practices" (p. 684) will be more desirable and set their prices higher. Logan presupposes that men who are muscular and offer penetrative services will benefit, while men who are less muscular and offer submissive services will be penalized. He hypothesizes that "hegemonically masculine physical traits" (p. 693) will be prized in the escort market.

In terms of methodology, Logan (2010) catalogues the height, weight, body type, race, and other features of escorts by body types (ecto-, endo-, and mesomorph). He then regresses these aggregated figures with listed prices to see which escorts set prices higher and which are penalized or have lower prices. He notes, "claims that escorts make about characteristics can be confirmed with pictures posted in the advertisements" (p. 687). Logan thus treats muscularity as the main indicator of hegemonic masculinity: "because muscularity is a physical signal of maleness and dominance, and it can be considered a proxy for strength and virility, the premium attached to muscularity in this market is consistent with hegemonic masculinity" (p. 694). Overall, he finds that "the premium for being a top is substantial, as is the penalty for being a bottom, again consistent with the theory of hegemonic masculinity" (p. 697).

Logan's analysis, however, manifests conceptual, methodological, and empirical problems. First, Logan reduces hegemonic masculinity to a single trait: muscularity. This represents a conceptual problem since theorists of hegemonic masculinity argue that it cannot be reduced to a psychological or physical trait. This also constitutes an empirical problem: even if it were possible to reduce hegemonic masculinity to a single trait, Logan ignores one very important part of the body. Logan ignores endowment, including shape and cut of the penis. Endowment is often a prominent item listed on male-for-male Internet escort websites (there are dozens of websites that Logan did not examine), and clients are keenly interested in it. My point is that it is not useful to reduce hegemonic masculinity to a single trait, such as muscularity. Second, Logan reduces hegemonic masculinity to a listing on a website and a picture that is posted. Reducing masculinity to a representation in this way is a methodological problem because Logan takes information that is a presentation of self or "cyber type" (Nakamura 2002) and treats it as a truth about escorts. It constitutes an empirical problem because escorts often manipulate these listings—posting enhanced and edited pictures—to secure a competitive market advantage (see the chapters below). Third, Logan fails to examine hegemonic masculinity as enacted or embodied through practices and interaction. This matters because Logan makes several claims about penetrative sex, or "topping," as being highly valued while submissive sex, or "bottoming," is assumed not to be. Logan thus fails to understand the complexity of power relations between men who have sex with men and the valuation of topping and bottoming in practice. The active versus passive dichotomy masks considerable complexity. There is a lot more going on in escorting with topping and bottoming than Logan accounts for. One escort I spoke with in Toronto referred to himself as a "power bottom." He said his services were highly valued and sought after precisely because he offered a bottoming service that other escorts did not. Thus, Logan bases his arguments on a mistaken active-versus-passive dichotomy that makes little sense in male-with-male sexual communities, and he presupposes that this is the starting point for setting prices. There is more complexity to pricing, masculinity, and sexuality than Logan accounts for, which is especially so when the issue of repeat clients is considered. Fourth, Logan fails to examine how masculinities change over time. His data collection provides a quick snapshot of one visual, online representation of masculinity. But as sociologists of gender point out, masculinities are in constant flux, so at the very least some longitudinal perspective would be needed to round out this research design.

Hegemonic masculinity cannot be operationalized as outward appearance or physical traits. If it could be, then Logan has ignored some important physical traits for male escorts, which are penis size and cut. Logan's work relies on representations rather than escorts' actual bodily practices. He reads the website photos and advertisements as authentic, one of the major flaws of online research. He also gives in to understanding tops and bottoms as reflective of power hierarchies and inequalities. Logan assumes that bottoming is feminizing and disempowering; yet escorts who offer bottom services do not equate bottoming with femininity and possess a market advantage in some local sexual cultures.

My purpose in sketching these texts and events is to point to a facialization of male escorting that is part of popular culture (and, evidently, sociology too). My sense is that these images are surfaces based on stereotypes. The rich texture of the sex and work of male escorts is effaced by renderings that are explicit (in the case of Hustlaball) and scientific (in the case of positivist sociology that likewise indulges in appearances). This overall faciality is what I want to prick and pull at in the coming chapters. I do so by emphasizing the mundane and the everyday sex and work lives of male escorts, and also by emphasizing the encounter as a key modality of interaction and touching. I want to get under the surface of male sex work to examine the bodily practices and interactions that ultimately make up the processes by which gender and sexuality become materially significant.

Chapter 3 | Theorizing Encounters

I want to know what the deal is when I go in. One client asked me "can you be aggressive," and I said "I can be aggressive." Well, easy, be aggressive then. But sometimes the connection with the guy is really good, the sex is hot, he is doing things most do not do, like giving it to me, giving me a back rub when usually it is being requested from you, he is taking his time and you are actually turned on, and it is like wow. . . . I form some kind of connection there. (Tyler, Ottawa)

Tyler's narrative here hints at two tendencies in the sexual encounter. One tendency is more closed, based on sexual stereotypes, as clients reach for a role at the start of an encounter. But a second tendency, which can emerge from the same set of interactions, is open and seemingly moves beyond the initial parameters set out by discourses and stereotypes of sexuality. In this chapter, I try to theorize these two tendencies in the encounter.

In the last chapter, I borrowed from queer theory to question the utility of identity as a starting point in the sociology of sexuality. The notion of gay and lesbian identities or a queer community is tricky because of how random the boundaries of community can be. There is too much congruence between fixed notions of gayness and the regulatory medical discourses of nineteenth- and twentieth-century sexology and psychoanalysis for such notions to sit well with scholars.[1] The sociology of sexuality should not start by presuming sexually united subgroups, as sexology does. Yet queer theory focuses overly on discursive effects and not enough on interactionist considerations of touching, too much on the radical potential of sex and not enough on materialist considerations of work and consumption. There are thus limits to what Steven Seidman (1995) calls queer textualism. Moreover, J. B. Noble (2006) suggests that we are now at a "post-queer" juncture, insofar as the word "queer" no longer signifies the plurality of possible ambiguous gender and sexual performatives. The word queer can also circumscribe the existence of power differentials within communities of sexual difference. As an alternative, I argue that the sociology of sexuality must move toward theorizing encounters, such as itinerant male-with-male sexual encounters in which the body is given over to a stranger.

Reconciling the works of Foucault with interactionist sociology provides a way of thinking through the two tendencies of the encounter. This chapter takes up that task. Ian Hacking (2004) has usefully claimed that the texts of Foucault and Erving Goffman complement one another. In this provocative argument, Hacking asks us to reconcile Foucault's writing about power with interactionism's focus on what people do. Whereas Foucault is concerned with how knowledge operates in discourse, Goffman is concerned with face-to-face exchanges. According to Hacking, Foucault lacks "an understanding of how the forms of discourse become part of the lives of ordinary people, or even how they become institutionalized and made part of the structure of institutions at work" (p. 278); Goffman lacks "an understanding of how the institutions he described came into being, what their formative structures are" (p. 278). But integrating their works proves challenging because it is not clear that they think about human relations in the same way.

Many scholars have attempted to recast Foucault's comments about discourse and sexuality. Earlier, I suggested that Butler's focus on performativity has not effectively brought Foucault down to the level of the encounter. To bring Foucault down to this level, we must use interactionism to understand the way that discourse is translated through gestures and touching. Discourse does not simply manufacture a subject who becomes a ventriloquist for cultural scripts; discourse is in part produced and modified by those bodies it operates on. Bodies translate discourse through their imbrications with others. I make this argument through a reading of the work of G. H. Mead, who is credited with creating the foundations of interactionist sociology. Rather than a sexed body, one that is discursively constituted, we have a sexing body, which through its reflexive and creative gestures transmutes discourse during the sexual encounter.

Foucault's writings regarding sexuality can be brought into conversation with interactionist sociology as Hacking suggests, but Goffman does not provide us with all the tools we need to discuss interaction. British anthropologists indebted to Durkheim influenced Goffman, and his focus on roles and rituals only represents one tendency of thought in interactionist sociology. To account for the open tendency in the meaning-making process, sociologists must reconsider Herbert Blumer's work. Foucault examines how we operate upon our selves as selves but places less emphasis on the influence of our interactions on others. He thus neglects the improvised and indeterminate swerves that encounters can take—swerves that Bulmer can help us to understand. Here and in chapter 5 I bring Foucault into conversation with interactionist analysis, including Goffman and Blumer.

Of the two tendencies in an encounter—closed and open—the closed tendency leans toward ordered and expected interactions, which are governed by the roles and rituals theorized by Goffman. This closed tendency is one of repetition or "sedimentation of corporeal style" (Diprose 2002:120). Conversely, the open tendency is toward unanticipated meaning-making and bodily practices, toward difference, openness to others, and coming together otherwise. These breaks or swerves result from interaction that Blumer theorizes. I delimit my discussion of the encounter to male commercial sexual encounters, although this theorization certainly has ramifications for interactionist sociology broadly insofar as I integrate Goffman and Blumer but also Mead to provide a more comprehensive interactionist theoretical posture.

As mentioned in chapter 2, sexual scripting theory has not emphasized unanticipated meaning-making or bodily practices, placing instead too much weight on the script leading up to the encounter and neglecting how the script breaks down or becomes altered through touching. Scripting theory does not allow for analysis of what is unanticipated in encounters. However, I conceptualize the encounter as productive of sexuality and of unanticipated eroticization. My use of Foucault allows for a discussion of how discourses of sexuality frame the way people think about their relations with others. But if discourses of sexuality constitute a subject, the constitution of the subject takes place in part through touching.

This chapter has four parts. First, I put Foucault, Blumer, and Goffman in conversation in order to understand the two tendencies of the encounter. Second, I discuss how bringing Foucault to bear on the encounter requires insight from the sociology of the body. The bodies in Foucault's writings are never fleshy, nor do the subjects in Foucault's writings seem to have much say about the discourses that shape their practices. Third, I discuss how Foucault and interactionist sociologists define power. I conclude by discussing how this conceptualization of the open and closed tendencies of interaction relates to itinerant sex and the specific logic of the lure in male-with-male sex where the body is given over to strangers.

Foucault, Sexuality, and the Encounter

In the *History of Sexuality*, volume 1 (1978a), Foucault detonates the idea that we "have" a sexual identity. Foucault (1983:203) tells the reader that his writings are concerned with the processes through which "we make ourselves subjects." What I take from Foucault is the idea of sexuality as a mosaic on which people strategically place themselves in power relations, as well as the way he discusses eroticism anew. I offer a thicker exegesis of his work, including his distinction between *ars erotica* and *scientia sexualis*, in chapter 7. Here, I outline what I take from Foucault in order to better understand encounters.

Sexuality is constituted through the desire to speak about it, which is why Foucault argues that we need to change the way we conceptualize power. Power has always been equated with the law, the sovereign, and the juridical. Moreover, power has always been equated with a negative relation, a negation, instead of a positive relation, a production.[2] For Foucault (1978a), desire is not repressed but is joined with power in an impetus to confess the truth about one's self and to take pleasure in knowing a truth.[3] The clinical setting is the confession's site. Foucault indicates that the confession leads to a form of pastoral power, whereby those who listen to the confession attempt to guide the soul of the storyteller toward certain ends.

Foucault's (1978a) project is therefore to provide insight into power beyond prohibition and sovereignty. He conceives of sex not in terms of repression or law, but in terms of power, which he defines as "the multiplicity of force relations immanent in the sphere in which they operate and which constitute their own organization" (p. 92). Power exists not in a central point, but "comes from everywhere" (p. 93) in complex strategical situations. It follows that power can always be resisted; there is always another action that may be taken upon an action.

His interviews (roughly between 1979 and 1983) offer a less genealogical vision of sexuality and are more normative.[4] Foucault (1997b) comes out and suggests that "the whole conceptual scheme that categorizes homosexuals as deviants must be dismantled" (p. 144). This is because male-with-male sex has become predictable, determined by identity: "the sexual act has become so easy and available to homosexuals that it runs the risk of quickly becoming boring, so that every effort has to be made to innovate and create variations that will enhance the pleasure of the act" (p. 151). Pleasure is imperative in Foucault's schema, but not because of some valorization of hedonism. Rather, Foucault values pleasure because pleasure evades categorization. The reason that Foucault rejects Freud is because Freud views classification of sexuality as the discovery of a truth.[5]

Foucault says very little about the touching involved in sex, but what he does say is interesting: "Sex is not a fatality: it's a possibility for creative life" (1997c:163). By "creative" I take Foucault to mean that the actual doing of sex is not always prefigured. In a sense, Foucault holds out that resistance to discourses of sexuality must account for the way we touch one another. Foucault associates pleasurable sex with new relational possibilities. For instance, Foucault equates bondage with new possibilities of pleasure, "a creative enterprise . . . the desexualization of pleasure" (p. 165). The conflation of pleasure and sex is broken down, and "very strange parts of our bodies" are introduced into our relations. These parts are "strange" because these touching encounters are often anonymous and less scripted than others.

Finally, in Foucault's writing, sex and sexuality constitute issues of ethical practice. Today "sexual ethics imply very strict truth obligations," which lead to our "constantly scrutinizing ourselves as libidinal beings" (Foucault 1997d:182). But erotic relationality runs counter to the deployment of sexuality. Indeed, erotic relationality can operate as a moment of itinerant pleasure. On one hand, Foucault is critical of discourses of sexuality as they lead to categorization. On the other hand, Foucault holds out that sex might entail something ethical. This ends up being friendship. Friendships between men entail a bond that is based on neither familial relationships nor conventional masculinity. The relations possible through friendship do not run alongside the deployment of sexuality, though they do not resist it either. An interesting case is the friendships that some male escorts develop with clients. The touching encounters of escorts and clients are often organized according to discourses of sexuality, yet the touching can turn to relations not grounded in sexual identity categories.

There are two similarities between Foucault and interactionists that I believe may be productive. First, both Foucault and interactionists reject the question of identity as a starting point. Instead, they both start with the question of the self as made up. Second, Foucault and interactionists employ a similar definition of power. Both begin from the assumption that power is not definable simply in negative terms (e.g., when exerted through physical force), but that power may also be productive and refers to the ability to produce effects in a network of relations. Although *The History of Sexuality*, vol. 1, contains space for understanding the deployment of sexuality as achieved through everyday confessions, Foucault does not take interaction as his object of analysis.

Whereas Hacking (2004) suggests that Goffman can be used to bring Foucault down to the level of the encounter, I argue that this theoretical move is not possible without Blumer. Goffman operates with a notion of interaction rituals that limits what the outcome of interaction can be. Blumer, however, places more emphasis on the unanticipated aspects of interaction. Most scholars are unaware of the extent to which Blumer differed from Goffman, and there are few documented exchanges between the two intellectuals. We find one of Blumer's only commentaries on Goffman's work in a 1972 book review, in which Blumer argues that Goffman's contributions are useful insofar as he "forces us to see order" (p. 50) in the way people comprehend and respond to one another. Blumer emphasizes Goffman's conceptualization of interaction as patterned and rule oriented. Interactions are ordered not as a simple matter of obedience; rather, people have developed skills at reestablishing order after an infraction of norms. For Blumer, Goffman's focus on interadjustment and ritual "distorts" (p. 52) the interactionist tradition, insofar as Goffman only emphasizes impression management. Goffman's is a "one-sided treatment" of the self that "sets up a static world," writes Blumer, since only focusing on patterned and ordered interactions "shuts out consideration of how norms and the patterned adaptations to them either come into being or deteriorate and pass away" (p. 53). The review illuminates the differences between the two: Goffman took individual efforts toward order maintenance and impression management as his object, while Blumer focused more on what is produced out of the interaction or how the terms of the encounter are always being struck anew. For Goffman (1959), we act to maintain a given definition of the situation. Obligations bind people to fashion their conduct in an expected manner (Goffman 1967). Interaction that exceeds the given definition of the situation must be realigned. It is Blumer who conceptualizes the open, creative tendency of the encounter.

This idea of two tendencies in the encounter can be further explained by situating the work of Goffman and Blumer in relation to G. H. Mead, who is credited with establishing the foundations of interactionist sociology. Goffman and Blumer draw upon Mead, although the two authors make different uses of him. The differences between Goffman and Blumer[6] can be clarified through Mead's (1967/1934) language of the "me" and the "I." The "me" takes the role of the other and is "a conventional, habitual individual"

(p. 197). This is a closed tendency insofar as it "controls the response of the individual" (p. 154). The "me" is the strain of thought Goffman emphasizes. In contrast, the "I" "reacts to the self which arises through the taking of the attitudes of others" (p. 174). The "I" is an "action over against that social situation within his [sic] own conduct." The "me" is associated with the closed tendency, the tendency toward taking the self as others would, whereas the "I" is associated with the open tendency, the tendency toward taking one's relations as a creative project. For Mead, "me" and "I" are abstractions that refer to operations of a group upon the self. The subject is its own object only insofar as the self is compelled and urged in relations with others. Mead does not focus on consciousness or inner experience. This is where he differs from Cooley as well as from phenomenologists.[7] My analysis extends Mead's focus on gestures across the chasm of individuals into the moment when their bodies come together: touch.

Meaningful language includes gestures, "the attitude of the body" (Mead (1967/1934:14), and the way bodies make meaning through movement. People translate meaning together through a conversation of gestures and continual readjustment to one another. This does not mean that gestures get read only as intended. In fact, Mead suggests intentionality is a false problem because in reading others during interaction we "translate these gestures into significant symbols" (p. 55). The gesture (or the touch) must be made sense of. There is no sole tendency toward repetition because the interpretation of acts requires translation of meaning. We often take the role of the other, "which is a tendency to act as the other person acts" (p. 73). In this sense, our conduct adjusts to the conduct of others. (This reference to ordered interaction is what Goffman takes from Mead.) We also have the capacity for reflexive consideration of the present. Gestures imply meaning-making in action. (This focus on unanticipated effects of interaction is what Blumer takes from Mead.) One makes meaning through "a process of intercourse with those about him" (p. 107). An interactionist account of itinerant male-for-male sex takes this last statement quite literally.

For Mead (1967/1934), there is no self prior to encounters. Instead, "there are all sorts of different selves answering to all sorts of different social reactions" (p. 142). The changes in our actions as a result of interpreting the gestures of others are aleatory insofar as "we shift from what we started to do because of the reply the other makes" (p. 141). The "I" is associated with "a creative expression of embodiment" (p. 222). The open tendency exists insofar as "the response of the 'I' is something more or less uncertain" (p. 176). Without this open tendency, "there would be nothing novel in experience" (p. 178).[8]

Here I pose two questions to bring interactionist sociology into contact with Foucault. The first question is about touch and discourse. If discourse is translated by touch, does discourse not provide a "me" by which to gauge one's interactions? The translation of gestures into meaning that Mead discusses is vital because it refers both to how discourse translates the self into a recognizable type of self (e.g., a "straight" self, a "gay" self) and to how discourse conveys meaning. We do not, however, have selves simply constituted by discourse. Instead, encounters create conditions for gestures and the imbrications of bodies to translate selves as well as to transmute and proliferate discourses.

Second, Mead (1967/1934) argues the subject is always enmeshed in what he calls "social control," defined as "the expression of the 'me' over against the expression of the 'I'" (p. 210). Is this expression of social control not similar to what Foucault referred to as subjectification? In the realm of sexuality, the expression of a sexual "me" (the closed tendency) over and against the "I" (the open tendency) is what Foucault would call a ruse of sexuality, a running alongside the discourses of sexuality. If, however, the unanticipated possibilities of the open tendency were not checked by obligations and habits, one result could be a different economy of bodies and pleasures.

Reconciling Mead's language of "me" and "I" with Foucault's discussion of discourse and sexual subjectification creates a queer Mead indeed: this Mead allows us to understand the mutable gestures that make up sexuality; this Mead has no time for identity or consciousness because his ontology of interaction moves with the creativity of the open tendency of the encounter; this Mead debases any fixed sense of the self and demonstrates how meaning is continually accomplished. Such a Mead could exist alongside a Foucault who views discourses of sexuality as proliferating and operating upon bodies; who situates the body as a nodal point of power; and who, like Mead, identifies two tendencies in encounters.

Difficulties still remain in reconciling Foucault with interactionism. For instance, Foucault is antihumanist insofar as he argues humans are not unmediated makers of meaning. My discussion here mirrors Foucault's cautions concerning representational practices and voluntarism. It is the subjectivist tradition in interactionist sociology that needs to be broken down since the subjectivist tradition stresses voluntarism and mentalism.[9]

The trick is to provide a sociological account of sexuality that emphasizes the creative and open tendencies of coming together without relying on a voluntarist notion of the subject or an instrumentalist notion of bodies.

Homoerotic Bodies

Foucault analyzes how sex is put into discourse. By contrast, I am interested in how discourse is put into the doing of sex. For Foucault, sexuality is aligned with power, but he does not provide us with a description of the ways power operates on bodies or the ways bodies operate in encounters.[10] Although Foucault accomplished much in bringing the body into view for historians and philosophers, he does not discuss the materiality of bodies or what Nick Crossley (2007) calls facts of the body. Foucault suggests that there is something specific about the way men relate to one another erotically, but he does not develop this thought further. Foucault's analysis of bodies thus remains incomplete, requiring that we flesh out the skeleton he provides concerning sexuality.[11]

To get closer to sex while keeping in mind Foucault's comments regarding the sexual mosaic and subjectification, sociologists must focus on bodies. Gary Dowsett (1996) argues that "an insidious form of heterosexism has emerged to rid research of an analysis of sexuality, as a multidimensional structure of power and praxis affecting all lives, as a product of iterative cultural production, an accumulation of experiences and meanings" (p. 34); in Dowsett's analysis, this heterosexism leads to the critical neglect of what bodies do. Dowsett asks that scholars reject the "plea for respectability" (p. 36) in most public health research on sex because such approaches eschew the body by reducing it to a set of indicators, erasing how people perform sexuality and gender. Bodies possess vital specificities in relation to pleasure—for instance, "a prostate is a prostate and uniquely male" (p. 37). Dowsett wants to render present this materiality of sex in sociological analysis. Unless scholars attend to bodily practices in sexuality research, Dowsett argues, gender and sexual performatives become treated as norms: "A norm is simply a social 'biopsy' performed at a given moment, which is then frozen for later examination, the body (politic) having moved on. . . . the norm is a concept that ignores the actuality of domains of contested power operating in the structuring of relations in any society" (p. 43).

The same claim can be made about sexual scripts. The script must freeze meaning to analyze it, but meanwhile the touching bodies have moved on. Paying attention to the specificity of bodies in male-for-male sexual encounters illuminates the ways that erotic relations prove irreducible to procreative, monogamous, heterosexual conventions. To understand how discourses of sexuality operate in the encounter, sociologists must be attuned to what people do with their bodies. While Dowsett's (1996) call for active bodies to be present in scholarship remains crucial, in later chapters I also explore the extent to which sociologists can assume that homoerotic bodies always share commonalities. Plus, male-for-male Internet escorting is not all about men indulging in the ambiguous pleasures of bodies coming together; power also operates in these encounters.

Problems of Power

There is a convergence between Foucault's notion of power as the ability to produce an effect and interactionist accounts of power. Power flows in actual situations and shapes the course of ongoing interaction. Power does not stand outside of any set of relations but circulates through them (Foucault 1983:220). Nonetheless, it may seem strange to discuss Foucault alongside interactionists because Foucault's method and writings seem to efface the human subject.

Given their interest in bodies and ongoing sets of relations, interactionists are best situated to study power as it operates in the everyday lives of people. Yet many scholars harbor myths about interactionist thought. These myths must be dispelled if interactionism is to be put into productive conversation with Foucault. According to Robert Prus (1999), the first myth about interactionism is that it concerns only the subjective realm. To the contrary, interactionists do not theorize the self as disconnected from others; indeed, they start from the premise that people are interconnected in particular settings. Another myth is that interactionists are only interested in "micro" sociology. To the contrary, interactionists believe we can only understand social organization by comprehending how it is generated from interactional sequences.

To analyze power (which Prus [1999] defines as the ability to shape or define a situation) according to an interactionist approach, sociologists must focus on the way people define situations and how these definitions shape the course of interaction. People usurp the agency of others in these sequences of interaction, but these attempts at usurpation can be diverted. In sexual encounters, the ability to define certain bodies or certain actions as allowable or pleasurable evinces power at play. The trouble here is the fallback to a voluntary subject or a "tactician" approach to negotiating power in particular contexts. Prus suggests that people in interactions are tacticians who attempt to work toward their own advantage or the advantage of their allies, referring to such engagement as "influence work" (p. 169). Such "influence work" defines the situation such that this definition compels others to see the situation the same way. Part of the work comprises scripting in order to develop legitimacy as a person others should follow in defining the situation. Prus arguably falls into the same trap he wants to avoid: he reduces meaning-making to the tactical decisions and bargaining ability of one participant.[12] This is not to deny that there is a tactical element to power at the level of interactionism, but, given the open tendency, strategy and tactics do not secure predictable futures.

This notion of strategy in interaction leads back to Foucault's discussion of power, sex, and sexuality. Butler (1990) critiques Foucault for pursuing an emancipatory discourse in his writing about Herculine Barbin, the nineteenth-century French hermaphrodite. Herculine was assigned the sex of female at birth, but in her early twenties was compelled to change her sex to male after confessions to doctors and priests. Herculine is uncategorizable within the heterosexual gender binary, which divides people into male and female. Foucault (1978b) connects Herculine's transgressive pleasures to female sexuality, which constitutes sex categorization. For Butler, Herculine's sexuality does not exist in an unregulated field of pleasures full of transgression; rather, the limits of Foucault's thoughts on the happy limbo of nonidentity end when Herculine faces scorn.

Foucault's treatment of Herculine opens the door to ambiguity concerning power and the body. In this formulation, power seems neither possessive nor possessed. Butler (2004b) argues that this ambiguity concerning power and the body results from Foucault's attempt to use a vocabulary that is neither structuralist nor voluntarist. Deleuze (1998:96) also points to this ambiguity: "if at the end of it Foucault finds himself in an impasse, this is not because of his conception of power but rather because he found the impasse to be where power itself places us, in both our lives and our thoughts, as we run up against it in our smaller truths."[13]

Following the Logic of the Lure

I contend that the encounter itself produces unanticipated parameters that shape the capability of people to exert influence and to define the situation. My aim here is to move beyond voluntarist claims concerning sex and sexuality by pointing to the importance of the encounter rather than questions of subjectivity, identity, or any individual sense of self. Plainly, the sociology of sexuality must start with what people do together. Yet sociologists also need a way to theorize elements of the encounter that are unpredictable and aleatory.

Itinerant commercial sex among men who have sex with men is common, especially in global cities such as New York, London, and Toronto.[14] I am not simply claiming that men who have sex with men are promiscuous; indeed, such a claim would be essentializing. As Patrick O'Byrne and colleagues (2008) indicate, the sociology of sexuality needs to undermine the promiscuity paradigm that has framed the way scholars characterize men who have sex with men. J. P. Ricco (2002) suggests that analysis should start instead with what he calls "the logic of the lure," urging scholars not to analyze individuals' desire but rather to follow the plot of anonymous sex. The logic of the lure refers not to frequent sex with new partners but to how such encounters are sought and carried out. Male-for-male Internet escorting encounters often follow this itinerant and anonymous logic of the lure. Sexual encounters between men in public are repeatedly unexpected, involving a relational logic that is indeterminate.[15]

The logic of the lure that Ricco (2005) underscores is an erotic relationality that does not start from the presumed ontological stability of identity but instead considers possible relations between bodies. Lauren Berlant (2009) has similarly called for queer theorists to stop thinking of men who have sex with men as a distinct subculture and instead focus on the diversity of sex practices. Sexual encounters are full of uncertainty and improvisation. Itinerant encounters and the fleeting nonidentity that follows are not "radical" in the sense that through them some broad change could be achieved. Nevertheless, encounters can provide creative openings in sexual categories.

Ricco writes that the logic of the lure we might call "queer" has three elements: first, becoming imperceptible; second, anonymous sociality; and third, itinerant encountering. Homoeroticism is always a relational encounter, involving selves that are open to others; it is never based simply on some fixed identity (Ricco refers to examples such as cruising). Tim Dean (2009) likewise differentiates between public sex in cruising locales, which is based on an ethic of openness to others, and Internet-based cruising, which eliminates the public element. Dean criticizes Internet-based cruising, which he suggests is a way of avoiding, rather than fostering, contact with strangers: "Cruising online makes finding a sex partner indistinguishable from Internet shopping—except that the sex partner arrives at your home address sooner and returns appear easier" (p. 194). Chris Ashford (2006) explores how the Internet contributes to a standardization of sex among men. And Donald Morton (1995) questions the "cyberqueer" who is all too willing to participate in capitalist production and consumption as long as the fun remains continuous and readily available.

I share these critiques of the reduction of cruising space to cruising on-line and of the promotion of gay and lesbian marriage in place of cruising. But I also think Ricco's (2002) focus on the itinerant and the anonymous can be extended to male-for-male commercial sex. Indeed, sometimes the same ethic of openness to others and strangeness that forms part of cruis-ing emerges in the encounter between client and escort.

This focus on coming together otherwise has implications for how we think about men's bodies, which we are used to imagining as secure corpo-real containers. Sociologists lack a solid description of male corporeality and the sexual specificity of men's bodies coming together, as well as the sorts of relations and practices that touching can make possible. What sorts of relations and practices can be generated by men's bodies coming together? It is exactly this coming together otherwise that Foucault (1997a:135) has in mind when he asks how to "use one's sexuality henceforth to arrive at a multiplicity of relationships." For Elizabeth Stephens (2004), every act of touching between men queers the boundary between so-called normal and pathological masculinity.[16] The queer male body generates and receives a flow of bodily fluids; it generates and receives a different order of pleasure, which disinvests men from heterosexual masculinity.

Itinerant encounters allow bodies to be in play in ways that challenge our understandings of how men come together—what Stephens (1999) refers to as "homoerotic possibility." She argues, "the penis, and specifically the ejaculating penis, *convulses masculinity*, confounds not only the limits of the body but the self, which swoons, spasms, loses itself" (p. 6, italics added). This loss is the loss of identity in the moment of coming together with others, the fuzzy imbrication of two figures. Convulsing masculinity suggests that the materiality of itinerant sex itself can undo sexual and gender identities through touching encounters between men.

Discussion

The following is a summary of the central claims of this chapter:

- According to Foucault, there are two tendencies in an encounter: a closed tendency and an open tendency. The closed tendency leans toward deployment of and adherence to discourses of sexuality. The open tendency leans toward unanticipated relations and friendship.

- According to interactionist sociology, there are two tendencies in an encounter: one that is closing and one that is opening. The two tendencies start with Mead's comments on the "me" and the "I." Goffman accounts for this closing tendency in his comments on roles and rituals. Blumer accounts for this opening tendency in his writings on meaning-making in action.
- Encounters are corporeal. Encounters involve bodies coming together and touching.
- Encounters involve power. Power, the ability to produce an effect and define a situation, emerges in the interaction between participants.
- Encounters may be itinerant. Those engaging in encounters do not necessarily need to be known by one another in any official, formal, or memorable way.

I began this chapter with the idea of bringing together Foucault and Goffman. My sense is that in fact Foucault should be brought together with diverse interactionist theorists—not only Goffman since he focuses principally on roles and rituals. Previous attempts to distil Foucault's comments regarding discourse and sexuality have not brought Foucault down to the level of the encounter. Despite Foucault's usefulness for understanding encounters, his work must be helped along when it comes to theorizing homoerotic bodies. Supplemented by other theorists of sexuality and interaction, Foucault can help us make sense of our most touching encounters.

Chapter 4 | A Note on Method and Storied Encounters

The Research Project

I have interviewed male-for-male Internet escorts in numerous cities in order to understand how these men organize their work and make sense of their interactions with clients. This chapter offers some descriptive details about the interviews I conducted, as well as the escorts themselves. At the back of the book, I include a postscript on methodology where I discuss issues of narrative and biography to justify how I have analyzed these men's words.

Four of the Internet escorts I interviewed were based in Ottawa, four more lived in Montréal, 13 lived in Toronto, one lived in Houston but traveled to Toronto and New York City for work, four lived in New York City, and four lived in London. One escort had moved from London to Toronto just prior to our meeting. I selected these cities because escorts often travel between them for work. (Nearly half of the escorts I spoke with had traveled to at least one other city for work.) The average age of these escorts was 34, with the youngest being 20 and the oldest being 64. All of the escorts advertised on websites dedicated to male-for-male Internet escorting, which is where I initially contacted them. These websites allow users to create a commercial profile, which potential clients consult. The profiles are searchable based on city location, escorts' features (e.g., ethnicity, penis size), and price (for more descriptive accounts of such websites, see Logan 2010; Lee-Gonyea et al. 2009). Of the men I interviewed, the average age posted on the website was 29 and the average time they had been working as escorts was 6.5 years: one escort had been in the trade for under a year, and four had been doing this work for a decade or more. Two of the escorts self-identified as black, four others as Latino, one as Lebanese, and the remaining 23 as white.

Only two of the escorts I interviewed began in the sex trade via street-level prostitution. A few had worked for brief stints with escorting agencies and massage parlors but left because they felt that Internet escorting provided more income and less management control. Two of the escorts had worked in the porn industry (films and magazines) and as models. For many men, escorting was not their only form of work: 20 of the 30 men worked other jobs. Their second jobs ranged from artist, counselor, store manager, model, and actor to psychologist and technology specialist. Of the 30 men, 23 reported being enrolled in or having completed college or university. A few had master's degrees and doctorates. Five of the escorts were enrolled in college at the time of our interview.

In my communications with escorts, I used the same scripted email in every initial message. This script provided information about my role as a sociologist and the aims of the research project. If I received a response, the second scripted communication I sent shared more information about the project. Male Internet escorts often receive emails from men who use such communication as a ruse in order to provide a context in which to pleasure themselves. Escorts refer to these individuals as "time wasters" or, as a sex worker in O'Connell Davidson's (1995) research termed them, "wank calls." All the escorts who responded to the more detailed note I sent then engaged in a series of email exchanges, sometimes 30 or 40 emails, to ensure I was not a time waster or a police officer.

Matt Pruitt (2008) considers it unlikely that escorts would respond to an email from a self-identified sociologist, finding lower response rates when he contacted escorts in this way compared with when he used deception as a recruitment strategy. I was unwilling to use deception to recruit, however, since my goal was not to have escorts complete a survey but to speak with me at length and in person. Pruitt also comments that using a first and last name in the title of the email leads to lower response rates. Nevertheless, I chose to use my full name because I did not want escorts to mistake me for a client. In addition to contacting escorts on their websites, I placed advertisements in queer-friendly publications. Only one interview was secured this way. I had an unshared phone extension at a university in Ottawa during the research so that I could assure those who called of their confidentiality and anonymity.

I emailed 550 escorts on three different sites (Canadianmale.com, boys2-rent.com, men4rentnow.com) and received 56 responses, which resulted in

Table 1. The Sample

Interview #:	City	Age	Start Age	Web Age	Years of work	Education	Other Work	Racialized Status	Pseudonym
1	OTT	44	32	37	12	-	-	black	Sam
2	OTT	39	25	-	-	college	-	white	Leon
3	OTT	34	24	27	10 (end)	college	-	white	Tyler
4	MON	22	19	-	3	university	-	white	Etienne
5	MON	30	25	28	5	university	artist	white	Claude
6	OTT	30	26	25	4	college	-	white	Bob
7	TOR	30	-	-	-	-	counseling	white	Bruce
8	TOR	39	26	33	13	college	store manager	white	Ricky
9	TOR	23	-	-	-	-	-	white	Gabe
10	TOR	42	-	31	-	college	film maker	white	Conrad
11	TOR	29	19	-	10	-	-	white	Eddy
12	TOR	33	-	-	(end)	university	psychologist	white	Steve
13	TOR	21	-	-	-	-	cafe manager	white	Ryan
14	HOU	24	22	-	2.5	university	tutor	Latino	Byron
15	NYC	24	18	21	6	college	model	black	Mike
16	NYC	44	27	-	17	college	clothing designer	Latino	Roberto
17	NYC	50	46	40	4	college	-	white	Donald
18	NYC	40	39	-	1	college, BSE, BEE	technology sector	white	Jeff
19	MON	33	31	23	2	-	-	white	Chris
20	LON	35	32	29	2.5	university	film maker	Latino	Ben
21	LON	36	32	34	4	-	personal trainer	white	Mark
22	LON	31	29	-	2	college	-	white	Jake
23	LON	56	46	48	10	college	porn, stage acting	white	Oscar
24	TOR	64	42	-	22	university	freelance journalist	white	Gerald
25	MON	36	33	34	3	college	accounting	white	Harvey
26	TOR	20	19	20	1.5	university	call center	Lebanese	Frank
27	TOR/LON	43	27	33	16	college	service economy	white	Garry
28	TOR	33	29	29	1/3	university	electrical engineer	Latino	Frederico
29	TOR	25	23	22	2	college	service economy	white	Sean
30	TOR	22	16	20	6	university	service economy	white	Josh
Average		34.4	28.3	29	6.5				

Note. 77% of the sample is in college or university. OTT = Ottawa; MON = Montreal; TOR = Toronto; NYC = New York City; HOU = Houston; LON = London.

30 interviews in total. Some escorts asked for remuneration that I could not afford to provide. One escort wrote back, "I will chat with you, for £900," while several others said they would chat with me for their hourly rate. Another escort in New York asked for $100 an hour. Initially I offered $50 remuneration for the entire interview, but eventually had to scale down to $35, for lack of funds. It is possible that only escorts interested in remuneration responded to my messages. But there was only one interview during which I sensed the respondent was there to take the money and run; not surprisingly his was the shortest interview (37 minutes). Most interviews lasted 80 minutes or longer as people generally love talking about their work. It is possible that I might have connected only with the more "active" escorts who are frequently online. John Oliffe and Larry Mróz (2005) claim that men need to be more actively recruited to research projects, and I may not have been assertive enough in my recruitment. Another limitation is that I am missing a complete data set as it concerns self-reporting on education and age.

Once we had exchanged enough emails to assure the escort that I was not wasting his time, we made arrangements to meet. Taking the first minutes to introduce myself as a sociologist studying sex work and to assure respondents that I would maintain their confidentiality and anonymity, I interviewed many men in coffee shops, where the background noise helped create a sense of such anonymity and confidentiality. I interviewed some escorts outside at bus stops and on park benches because they felt that these locations offered anonymity and confidentiality. I also interviewed four of the escorts in their homes, since this location was more convenient for their schedules or, again, offered sought-after anonymity and confidentiality. All interviews were conducted in person, except for the interview with the escort from Houston. A face-to-face interview encounter is more complex than a telephone chat as gestures may strongly influence what is verbally communicated.[1] All interviews were taped and transcribed. In this book, the names of the escorts and certain details that could be used to identify them have been altered to protect their anonymity.

The questions I asked in interviews were generated by broader empirical questions I set out to address. As I mentioned earlier, literature in the sociology of sex work has not fully examined how the labor process of male-for-male escorting has recently changed, nor has it investigated how the labor process of male-for-male Internet escorting differs from that of other sex work. I address these empirical questions concerning the sexual entrepreneurialism of escorts in chapter 6. In an earlier chapter, I also critiqued sociological understandings of sex that overemphasize interaction scripts, presenting a discussion of Foucault and interactionist sociology to conceptualize the way sexual encounters are socially ordered as well as the way encounters provide moments of emergence when sexual scripts mutate and are undone. I address this empirical question concerning the two tendencies of sexual encounters in chapters 5 and 7. As I explored in chapter 2, gay and lesbian studies tend to reduce sexualities to particular fixed identities. Although queer theory purposefully addresses questions of fluidity and identity, it places little emphasis on aging and sexualities. In this book, I try to make sense of how age-graded sexualities influence the work of male-for-male Internet escorting, addressing this broad empirical question about aging and sexualities in chapter 8. In chapter 3, I argued that the sociology of sexuality should explore how bodies come together in sexual encounters and how discourses of sexuality are translated through touch. This empirical question is investigated in chapter 9 through my analysis of escort narratives about body work and body trouble. I provide more information on interview techniques, as well as how I made sense of the interview transcripts, in the postscript.

A Note on the Sample

I have never done drugs. I have rarely smoked pot. I drink occasionally. But I do not do drugs with clients. I know guys who party with clients, they will do powder off the table. I just do not think it is a good idea. You want to see them quickly, get them to talk, get as much money as possible. It is more exciting for some of them that I am clean, because they cannot believe the way that I treat them. They want me to come back, they are getting better quality for what they pay. You get repeat clients if you are clean. (Byron, Houston)

One issue that has shaped this research project and the story I can tell about the work of these men is their socioeconomic position relative to other men involved in commercial sex. A majority of these men enjoyed success in postsecondary education, and several of them worked other well-paying jobs. The socioeconomic position of these men shapes the kinds of claims I can make about their relations with clients and their work. In chapter 6, for instance, I discuss the role of the Internet in labor process as well as these escorts' sexual entrepreneurialism—issues that do not arise in on-street sex work. In chapter 7's discussion of intimacy, I describe how some of these men's encounters with clients involve elements of friendship. And in the excursus on stigma, I show the lack of "bad stories" about violence, poverty, or drug use among these men. Reasons for this lack may include the socioeconomic position of this sample of escorts and the average age of these escorts, which is higher than other samples of male escorts.[2] Many of these men report it as their "choice" to enter escorting; the other side of the story, working without choice, is not my focus here.

The claims I make in this study would differ if I had greater representation from poorer strata of male-for-male Internet escorts or a mixed sample of male-for-male Internet escorts and on-street workers. Yet it is precisely the selectness of this sample that makes *Touching Encounters* a unique story—one that has not received much space in the sociology of sex work, perhaps because criminological and public health research tends to focus primarily on female sex work and on-street sex work. Despite this latter focus, there has recently been a welcome shift in the sociology of sex work to focus on erotic dancers, agency-based workers, and other sectors of the commercial sex industry.[3] I hope that the story I contribute in *Touching Encounters* enriches the sociology of sex work in a similar way.

Storied Encounters: Talking about the Self after Coming Together with Others

My approach to research methods emphasizes what is produced out of encounters. From preinterview communication, to the interview, to postinterview correspondence, to production and analysis of transcripts, to writing, editing, and speaking about the research process: all research is grounded in relational encounters. But interview- and narrative-based research only allows readers and researchers to access a storied version of the encounter. And so I want to add one final proposition to my conceptualization of the encounter: The encounter affects the stories that we can tell about our relations. We do not forget what our bodies have done, even in itinerant and anonymous encounters. Even a meandering interaction can prove formative for the stories people tell about their relations. People's elaboration of past encounters requires interpretation, and interpretation is fundamental to storytelling insofar as it is the communicative link between past and future. Earlier I suggested that emphasizing corporeality in the sociology of sexuality is one tactic for unraveling the masculine subject that sociology has privileged for so long. But this emphasis leads to the question of what social scientists can really know about corporeality, given the limits of qualitative research, especially interview-based research. I argue that while the touching encounter exists in interaction, the storied encounter elaborates on this interaction.

Ken Plummer's (1995) work on sexual stories anticipates this argument. According to Plummer, sexual stories are produced in "social contexts by embodied concrete people experiencing the thoughts and feelings of everyday life" (p. 16). "Coming out" and HIV/AIDS stories, for instance, are only possible to tell at particular historical moments. As Plummer notes, "the notion of gay identity only becomes a possibility once there has been a breakdown in traditional notions of the self. In the past, the possibility to choose to possess a gay identity simply did not exist" (p. 93). Sexual stories can also try to make sense of how sex intersects with work.[4]

My purpose in this book is to draw from the narratives that escorts share about their encounters with clients to undo conventionally held ideas concerning the sex and the work of sex work. In sharing these narratives, I underscore the ways that biography, touch, and escorting are interwoven in queer ways. The sex of escorts' work is partly the sex of their everyday lives. Biography cannot be separated from sex work; sex and work do not have to be held apart because there is often no "private" sex life to go home to. Encounters with clients thus become part of the life histories of these men. But I am also suggesting that there remain limits to knowing about touching encounters through interviews and narrative research. As Andrea Doucet (2006:63) puts it, "certain projects and certain sites of research do not lend themselves to knowing subjects but rather to *knowing only their narratives*" (italics in original). Narrative only allows access to a storied version of the touching encounter. In this sense, the storied encounter deals with the touching encounter in a narrativized form. I elaborate on these issues in the postscript.

Five Lives

The purpose of this excursus is to challenge stereotypical understandings of men who sell sex. For instance, Marlowe (1997) suggests male sex work is different from female sex work primarily because "many gay men have learned not only to accept but also take pride in sexual deviance" (p. 141). Marlowe also writes that "boys who engage in casual sex are considered to have a normal and healthy sex drive" (p. 142). That is, they are not stigmatized but envied. Marlowe believes that male sex workers cash in on and exploit older and less attractive male clients.

Such assessments of men who have sex with men and men who sell sex are limited. The life history narratives of male-for-male Internet escorts are often varied and suggest their diverse reasons for getting involved in sex work.[1] Below I offer life history vignettes for five of the respondents, each from a different city. These sexual stories often focus only peripherally on sex. What is more, the biographies of the men I interviewed are interwoven with sex and work in queer ways, their sense of self often emerging only after coming together with others.

Etienne

I met Etienne at a coffee shop north of the gay village in Montréal. He insisted we meet at a coffee shop known as a community-organizing center. I quickly learned from talking to Etienne that his escorting work is connected to his life as an activist, or, put differently, that his life as an activist and his life as an escort emerged at the same time. Aged 22, he was one of the younger escorts I spoke with. Here is Etienne from Montréal sharing a narrative about starting out in escorting:

It's been three years now. I started when I was 19. I started because there was a student strike in 2005 and I lost my apartment; I lost everything for participation in the strike. There I met gay anarchists in the strike who were doing sex work

and were living by it. For the first time we discussed work, it was the first time I
was thinking about what I want to do. I also had my first jobs being paid minimum
wage and having to work 30 hours a week just to pay my rent . . . . I decided to let
up school after the strike. I would have been stuck at this point, like I would not
be able to get better jobs because I did not want to go at first to school. It was a
way to make money and not work that much. Having work that was full of human
relationships, you're producing something but it's a relation, so it's different. I was
good for it. The first time I did it I did not place an ad or go on the street, but I did
a massage for a guy once and he proposed to pay me for it as work. And he called
me back the week after proposing another massage. I said, "OK" and it became like
a treat, and I discovered I like to do it and it was not hard and it was not a big deal.

Etienne and I chatted for hours about anarchism and about sexuality, the politics of sex, and the meaning of work. He took the politics of his work seriously. He is a member of the Pink Panthers, an anarchist group concerned with sexuality. About the Pink Panthers, Etienne says:

Basically it's to get sex work recognized as work, not that much to have the state
interfere with what we are doing between our clients and ourselves but just to not
criminalize, offer social services so HIV won't get everywhere. It's not that contra-
dictory to work, like I'm living on the fact that sexuality is made a commodity as
any other. But at the same time I don't think it is sex work that is not good, I think
it is work. As long as I have to work to live, I prefer sex work to anything else. And
with the Pink Panthers it's more than that. We're doing movies; we're doing some
demonstrations. We confronted [the Canadian Prime Minister] Harper when he
came to Montréal. Queer radicals and people who have social critique must have
reflection on sexuality together.

Etienne's entry into massage work and escorting was accompanied by a swerve in his life. After leaving school, he came to live communally among other activists; activism informed his thoughts about work, which informed his work practices and the way he tried to establish relationships with clients. He wanted clients to be aware of what they wanted and what was possible for him to provide because he did not want to exploit them. As he says, "my work is to make slavery a fun experience by sexualizing alienation." He did not want to live in Montréal's gay village because he found it pretentious and geared toward stereotypical body images. Of all the escorts I spoke with, Etienne offered the strongest critique of capitalism even as he forwarded a no-tion of the collective laborer and a sense of solidarity with other sex workers across gender boundaries and class.

Bob

Escorts have diverse experiences of starting out with this work. I met Bob from Ottawa in a coffee shop. I remember riding my bike way east of downtown; it was a long ride. Bob was late and I was waiting around, hoping I was not getting stood up. He arrived. We quickly went to a different location for the interview because he recognized someone inside the shop. Compared with Etienne's, Bob's first years of sex work were quite different:

I started about four years ago. It was with the drug trade actually at first and it went from there along, you know, someone I knew was doing it connected me with a few people and taught me about going here and going there. And so I went for a couple of years like that and I was burned right out and couldn't keep going. I sobered up and kept it. I left for six months and then considered running it as a business you know much more stable and more like an escort service rather than just cruising around. And it's really taken off. I've done quite well since I started like that so I can't complain.

As Bob put it, his start with sex work had him "homeless on the street, wrecked on dope, selling my ass, and there was no help." The vocabulary Bob used to describe what he does now was more entrepreneurial than in Etienne's narrative. Bob works in Ottawa, which, according to escorts, is more closeted than other cities such as Montréal. Ottawa is a persnickety city compared to the sexy, seedy Montréal: this difference is how escorts narrate their sense of place in Ottawa. Ottawa is also a government town, and many of Bob's clients are military officials, bureaucrats, lawyers, government employees, and executives from abroad. Bob went from having some run-ins with police over drugs to being a traveling, professional escort who is paid to snuggle and sleep with Ottawa's elite. Because he also meets many clients who are in Ottawa on official business, he has established a list of contacts the world over. These clients sometimes invite him to work the weekends in resorts or other destinations. Yet the result is not always fun in the sun:

A regular of mine, one of my first ones ever, a nice guy, he took me to Mexico with him, and he dropped dead of a heart attack on the beach while I was there. I didn't know what to do. His son was my age and I knew him outside of the whole thing and we got along so he came down and dealt with it all but thank God because I ended up like what do I do? What happens here? Am I stuck in Mexico? He's got all the tickets and everything. It actually worked out and his son knew everything too so it wasn't a hidden thing so it got dealt with but after that I was nervous about

doing trips with anybody anywhere. You could see the few weeks I had seen him
before, he was stressed out getting angrier and angrier and started working from
home rather than going into his office.

This narrative is significant for two reasons. First, it describes how interwoven the
lives of the escort and the client are, providing a significantly different picture than
the stereotypical image of the sex worker. Some sex work scholars conceptualize sex
workers as performing a detached customer service, as having no connection to the
client, and as severing their private life from their work life. Here, Bob demonstrates a
concern for the client's life, which came to an unfortunate end during an extended sex
work session out of country. This leads to a second point: Bob's biography is linked to
escorting. These men cannot simply block out what happens at work; the public life
of their working self cannot be bracketed off from the so-called private self, which
means that the division between public and private self that some sex work scholars
focus on constitutes only part of the story.[2] Work is usually a place where attempts
are made to conceal sexuality; however, with male-for-male Internet escorting, the
"private" of the sexual and the "public" of work fold into one another.

Ricky

Ricky's narratives also demonstrate the imbrication of escorting with biography. Ricky
is a prominent figure in Toronto's Church Street gay village. Ricky also manages a
store supplying leather bondage gear, a job he is not sure how long he will maintain.
He has spent time volunteering for sex activist groups in Toronto as a safe-sex advocate. At age 39, Ricky was not the oldest escort in this study, but his 13 years in
the industry made him one of the longest-serving escorts I spoke with. Ricky worked
as an escort pre-Internet and post-Internet, so he has many stories to share about
changes in labor process inside and outside the sex industry. He also had considerable
work history beyond escorting to compare with escorting:

I was working a job that I hated, which has happened most of my adult life. I tend
to not fit into corporate type jobs. I've done them. I'm generally otherwise in retail
management. I've gone to college for it. I went to college later, like when I was
around 30. Even at a young age I would start off doing jobs in sales and retail and
that kind of stuff and I get bored easily and also I'm not good for corporate struc-
ture. I like the money that they offer but I can't follow the rules, I find a lot of cor-
porate jobs waste a lot of time doing stupid things that don't help selling at all. So
I left the job that was my first job ever, downtown Toronto. And I was working for
a sex shop and at that time I started seeing a man named Nic. . . . You may come
across him because he's a big name in prostitution and prostitutes' rights. He was

a big activist. He's passed away since . . . while I was seeing him. He did it all his life. He did porn as well. He didn't get me into it at all. I didn't tell him I wanted to start doing it. I joined an escort agency without him even knowing it. Just to get an income going, and obviously he said, "Why didn't you ask me? I would have helped you get into it more easily" and then did it for a couple of years, at that time I was 23. Then I got a job again because I got bored of that because back then it was all done by phone and cell phones were not around, it involved sitting at home all day waiting for calls. Most of the calls were time wasters.

For Ricky, the time spent on the computer or on the phone arranging the encounter with the client can be as boring as any other work. In contrast, the touching encounter itself is something Ricky enjoys. He treats these touching encounters as an extension of his sex life. As his narratives suggest, there is fluidity between his work sex life and his so-called private sex life. Though his sex life and his work life overlap, there can be difficulties in achieving relationships with other men:

Do they want a boyfriend who's an escort? I'm loosely dating a man right now, we've become good friends, we have good fun sex. We like each other a lot. He's attractive, he's intelligent. He's making about 100K a year. I have a job now, but when he met me I was an escort and I'm worried is he going to use me for a while for sex and have a good time, which isn't a bad thing, then say, "Yeah, I can't date a man like this." So I have to worry about that. Is it possible to be able to fall in love with me with my career choice right now or not? So that is a big deterrent for wanting to be honest about what I do with someone in my life.

Ricky's story raises a common issue among male-for-male Internet escorts: keeping secrets. Secrets need to be kept to ensure the anonymity of clients, but also, as Ricky's narrative points out, to manage who knows what about him in Toronto's gay village. During our interview at a pub on Church Street, many people waved to Ricky and asked him what he was up to. Our chat went on for over three hours not only because of these interludes but because Ricky liked talking about his sexual encounters. The interview encounter can provide a confessional opportunity. Being notorious and popular in downtown Toronto feels good, but, as Ricky's narrative indicates, being known can also hinder him from establishing relationships beyond escorting.

Roberto

Living in downtown Manhattan is expensive. Roberto has spent a lot of time going from job to job, not out of boredom but from economic necessity. His family still resides in Brazil and he sometimes sends money back to support them. His mother knows what he does to earn the money. We spoke in Roberto's Manhattan apartment. It was a mess because he was painting, so we sat on a couch covered by drop sheets. The way Roberto talks about his escorting being "on and off" reflects a consistency among male-for-male Internet escorts, who often work as escorts in conjunction with other jobs. Some men leave escorting and take on full-time work. But they usually come back:

I'm 44 now and I started when I was 27, but it's been on and off. I stopped it and I went back and sometimes I would be doing this part time and doing something else. I've always been legal here. I arrived in '86 and by '88 I already had a work permit, so I worked, I used to work in restaurants. It was hard work, but even back then people used to look at me and they thought I was already escorting. I guess because you're Brazilian, young and good looking so they assumed that I was doing it. And I thought, when I was younger I thought it was flattering because I never saw myself like that. And I actually thought, "hey he thinks I can do that." But little did I know. I worked really hard and eventually I was working the Upper East Side, this Greek restaurant making good money and some drama happened and the owners were jerks and they stiffed me my tips, and I lost my job. So I collected unemployment and I went to look for work but when I went to look for work they were very strict. I started getting facial hair and they don't want that. They wanted clean cut. A friend of mine said to me, "Why don't you try hustling, you know you can make money?" I knew guys that did it, and as much as I made good money in restaurants it's not the same amount of money. At the same time I met my lover. Actually I had already met him for about three months when this guy told me that. So I started, I tried and I said to my lover, listen, because my lover was American. He owned his apartment, he was vice-president of a company and his life was set. And I was like, I don't know if this is going to work but if it works that's what it's going to be. You've got your life and I have to get my life. I need money. So it worked out. And I was with him for five years so I wasn't doing as much but I was doing that pretty much full time, but I wouldn't do it when I was with him. After we broke up, then I went to college. That's what I was doing because I needed the money to go to college. Then when I got out of college in 2001, I continued doing it and started graphic design. It's been on and off.

As with other male-for-male Internet escorts, a boyfriend lingers in the background. This presence of a relationship does not mean, however, that sex with the boyfriend becomes "real" sex and the sex at work becomes feigned. Not all of these men make a distinction between their "private" sex lives and sex they have at work. Roberto suggests that escorting was his way out of the cycle of hardship that came with working on the lower rungs of Manhattan's restaurant circuit. He put himself through college but still works as an escort and says he will do it until his company gets off of the ground.

Jake

When I spoke with him Jake was living in London, but he grew up in Scotland. He had been having sexual encounters with men for several years, mostly in parks and public washrooms. Itinerant sex can involve ambiguity and excitement, but park sex can also be terrifying because the police are keen to make arrests. The sexual encounters of male-for-male Internet escorts are also itinerant: they do not always follow pervasive sexual scripts. Jake's story about entering escorting evinces the itinerant and unpredictable character of male-with-male sex. When Jake talks about "doing it for cash," he means that escorting is in many ways an extension of the kinds of sexual encounters he was previously engaged in, those marked by anonymity and itinerant meetings:

The very first time I had slept with a bloke, it just kinda happened by chance, the first or second bloke I had met, someone I had already slept with beforehand, no money involved, but the second time around he wanted a bit of work done, he wanted his flat painted. The one time I had met him before was to do master-slave domination, corporal punishment, I was suggesting that he pay me, so it became more, there was a weekend of role play and he paid me for that, the corporal punishment. Not sure if that was the first time it was for cash, but the second time it was a guy I had slept with before and we were trying to meet up again and we were not able to, and then he suggested that he pay me for it so that we could both get what we wanted, because by that point on my profile online it said that I would be interested to do it for cash, so we met up again, master domination, him being in the more dominant role, so it was the stuff we had done before, the last time we had met, but then he paid me after. Those were the first two times. Then I did not really do it. I wanted to, but I was sleeping on a friend's couch. I had accommodations before, but that came to an end, and I still wanted to stay in London, so I crashed on his couch for a couple months. It was difficult, it was not a stable set up. I did not pursue it completely and I did not have access to a computer, I only had online access in an Internet café, so I was not online often, so it was not stable enough and there was not enough opportunity. I had an office job for a couple months, I was doing the medical experiments, and then I said I wanted to try it again, so I set up the profile online and I guess the first proper work would be then, a bloke I met online who said he was looking for a massage, said he would pay for it, and it went on from there. That was the first time after I set up. That was the first proper one. The other two times, it was more opportunistic.

Jake now lives with his partner, who is fully aware of and supports his work. Jake's lack of stability at that point in his life course made it tough for him to do the work regularly. Not having access to the Internet made it difficult to arrange encounters, although living in London provided Jake with a market for his interest in bondage activities.

In this excursus, I have introduced a few of the work and sex lives of escorts who shared their stories with me. All of the escorts have diverse stories about how they entered the work. The male-for-male Internet escorts I spoke with offered strikingly different life history narratives compared with one another but also compared with the kinds of stories that people in other sectors of the sex industry offer. I've also argued that encounters shape our understandings of others as well as the stories we tell about our relations. Biography and escorting are interwoven in queer ways, insofar as escorts approach the sex they have at work as part of their overall sex life. It is important to allow these narratives their own space because otherwise they become lost in the analysis of substantive topics such as interaction, work, sex, aging, and corporeality—topics that the following chapters take up.

Chapter 5 | Interviews as Encounters

Sexuality, Reflexivity, and Men Interviewing Men about Commercial Same-Sex Relations

The Line between Escort-Client and Escort-Researcher

The encounter between the Internet escort and client parallels the encounter between escort and researcher. Clients contact the escort by email after consulting the escort's website; I also contacted the escorts by email. The escort and client exchange a few emails to make sure the client is not a police officer, and then they swap details about where and when to meet; likewise for the escort and researcher. As with the encounter between escort and client, the beginnings of my encounters with escorts consisted of questions and confessions. The escort and client spend an hour or longer interpreting each other's words and gestures, figuring out what to say and do next; similarly, the escort and researcher spend time interpreting one another and assessing one another's moves. The client hands over money to the escort for the time spent. I handed over remuneration for the interview. Following both encounters, an email comprised of kind greetings might be sent.

Key differences exist between these encounters, of course. The client's initial email concerns what sexual services are available, whereas I initially sent messages to see if escorts would talk with me about their work. The client wants his anonymity guaranteed, whereas my job is to secure the anonymity and confidentiality of respondents. The client and escort often meet in a bedroom, whereas my meetings with escorts almost always took place in cafes. The client and escort engage in sex, or maybe they snuggle, eat pizza, and watch a movie, whereas the escort and I engage in a focused dialogue concerning his past work experiences. The client tells the escort in a message the next day, "you were fantastic," whereas I am keen to know if the escort recalls any other stories.

In this chapter, I consider the epistemological issues that arise in interview encounters between men when sex and sexuality are being discussed. Because both researcher and respondent have the capacity to shape the encounter, interviews are performative collaborations.[1] Both respondent and researcher try to make sense of what is being said and done in order to conjure up the next thing they will say and do. In what follows, I analyze moments when, as the researcher, I was sexualized by respondents, focusing on how my verbal and bodily responses to such moments of sexualization shaped and modified the meanings produced through the research encounter. I draw from the work of Goffman (1961) and Blumer (1969) to theorize interviews as encounters and to conceptualize these instances of sexualization as moments of emergence that shape the interview's outcome. Goffman and Blumer help account for any encounter's dual tendencies: on the one hand, the tendency toward following scripts and falling back on set roles and, on the other hand, the tendency toward unanticipated consequences of interaction and spontaneous meaning-making.

When sex, sexuality, and other touchy subjects, such as intimacy and the body, comprise topics of an interview, issues of reflexivity arise and the researcher may become the object of sexualization. In her research with male clients of female sex workers, Sabine Grenz (2005), a female sociologist who conducted fieldwork in Germany, found that she was sexualized in her encounters with respondents, even in correspondence prior to the interview. I similarly found that many escorts related to me in a sexualized manner. And why not? After all, the interview is an itinerant coming together, not unlike escorts' encounters with clients. My analysis here focuses on how my responses to the words and gestures of escorts influenced the course of our interview and how, at times, I attempted to redefine the interaction as a research encounter when respondents wanted our meeting to become a touching encounter.

Anthropologists have written a great deal about the way sex and sexuality matter during fieldwork and during the interpretation of field notes.[2] They identify honesty about sex and sexuality as part of the reflexive turn in anthropology. Sociologists can learn from these debates, especially since there remains a tendency in sociology to neglect the fact that male researchers interviewing men are sexualized as well as sexualizing individuals. Erich Goode (2002) suggests that sociologists have remained largely silent about the sexual politics of research, writing hardly anything about men interviewing men about sex. Although Michael Schwalbe and Michelle Wolkomir (2002) have written about the specifics of men interviewing other men, they do not consider the issue of men interviewing men regarding same-sex relations or the diversity of men's sexualities. The first question that escorts often posed to me at the start of interviews was, "Are you gay?" The question seeks a singular identity declaration and overturns established researcher-respondent roles. The respondent's demand for the researcher's confession of sexuality shapes how the respondent bestows status upon the researcher as a sexuality insider and bears consequences for the dialogue that emerges. The respondent's reflexivity is thus as important as the researcher's reflexivity in shaping interviews.[3]

This chapter is organized in four parts. First, I compare Goffman's (1961) and Blumer's (1969) writings concerning the encounter to produce an interactionist conceptualization of interviewing, suggesting that the unanticipated elements of research encounters are as important as anything that is scripted. (Try telling this to an ethical review board!) I then emphasize respondents' reflexivity by analyzing both the propositions and moments of sexualization that occurred during my research. I conclude with a discussion of how understandings of sexuality are produced and contested in encounters, including research encounters.

Theorizing (Interview) Encounters

Researchers do not have complete control in the interview nor should they seek authority over respondents.[4] Posing as an authority can deter the respondent from providing lengthy stories. Establishing rapport in an interview is complicated, since one never knows how certain words or gestures might be interpreted and shape the ensuing dialogue. Given the possibility of unanticipated power shifts and identity play in the interview, how should we conceive of research encounters? I draw from Goffman's and Blumer's accounts to provide such a conceptualization.

In Goffman's (1961) notion of the encounter, there exist certain rules: "an encounter exhibits sanctioned orderliness arising from obligations fulfilled and expectations realized . . . therein lies its structure" (p. 19). For Goffman, there is a "boundary between the wider world and the mutual activity embedded in a focused gathering" (p. 33), though "the barrier to externally realized properties [is] more like a screen than like a solid wall." He believes that "the screen not only selects but also transforms and modifies what is passed through it." The screen is an interaction membrane: "If we think of an encounter as having a metaphorical membrane around it . . . the dynamics of an encounter will be tied to the functioning of the boundary-maintaining mechanisms that cut the encounter off selectively from wider worlds" (p. 66). Following Goffman, we may understand an encounter in terms of its interaction membrane, which sets it on a path. The tendency in Goffman's version of the encounter, therefore, is toward following scripts and falling back on set roles.

Goffman commonly comes to mind in discussions of encounters because he is touted as an interactionist. Yet Goffman was more indebted to Durkheim's ideas concerning rituals than to the so-called Chicago School in that Goffman's characters are not actual but ideal.[5] Sociologists have treated Goffman's studies as ethnographic when they were a step removed from ethnography. What Goffman does provide is an account of how our adherence to scripts and roles leads to the maintenance of everyday orderliness. For example, roles that frame the research encounter, such as researcher and respondent, are inescapable and constantly negotiated. Unlike interactionists, however, Goffman manifests little concern about how scripts and roles are undermined or change over time. His notion of an interaction membrane, which he grants independence beyond the encounter itself, is not entirely compatible with an interactionist emphasis on the productiveness and unpredictability of meaning-making. For Goffman, the interview encounter is rule-bound.

To account for what is unanticipated in encounters, we must look to Blumer. For Blumer (1969), meaning does not emanate from the intrinsic properties of an object, nor is it assembled out of individuals' psychological elements. Rather, meaning arises from interaction: "The meaning of a thing for a person grows out of the ways in which other persons act toward the person with regard to the thing" (p. 4). Interactions are not rule-bound, since "it is the social process in group life that creates and upholds the rules, not the rules that create and uphold group life" (p. 19). Blumer does not rely on some notion of rules or roles because he is not concerned with forecasting the outcome of the encounter. Individuals may hesitate, procrastinate, be more "me" or "I" oriented, resist and fail to fit into joint actions (Blumer 2004:97). Certainly there remain problems with Blumer's depiction of encounters. It is important to acknowledge that encounters are situated in particular cultural and material configurations; the subject is not voluntaristic. It is also important not to let Blumer's empiricism lead to qualitative realism.[6] Drawing from Blumer, however, we can emphasize that the respondent has a capability to shape the course of the interview, so that what exactly will be produced from the encounter is unanticipated.

Speech acts and conversations of gesture between researcher and respondent during encounters thus constitute examples of meaning-making in action.

What if we did away with understandings of research encounters that position the researcher as providing fixed rules for the game? Then we would valorize the respondent's reflexivity and be able to claim that reflexivity is part of the encounter's relationality. Indeed, the researcher does not possess predetermined power in the interview encounter—and the respondent certainly exercises reflexivity in his interactions. However much scripts and roles may guide our interactions, there nevertheless remains an open tendency to research encounters. We can never fully anticipate the meanings that will be forged during an encounter.

Propositions

During the interview, both the researcher and the respondent fashion a sense of self through talk and gestures, a sense of self that may be sexual and gendered. A different set of gender dynamics inhere when women interview men compared to when men interview men, and these gender dynamics are further complicated when we consider sexuality. How did the men I interviewed perform a sexual and gendered self during our encounter? How did I?

Much contemporary literature concerning gender and men takes for granted the idea of hegemonic masculinity. Hegemonic masculinity, defined as the valorized masculinity in any context, usually gets portrayed as competitive, individualistic, brawny, violent, and tied to heterosexuality.[7] Whereas men sometimes aggressively display masculinity when being interviewed by women, I did not experience such hostility in interviews with these men. Nor did I experience what could be construed as a masculinity contest. Schwalbe and Wolkomir (2002) argue that masculinity is both displayed and threatened by the interview process. From this perspective, hegemonic masculinity pervades all relations between men. Oliffe and Mróz (2005) likewise hold that men are stoic during interviews, unable to talk about emotions and intimacy because of threats to masculinity. But these authors do not focus on same-sex relations when men interview other men, so they end up assuming that relations between queer men involve a contest over hegemonic masculinity.

For Steve Garlick (2003:156), "research into men and masculinities has failed to seriously engage with some central insights of queer theory." One limitation of the masculinities literature is its failure to understand how the language of masculinities depends on a heteronormative sense of male sexuality: "the failure to problematize the construct of the 'male sex' has led to much attention being given to the notion of 'masculine sexuality' and the way it is expressed through sexual intercourse, without consideration of the way this concept is reliant on heterosexuality" (p. 158). Heterosexuality produces a sense of universal masculinity. But meanings of sexuality among men who have sex with men are not all determined by the pursuit of hegemonic masculinity: "Gay men are left out of the configuration of 'male,' 'men,' and the 'masculine' altogether. . . . The prevailing formulation of masculinity represents a failure to engage with the creative meanings and embodied experiences evident in nonhegemonic sexual cultures" (Dowsett et al. 2008:124–25). Queer masculinities do not always pivot on competitive, individualistic, and brawny ideals. Sexuality matters when men are interviewing men, and hegemonic masculinity is not the only, or even the primary, script operating in such scenarios.

When researchers interview men about same-sex relations, they must respond to specificities of talk and gesture concerning queer sexualities in a way that respects the respondent's definition of the situation or the result could be diminished rapport between researcher and respondent. If not wholly scripted by the pursuit of hegemonic masculinity, what, then, are these specificities of talk and gesture concerning queer sexualities? Grenz (2005:2091) describes how the encounter between escort and researcher occurs in a "context that creates the desire to confess," and I now focus on how not only the respondent but also the researcher is invited to confess something about the self. At the beginnings of interviews, respondents often posed the first question to me: "Are you gay?" The question is a proposition, an invitation to create a certain image of myself, perhaps one the escort is more comfortable with, though I cannot know what the escort is expecting in advance of my speech acts. Given that both researcher and respondent affect the course of interview encounters, the question "Are you gay?" is fascinating not only for how it seeks out a singular identity declaration but also for how it momentarily overturns established researcher-respondent roles.

This confession of sexuality demanded from the researcher shapes how the respondent bestows meaning and status upon the researcher as an insider or outsider. While I agree with Schwalbe and Wolkomir (2002) that it is sometimes valuable to let the respondent ask the first question, the stakes are high with this specific question since early in the interview I am not yet familiar with the respondent's sense of self or with what kind of language he uses to describe his life. Responding one way or another could create a scenario where the respondent is more or less open. Often the question was posed before I had a chance to talk to the respondent about confidentiality and anonymity and before I had a chance to turn on the tape recorder. I remember feeling stuck: what should I do? Should I scramble like a desperate fool to start the tape?

The meaning of gay in this case is not fixed but is up for grabs. What "gay" will mean and how it will shape the interview is immanent to that encounter. I could not assume "gay" had the same meaning for each respondent. Rather, I had to be aware of the different and uneven language used by men concerning sexuality. Julie Mazzei and Erin O'Brien (2009) believe that an important part of reflexivity during the interview is knowing the gender and sex script a respondent is operating with and accurately following that script to create a successful definition of the situation. This represents another example of the trouble with contemporary scripting theory. Researchers need to listen actively for the language the respondents use to talk about themselves. But how can researchers know the script prior to interaction? We cannot assume that particular forms of masculinity determine sexual scripts, nor can we assume that there is a stable script operating as a baseline throughout the encounter since meanings are handled in, and modified through, interaction. The encounter between researcher and escort has an open tendency, which is not scripted, insofar as what will be said and how what was said prior to any performative utterance influence later utterances. Claims regarding sexuality during interview encounters influence the breadth and depth of the speech acts and conversations of gesture that follow. These confessions of sexuality during interviews can be conceptualized as a "constitutive hermeneutic" (Walby 2007) created by respondents, a frame that shapes the interview. Using the "gay" signifier in one way or another, even among self-identified gay men, can close down the dialogue, precisely because of the open tendency in the encounter as well as the volatility of any signifier. Introduction of a speech act or gesture into the conversation between researcher and respondent can prompt unanticipated consequences for the rest of the dialogue.

Some respondents were dismayed when I told them, "I have slept with all kinds of people," my preplanned answer to their "Are you gay?" question. I wanted to be honest, and I wanted to provide the same answer to all escorts, regardless of whether I knew a more coherent response would have further opened lines of communication between us. Alison Rooke (2009:154) reminds us that a commitment to queer theory during the research encounter entails "an epistemological openness and attention to one's own sexual subjectivity and the performativity of self." To respond in the affirmative would in some ways work against queer theory's emphasis on unstable identities. Plus, if I did respond in the affirmative, it might have created a scenario where the respondent began to explain less and rely more on hypothetical "bonding ploys" (Schwalbe and Wolkomir 2002), such as "you know what I mean," which I wanted to avoid. If I responded by assuming the "cute, young, dateable guy" performance of self, it could create a sexualized rapport.[8] Sexualized rapport can be distracting and does not often generate the kind of dialogue a researcher is aiming for. I wanted to see how ambiguity concerning identity would be interpreted in the research encounter.

With some other respondents, my hesitation to position myself as gay posed not a problem but an opportunity to pursue a new conversational trajectory:

Ricky: I assume you're gay.
K: I've had sex with . . .
Ricky: Me, too, I've had more sex with women than most of my straight friends.

In this exchange, I did not even finish uttering my standard answer to the "Are you gay?" proposition. The respondent read hesitancy right off my body and was able to infer a response that corresponded with what I was going to say. This example demonstrates how much the body matters in research encounters insofar as gestures are communicative.[9] This anticipatory moment shaped the course of the interview, opening up a discussion of sexuality that moved beyond consideration of male-for-male relations in terms of a simple "gay" versus "straight" dichotomy.

Another example of how speech acts can shape the course of an interview concerns my use of the term "sex work" to refer to the activities of male-for-male Internet escorts. Some escorts accepted this term without question; they thought of what they did as work. When I was interviewing Jake in London, however, and I asked him at the start of the interview how he became involved in escorting, he responded, "I do not like the word escort, it is too coy, prostitute, whore, something like that." I decided to follow up:

K: What do you think of the terms *sex work* and *sex workers*?

Jake: Sounds like shat. It is moving away from prostitute, the connotations and the history; sex worker sounds quite cold and mechanical, but maybe that is what they are looking for, a word stripped of all kind of history. I would not want to be classified as a sex worker, I like words that are a bit more colorful, prostitute, whore.

Just as some of these men identified as "gay" whereas others refuted that identity category, some of the men rejected the category of "sex worker." As researchers, we must be aware that introducing a word into dialogue can have unanticipated consequences. Attributions of identity to the self or another can shape the course of what will be said in the interactions that follow. Luckily, Jake was not offended by my inference in this instance, and the interview carried on for over two hours.

Whether in relation to sexual identity or work identity, the researcher needs to take care when assigning labels to the respondent. Not explicitly addressing the "Are you gay?" question created a new set of meanings that either opened up the discussion of sexuality or closed down the possibility of the respondent's reading me as a sexuality insider. I could not even assume agreement about the word "escort." A chilly distance between researcher and respondent can emerge if the researcher is not careful about introducing words and gestures that might hasten the encounter's closure. Considerations about specificities of talk and gesture assume particular importance during the first few minutes of any interview encounter. This is because the meanings that will be forged during an encounter cannot be fully anticipated. Indeed, the researcher's and respondent's identities are in part an outcome of the encounter rather than predetermined.

Sexualization

"Kevin, it was my pleasure meeting you. I look forward to hearing from you when you start writing. Take care of yourself. Oh and by the way . . . . you are a sexy man! LOL, Harvey, Montréal."

Recognizing encounters and storytelling as joint actions constitutes a key component of interactionist approaches to theorizing such goings-on.[10] What we say and do as researchers influences what the respondents say and do and vice versa. The self, as Grenz (2005:2103) remarks, "is not to be seen as the 'real' or 'inner' truth of the respondents but as something constantly reproduced in the interview setting through the content of their stories as well as through our interaction." Notions of the sexual self are negotiated in the encounter. Associating oneself with the "gay" signifier can have consequences for the rapport between researcher and respondent, as can the purposeful act of muddying the waters during talk about sexuality in interviews.

Although the researcher self-presents as a sociologist, the respondent may position the researcher as a sex object. Sexualizing the encounter is a sort of power the respondent can wield at any moment. The researcher's body is open to sexualization, especially in the interview encounter, where it is being viewed and is moving in relation to the respondent's gestures. Gestures interpreted as nonsexual may be taken in another direction. I purposefully wore business attire for the interviews: black shirt, black pants, black shoes, and horn-rimmed black glasses. Whereas my intention was to seem professional, my appearance could have been interpreted otherwise. Some of these men clearly wanted to turn the interview into more of a touching encounter. During interviews, I was often propositioned to receive sexual favors, as in the following example:

K: Do you think you could walk me through, because not everyone does this kind of service, like a typical S&M scene?
Ricky: I could show you.
K: You could show me . . .
Ricky: A simple S&M scene? Those words don't go together.
K: OK, yeah, not a typical S&M scene, but what exactly does the work of that consist of?

It is reasonable that escorts would break from the respondent role and sexualize me before, during, or after the encounter since much of their work with clients involves sexualizing and being sexualized. I obviously bumbled the initial question, but his response, "I could show you," was accompanied by an impassioned stare and the curl of a smile in the corner of his mouth. In my "you could show me" response, my tone was clearly hesitant in a way that indicated not discomfort but acknowledgment that he had departed from the researcher-respondent interaction script. I read his response, an insertion of "simple" in place of "typical," as an attempt to reassert the script in our researcher-respondent interaction, which he had attempted to reconfigure. I then had an opportunity to reframe my question to indicate that I was interested in talking about the performance elements of S&M as a kind of work. This escort apologized in an email the following day for deviating from the respondent role—an apology that I was not expecting (and thought unnecessary) but that nonetheless draws attention to the palpability of roles in research encounters.

What we say and do as researchers during the interview encounter moves the dialogue in certain directions. For instance, Grenz (2005:2095) "had to take care not to be too friendly and not to have too much rapport, which in other interview settings would be considered a necessary prerequisite for successful research." During interviews, I too felt I was policing my own gestures and speech to hinder respondents' sexualization of me, not by drawing explicit attention to what the escort was doing or saying but, in a more Goffmanian sense, by trying to define the situation as a research encounter through my own gestures and talk. A touchy gesture was the hug. I would often hug the men after handing them remuneration when saying goodbye. Many times this hug was taken as an indication that I wanted to get closer, whereas I meant the hug as a parting sign. After we hugged at the end of our interview, one escort in Toronto walked me to my hostel, requesting more hugs at each red light we waited at. When he suggested that he accompany me upstairs, I had to explain that I was not in a position to have intimate relations. Nevertheless, I did not want to offer a distanced parting sign such as a handshake; the encounter seemed to demand a kinder action.

Other times, at the end of interviews, escorts asked me to come back to their house and "hear more, first hand," as Jeff from New York put it. It was easy enough to say I was late for another interview or to explain that the line between client and researcher could not be breached. Readers might assume that sexualization was more common when I interviewed escorts in their homes, but this was not the case, perhaps because these men did not think of their homes as sexual settings. My point is that any smile or movement of the hand can be interpreted as sexualization in research encounters, even if it is not intended to be.

Sexualization may start before the meeting between respondent and researcher. Grenz (2005) reports that sexualization surfaced during initial phone communications. I experienced a similar set of ethical issues. Some respondents, it seemed, honestly mistook my clearly scripted cover letter for an alluring note from a client, probably without even reading it, and so responded to me with a note about prices and services. I deleted these messages. Some responses, however, were ambiguous. For instance, one escort wrote back, "let me know when you're in town, we will set it up." In such cases, I responded again with the scripted cover letter, hoping that the escort would read it and write back indicating an interest in the interview. One of the first respondents I heard back from, calling by phone in response to an ad in a local newspaper, tried very hard to create a sexual scene. He left messages on my university telephone such as "I can give you head after we talk, you can fuck me if you want." I refused to respond to his calls. He called three or four times a day, for a week. When he continued to leave sexualizing messages, I eventually had to take a stern tone with him to communicate that I thought he was being inconsiderate and was missing the point of why I wanted to talk to him. I was trying to portray an identity as a professional sociologist conducting a rigorous study about male-for-male Internet escorting, but he continued to configure me as a client. The point is that respondents can read different identities onto researchers before and during interviews, subverting our attempts to position as researcher.[11] Researchers are able to present multiple selves to respondents, but this does not mean our self-presentation will be interpreted as we wish.

Another time, I placed an ad in a local newspaper trying to find clients of male-for-male Internet escorts to talk to about their experiences of purchasing sexual services. One man called, and we spoke for about 20 minutes. He suggested that he was deriving pleasure from our conversation, that "even just talking about it with you kind of makes me hard." He asked me if "I get off" from the interviews. I explained the purpose of the research and asked him if he wanted to keep talking. He said no, hung up the phone, and we never spoke again. When sexualization did occur, I negotiated these interactions with a constant Goffmanian concern for roles, insofar as I had to reinforce my position as researcher through verbal and nonverbal communications. Part of this decision not to be "touched" by the field was to prevent the academic stigma that would accompany such a deviation in research design. Despite these presentations of self as sociologist, however, sexualization continued. In email correspondence after one interview, I wrote to the respondent: "Kevin here. Thanks for meeting with me yesterday. It was great to talk to you about your work. Hope all is well. Kevin." Roberto wrote back: "Pleasure was mine. Sorry I had to leave and thank you for the tip. If there is anything else I can do for you let me know. . . . I would love to."

This escort had to leave our interview encounter because a client had called his cell phone and asked if he was available. He said yes and left a minute later. There was no overt sexualization during the encounter. In his email, however, the remuneration of $35 I gave to him was construed as a tip, the kind a client would leave after a session. "If there is anything else I can do for you let me know. . . . I would love to" could imply further elaboration on what he had said about his work through written correspondence, but it could also imply sexual favors. The script of researcher and respondent is broken down, although the meaning here remains ambiguous. In this relationship between ambiguity and power, meaning swerves or follows an unanticipated trajectory.

Understandings of sexuality are both produced and contested in encounters. Grenz (2005:2111) writes of her interviews with male clients of female sex workers, "instead of simply giving men an opportunity to talk about commercial sex, the interview provided space to discursively reproduce sexual identity on both levels, through the actual content of their stories as well as through our interaction"; the same holds true for my interviews with these men. One proviso is that discourses of sexuality do not simply float around as suggested by the metaphor of scripts. Who is conducting the interview matters for how the self is constructed through gestures; my own body and tone were involved in meaning-making and identity construction during these encounters.

Qualitative research purports to get closer to its objects of analysis than other forms of research, but one question remains: how close should researchers get? Sex with escorts would alter my understanding of them as people. But would it better help me understand how they talk about their work and their clients? In anthropology, researchers hotly debate such questions about sex and knowing, and sociologists can learn from these debates. Commenting on the pervasiveness of sex and sexuality during anthropological fieldwork, Kate Altork (1995:121) contends that "protecting oneself from being 'touched' by the field, might be unnecessary in certain circumstances." Ralph Bolton (1995:149) adds that touching forms an essential part of research: "I cannot imagine doing fieldwork without sex." Active participant observation may extend a researcher's understanding of sexual conduct, but not all research with sex workers takes sex as the object of analysis.[12] Given that my research is about how escorts organize their work and make sense of their relationships with clients, it is not clear how much having sex with escorts would contribute to analysis. Nor do all anthropologists hold that sharing one's sex or sexuality is necessary. Commenting on her experiences of marrying and then divorcing a key informant, Katherine Irwin (2006:106) writes, "becoming intimately close to setting members can do more harm than good." For this reason, Joseph Carrier (1999) had sex with men associated with the research setting but not with respondents. Moreover, researchers who study sexuality and sex work can be stigmatized in academia for getting too close to a sensitive subject (see Bernstein 2007a; Brewis 2005). How close one gets in the field depends on what the object of analysis is. To touch or not to touch hinges on whether there is an epistemological gain. Just as preventing oneself from being "touched" by the field might be unnecessary, getting close to respondents is not a requisite of reflexive research. The point of this project is not to provide an ethnographic account of escort-client sex, but a storied account of escorts' work and sex lives.

Discussion

This chapter contributes to debates concerning epistemology and interviews by showing how researchers' confessions and attributions of identity can create a constitutive hermeneutic that shapes the research encounter as it happens. By not affirming a fixed identity in response to the "Are you gay?" question, I sometimes opened up an opportunity to talk about sexuality beyond binary identities, although sometimes such purposeful ambiguity closed off the dialogue and discouraged rapport. Homoeroticism cannot be expunged from the encounter when men interview men about same-sex relations; swerves toward sexualization continually enter through gestural conduct and speech acts. Sometimes indications to reaffirm the escort-researcher boundary are necessary, a necessity that speaks to Goffman's conceptualization of roles as integral to encounters.

The logic of the research process concerning sex work mimics the logic of the lure between sex workers and their clients. Clients contact escorts by email. A time, place, and rate are agreed upon. The encounter occurs. Money is exchanged, and the encounter ends. Much the same could be said about my relations with the escorts I interviewed. Yet, as Blumer suggests, a script does not predetermine the encounter; the meanings of an encounter are instead produced through interaction itself. The researcher has an agenda-setting power, and yet the respondent can swerve the encounter toward propositions and sexualization, a swerve resulting from meaning in the making.

In this chapter, I have focused on the specifics of men interviewing men about same-sex relations. Schwalbe and Wolkomir (2002) claim that it is common for men to position themselves as autonomous, in control, and rational during interviews. Other scholars have commented on how men sexualize female researchers during the interview.[13] I did not find that the male-for-male Internet escorts I interviewed were trying to position themselves as autonomous, in control, or rational during interviews. My interviews thus suggest the difficulty of making generalizing claims about what interviewing men is like, as though all men share some underlying attribute that manifests during research encounters. While we can assume that interviews provide an occasion for both the researcher and the respondent to fashion a sense of self through their talk and gestures, we should not assume that men consistently pursue hegemonic masculinity.[14] Furthermore, men's sexuality cannot be treated as an extension of gender. If gender identity is not stable during an encounter, neither is sexual identity. In other words, "the very idea that types of people called homosexuals or gays or lesbians can be called up for interview becomes a key problem" (Plummer 2007:21).

Theoretical assumptions have methodological consequences. When we treat interviews "not as question-and-answer sequences but as interactive sites for meaning-making, interviewers can no longer be regarded as passive listeners and neutral recorders" (Järvinen 2001:280). Elspeth Probyn (1993) has called for a way of speaking about sexuality that neither privileges the researcher (as in self-indulgent accounts of reflexivity) nor speaks for the other: the way to accomplish this balance is by emphasizing the interactional features of the encounter. The respondent's reflexivity, then, is as important as the researcher's reflexivity in shaping the conversation to come. Rooke (2009) contends that researchers are required to understand the erotics of knowledge production, and I hope this chapter has contributed to that reflexively queer ambition. If researchers do not take seriously the idea that meanings are construed in, and modified through, interpretive processes, then they fail to consider the impact of their own bodies and words in the research encounter.

Chapter 6 | What Male-for-Male Internet Escorts Say about What They Do

I know what it is to really have to work. This is work too. I have to find clients.
But it is easy work. I have done work, I have been to university, I have tried many
things, I know this is easy. What you get from this and what you get from a day job,
there is a big gap. (Chris, Montréal)

Instead of thinking of the escort-client relation as deviant behavior or as a pure economic exchange, I suggest that escorting should be conceptualized as a corporeal interaction, a site for conversations of gesture and confessions of the self. But escorting is still about work.[1] This chapter examines how the work of male-for-male Internet escorting is organized. Escorting as self-employment has been shaped in part by the availability of computer and Internet technologies, which have fused commercial sex with entrepreneurial e-business.[2] I build on the contributions of other sex work scholars to claim that the analysis of labor process can help sociologists make sense of work conditions, work tasks, and sex workers' relations with clients.[3]

In sociology, the literature referred to as labor process theory (LPT) has focused on workplaces, such as factories, with a highly structured and hierarchal division of labor. LPT analyses typically focus on workplace antagonism, deskilling, and worker subordination. LPT, such as the work of Harry Braverman (1974), originally dwelled on structural issues of control, while recent accounts have focused on a broad range of issues, including emotional labor.[4] My analysis starts from the assumption that labor processes are "specific to particular work settings" (Wardell 1999:9). I contend that LPT should be extended to consider the work of self-employed entrepreneurs. My analysis explores the individuated labor process of one form of nonstandard work, where, instead of a typical employer-employee relationship in an organization, the exchange of labor power for pay is constrained and enabled by Internet use. Thus, I examine the logic of competition germane to capitalist labor process outside formal organizations.

In addition to exploring how the Internet makes possible new sex work arrangements, I supplement LPT by conceptualizing the central role that the sexualization of men's bodies has introduced in nonstandard work. The commercial encounter of male-for-male escorting involves touching between men who are often strangers. Sexualization refers to a process by which a male figure is approached as both a sex object and the focal point of an encounter. Male escorts' sexualities are partly compelled through an entrepreneurial, individuated labor process, raising interesting questions about the management of appearances for competitive advantage in commercial sex relations.[5]

Beyond suggesting that LPT must be supplemented through accounting for the sexualization of men's bodies in nonstandard work, this chapter considers how far the idea of sex work can be extended given the diversity of labor processes in the commercial sex industry in its various sectors. The use of the term "sex work" signifies an effort to redefine people involved in commercial sex as workers who should be granted the protections that other workers enjoy. Yet the ambivalence of many male-for-male Internet escorts about the idea of sex work suggests that sex worker activism develops unevenly among different sex industry sectors, thus presenting a challenge to sex work organizers in generating solidarity among people who sell sexual services.

I begin by engaging with debates about labor process. To understand some forms of nonstandard work, I argue that LPT must account for the work of self-employed entrepreneurs as well as the sexualization of men's bodies. Second, I analyze the narratives of male Internet escorts. I discuss elements of labor process such as entering the trade, work conditions, tasks, advertising, and pricing. I focus on escorts' narratives as a way of understanding how their work is organized. As Studs Terkel's classic text about working revealed in 1972, narratives provide data about how workers complete tasks and relate to clients. One paradox of what male escorts say about what they do is that some of the men reject the idea of sex worker solidarity while using labor vocabulary. Male-for-male Internet escorts manifest diverse understandings of sex work, but few locate themselves in the sex work paradigm, thus raising questions about sex work organizing and solidarity.

Labor Process and Male-for-Male Internet Escorting

I have had regular jobs. I plan to again. But for now it is nice not having a retail store manager telling me what to do. I do not have to deal with crap. I was a call center phone operator, a grocery store clerk. Dealing with clerks, 20 customers, learning about the whole organization and the whole goddamn store. My work is different. I am awkward around some straight people, but with gay men I'm in my element. I can be the life of the party in gay spaces. In this job, I work with gay men or closeted gay men, in their homes or hotel rooms, I know how to talk to them, and I know how to please them. One at a time in a private space. This suits my skills and talents better than a straight desk job. (Frank, Toronto)

Frank's narrative indicates how male-for-male Internet escorts make sense of their work in relation to other jobs they have had as well as jobs they hope to have in the future. Some sex workers select commercial sex over the labor process of service-sector work, and Frank's narrative certainly underscores the difference between escorting work and work in a retail store, a grocery store, a call center or a "straight desk job." How can we theorize this difference in labor process?

Capitalist labor process involves the design, control, and management of labor for the purpose of extracting surplus value. Labor process theory (LPT) focuses on how employers and managers control the direction and tasks of labor. Conceptualizations of the elementary forms of labor process are tied to Karl Marx (1976:174), who argued that "the elementary factors of the labour-process are 1. the personal activity of man, i.e., work itself, 2. the subject of that work, and 3. its instruments." Marx's definition shows how capitalist labor process becomes a primary means by which people are brought into social relations. In what follows, I discuss work conditions, tasks, and relations with clients as the elementary forms of labor process in sex work.

Reevaluations of LPT emerged in response to Braverman's (1974) argument that LPT's focus should be objective processes of managerial control rather than work as experienced on the shop floor. Michael Burawoy (1979) prompted a reflexive turn in LPT by claiming that many analyses of labor process are too structuralist. He demonstrates how worker agency sometimes aligns with consent to labor processes. Paul Thompson and Chris Smith (2009) likewise write that accounts of labor process germane to "industrial sociology" are limited in light of new technologies' impact on work, the shift to a service economy, and mobilization of emotional labor. Since Burawoy's intervention, LPT has encompassed debates about subjectivity, identity, and gender.[6]

One criticism of LPT is that it does not help develop a broader sociology of work. LPT seems to be "dictated by what appears to be an iron law of surplus extraction" (Streeck 1987:284); for this reason, critics argue, LPT is too narrow. Forms of work "not felt to be of strategic political relevance" (Watson 2003:46) have been excluded from LPT's purview. Yet there may be ways to extend LPT while remaining in dialogue with its core theory. As Thompson (1989) suggests, there should be no "fixed orthodoxy" (p. 213) of LPT.

These debates in LPT raise a key question: what kind of work is sex work? Most sex work is capitalist labor since in escort agencies and erotic dance clubs an owner directly benefits from the labor of others.[7] LPT can be applied to the work of escorts who work for an agency or that of erotic dancers in a club since agency and club managers clearly extract surplus value from sexualized labor. With Internet escorting, however, there is no organization that controls the work and there is no owner who directly benefits from the extraction of surplus value.

Despite the question of surplus value, I want to make the case for applying LPT to the work of self-employed entrepreneurs. The chief reason why LPT should focus on the entrepreneurial self-employed is that these workers "further the cause of post-industrial capital through their own volition" (Jones and Spicer 2005:224). Escorting involves self-valorization, where the generation of capital exceeds the effort and capital invested in aesthetic labor and body work. As Loïc Wacquant (1995:67) notes, the "body is capable of producing more value than was 'sunk' into it," but this surplus is not necessarily extracted by an owner of a formal organization. Though Internet escorts do not work in organizations, flows of capital nevertheless crosscut their work.

Work is conventionally conceived of as full-time and related to manufacturing, yet this kind of work is increasingly rare. There exist many ways of categorizing new nonstandard work, including " nonconventional" and "atypical." Male-for-male Internet escorting is nonstandard work. Escorts are not represented by agencies and are largely unaware of each other as "competitors," meaning that Internet escorting operates according to an individuated labor process and is similar to "self-employment" and "dependent self-employment."[8] Self-employment refers to work in which the worker makes decisions autonomously but has no office support. Dependent self-employment signals work that ties the worker to an agency or a clientele, where the cost of switching from the client pool would be a burden. Some escorts use this labor vocabulary in describing what they do:

You're self-employed, and you're also not self-employed. . . . you're dependent on whether or not someone is interested in you, whether or not they want to see you again, whether or not they like your pictures online, whether or not they liked what you had to say in an email. (Claude, Montréal)

Despite its clandestine nature, Internet escorting occurs within broader commercial networks that impact how this work is organized. Although escorting does not happen in an organization where workers are constituted en masse and surveyed by a manager, entrepreneurs are motivated by a corporate ethos and seek to accumulate capital on their own. The sociological study of entrepreneurs is underdeveloped, and I suggest that LPT can provide analytical guidance for broadening the study of entrepreneurial work to encompass sex work—precisely because such work involves surplus value, although it is not directly extracted by an owner or operator of a work site.

LPT can be extended by focusing on nonstandard forms of work that exist outside the "restrictive logic of wage-effort bargaining" (O'Doherty and Willmott 2009:946). Part of reorienting the focus of LPT involves analyzing how control in the labor process comes not from "above" but from "below" in freelance work enabled by new communication technologies and how surplus value in the labor process is collected not from "above" but from "below" by the entrepreneurial self-employed. LPT need not focus only on work where employers control labor but can also be used as a lens through which to analyze forms of self-management. I use LPT, then, to examine how the logic of accumulation and competition germane to labor process may be relocated outside of organizations, in entrepreneurial settings. LPT should pay attention to Internet escorting as an activity that breaks from capitalist extraction of surplus value only to revalorize the same process, positioning aesthetic labor as a commodity.

Male-for-male Internet escorting is distinctive in placing the sexualized male body at the center of the labor process, thereby troubling conventional understandings of masculinity and work in which men's work is generally associated with manual labor. Indeed, working men's bodies are thought to represent a working-class habitus and are assumed to be heterosexual. Men's work has also been tied to family through the notion of "breadwinning," construed as a man's ability to bring home money to pay for family expenses. Yet heterosexual, breadwinning masculinity is less and less associated with nonstandard work. Male-for-male escorting involves aesthetic labor, where escorts are pressed to work on the body's appearance for pay. Male-for-male escorting is also a form of body work[9] that involves men erotically touching the bodies of other men. Male-for-male escorting erodes the link between heterosexual masculinity and work as breadwinning masculinity is replaced by the fluidity of queer sexuality, and the escort's body is sexualized as a matter of labor process. In this chapter, I draw from Chris Warhurst and Dennis Nickson's (2009) account of aesthetic labor and appearance management to discuss the work of sexual entrepreneurs. But whereas Warhurst and Nickson use the concept of aesthetic labor to indicate how organizations hire employees with particular appearances, I focus on the work of self-employed Internet escorts, extending LPT into a hitherto neglected realm of work.

Contemporary societies are marked by a shift toward exploratory sexuality, a loosening of kinship bonds typical of heterosexual relations that Bauman (2003) refers to as "liquid love." This unyoking of sex from family and its location in the marketplace lead to malleable identities and pervasive individualization. The sexualization of men's bodies as an element of labor process results partly from the rise of recreational sex and the creation of niche gay commodity markets. Sex today serves many purposes, including the exchange of labor power among men. What makes male-for-male Internet escorting remarkable for sociologists is the male body's centrality to the relation between escort and client. LPT has begun to account for emotions and the sexualization of women's bodies, yet the sexualization of men's bodies has not garnered critical attention.[10] Here, I distinguish between considerations of men performing "women's work" or analyses of gay men's work experiences of gay men and the sexualization of men's bodies as a feature of labor process, arguing that LPT must broaden its critical reach to encompass this latter category of analysis.[11]

What Male-for-Male Internet Escorts Say about Entering the Trade

Getting Started

These men's stories about their entry into escorting challenge common stereotypes about sex workers. David Luckenbill (1985) argues that entry into male sex work occurs as a solution to desperate living or as an exciting adventure. By contrast, these men's stories suggest that escorting and other forms of work share the same impetus: the need to exchange one's labor power under capitalism. For instance, before becoming an Internet escort in Canada, Sam from Ottawa advertised his abilities as a manual laborer in a local newspaper somewhere in the Caribbean. He began receiving inquiries from potential clients about whether he conducted erotic massage:

At first, I was a bit scared. You know how people think about this job. So, at the beginning I said no. But it kept coming with every ad. There would be a call now and then, because I was putting my phone number in the ad. I was not ashamed to be looking for work. (Sam, Ottawa)

Sam found that erotic massage (and then escorting) did not subject him to external rules or employer surveillance. He perceived entering the trade as a decision to secure the best income available to him at the time: "People were offering me money to do the work for them. I came to find myself in a position where I am making rules." Unlike Sam, some escorts start out in escorting agencies. Sex workers in Luckenbill's (1985) study either left the escort agency they worked at because they felt controlled by management or they were fired because they did not follow the rules. Whitaker (1999) also discusses some of the ups and downs that come from working for agencies. A few of the escorts I spoke with had quit agencies because of pressure from the employer:

My first client in Ottawa was through an agency. There was added security. The agency knew the guy and his place and contact number; if anything happened there would be a safe out. But the guy running the agency was an asshole. He made me sick to my stomach. I did not stay there for long because I felt degraded. . . . I felt like I was a number. They were not respecting my existing work schedule. (Tyler, Ottawa)

After getting into Internet escorting, these men found that the lack of employers' rules was a welcome change compared with other work—and other forms of sex work, too.[12]

Consistent with sociological claims about conventional working lives being replaced by erratic postindustrial job changes,[13] some men entered escorting after losing other jobs. Frederico moved to Ontario from Mexico a few years before I interviewed him. He had been working in the automotive sector near Toronto. When the manufacturing plant where he was working closed, he found himself without income and with credentials valued only by an ailing industry. Frederico had always been interested in sex with men but had never considered commercial sex relations prior to being laid off. "These times are difficult for manufacturing," he says. Frederico continues to look for other work while living off escorting during this transition.[14] Other men sought a second job, indicating that escorting is, for some, temporary work. Some men start escorting merely to supplement their income:

I started this when I was 46. My regular job, I make $80,000 a year, and my first year of escorting I made in excess of $10,000. . . . . I didn't rely on that as my primary but it was a good supplement, good part time work that didn't require as many tedious hours as a part time job at a bookstore. (Donald, New York)

While some men become involved in escorting when they are older and have a steady income, other men started out in the more perilous business of on-street propositioning:

When I was 18 was probably the first time on the street; I was propositioning. Then it became a little more structured. The difference would be post-Internet; it created more professionalism with people who have websites. They go to the gym. They are into fitness. They do porn. I don't do any of that. Their website is slick. They charge a lot of money and are more like a companion. I fall in the middle. I'm not a pro but I'm not a scam artist. I do it for extra money. It doesn't pay my rent. (Conrad, Toronto)

The men I spoke with are employed in other jobs, have Internet access, and accept clients depending on income, resonating with what Bernstein (2007b) refers to as "middle class sex work." Commercial sex is now accepted as a way to make money due to a shift to "a recreational model of sexual intimacy" (p. 141), creating new possibilities for the sexualization of men's bodies. The men I interviewed seek out the best earnings/hours-worked ratio.

It's an efficient way to make money. Rather than working four hours and coming home with 45 dollars like at my day job, plus my commute, I can work for about an hour and fifteen minutes, come home, and I've got 200 bucks. (Frank, Toronto)

What makes escorting so efficient is the Internet. The hardware and software required to communicate with clients are the "instruments" of the labor process for self-employed sexual entrepreneurs. The profiles created by escorts are searchable based on city location and aesthetic features of the escort, meaning that clients sort escorts based on categories of sexuality and body type. Escorts accentuate certain parts of their bodies using pictures to leverage a competitive advantage.

Work Tasks and Conditions: Escorts as Sexual Entrepreneurs

Male-for-male Internet escorting is not tied to any formal organization, but it is organized according to the anonymous, just-in-time relations enabled by the Internet. Thompson and Smith (2009) contend that communication technologies like the Internet make possible work that is no longer tied to a particular locale. Male-for-male Internet escorting is part of the circuit of global capital enabled by such technologies. Escorts' clients are often traveling members of the transnational capitalist class, such as chief executives, looking for a one-night mate in each new city.

Establishing a connection with a client requires hours in front of a computer creating online advertisements or finding clients in online chat rooms. Whether escorts use specialty sites or chat rooms, the escort controls when work happens: "When I am not available, I am not available. I am on a couple of gay sites. When I am online, I am available. Guests who come a second time usually have my number" (Sam, Ottawa). While a "new breed of e-pimps" (Kilvington et al. 2001:90) may have emerged in other online sectors of commercial sex, this is not the case with male-for-male Internet escorting. Escorts select clients based on email correspondence. Screening occurs via the process of reading correspondence and looking for cues to ensure the other person is a serious client, not a police officer or a time waster: "I screen based on gut feeling. When I talk to someone on the phone, or by email, if the language and the words do not sound right, they are screened right away" (Tyler, Ottawa). Working at a computer and dealing with emails are constant tasks among online escorts. Indeed, this clerical activity of booking clients is the foremost task in online escorting.

Robert Weiss and David Riesman (1961:79) wrote that "in a society where most men work, the job furnishes a metronome-like capacity to keep in order one's routine of waking and sleeping, time on and time off, life on and life off the job." For male-for-male Internet escorts, the timing of the work is undisciplined and no formal organization regulates the work. But some of these men are "on call" at the whim of clients. Clientele surges, for example, during the week of Gay Pride celebrations, yet over time the number of clients rises and falls:

I'll have a day or two where my phone is ringing off the hook and I'm seeing four or five clients in a day, then I don't get a call for a week . . . either everybody wants to get laid or nobody wants to get laid. . . . I always had jobs where I worked specific days of the week before. I thought, I'll book one or two clients today, one or two clients tomorrow, one or two clients the next day, you know, have a couple of days off. It doesn't work like that. (Claude, Montréal)

Rather than having a boss or manager dictate work tasks, escorts provide on demand the kind of sexual event that clients want. The escort owns his sexualized body and labor power until he negotiates their sale to the client. Not only is the work unsteady, but the rapport the escort attempts to create with the client does not always lead to that client becoming a repeat client. Repeat clients allow escorts to build up a clientele and to start escorting full-time. This uncertainty about clientele parallels the labor uncertainty faced by independent contractors.

Further signaling an individuated labor process, escorts tend not to know one another. One escort from Ottawa (the smallest city in this study at one million people) mentioned that he knows a couple of escorts and they occasionally meet to discuss clients: "It's a small community here and so we compare notes every once in a while. If a client is an asshole it gets out" (Bob, Ottawa). In Ottawa, the small number of escorts and the limited clientele make for a competitive market: "summer gets rough, all the kids come in and it can get competitive. When I started there were two in a chat room, now there's 20" (Bob, Ottawa). Some remain unaware of other escorts but occasionally meet in group encounters:

Met one guy. I did a three way with him and a client. I spoke with him in the shower afterwards, but we have not spoken since. I did a three way with another client but we did not speak after. We might have swapped numbers in case he was looking for another three way. (Frank, Toronto)

Most male-for-male Internet escorts tend, however, not to know one another unless they are "co-workers" who facilitate group encounters to make more money. Only one escort I interviewed knew several other escorts. He referred clients to other escorts by email or phone:

I got business cards. Whenever I go to a new city, Las Vegas, San Antonio, that is how I get other guys to work for me, I try to get Latin guys or dark-haired guys, a dark complexion and tight body like mine. I have an ad with more than one city on it, so with those cities if someone calls but I am not there I can give it to my friends. Get a kickback. I have not seen many guys in the last two years cause I do more referrals. (Byron, Houston)

This narrative substantiates Jo Phoenix's (1999) claim that some sex workers embrace the ideal of market entrepreneurship; it also suggests that the labor process compels sexualities insofar as particular sexualized features of the male body are isolated and made the basis of exchange.

Because Internet escorts are not represented by agencies, they must be entrepreneurial in order to make money. An entrepreneur assumes the risk of an initiative to make profit. The risk for male-for-male Internet escorts is that they will not locate clientele interested in their bodily features. I refer to the activity of promoting such individualized features as sexual entrepreneurialism. Frederick Lane (2000) discusses "sexual entrepreneurs," such as porn filmmakers, who create images that become popular among consumers, and Sari Poel (1992) uses the term "top whores" to underline a similar idea. Escorts as sexual entrepreneurs meet a demand for specific kinds of touching. These escorts offer sexual services based on clients' sexual preferences for particular fetishes. Key aspects of sexuality for Internet escorts, then, include signaling their sexual persona, suggesting what sexual activities they will engage in, and fashioning their bodies to be fit for these activities. In this way, client demands compel the escort's working sexuality. Sexual entrepreneurialism also requires that escorts' pictures accentuate bodily features so that these may appear online:

I model, so sometimes I can use my modeling pics. . . . it's good to get new pictures often at least every month when you're escorting because people get tired of you. . . . your new pictures look better, they'll be like, "Oh he's looking really good." And they'll probably call you again. (Mike, New York)

It is difficult to pitch it right because you can give people the wrong impression just by putting a certain picture or piece of text up. A lot of my stuff I have leather on but if I use a leather picture for my main image the only people I will get are the leather people and the people who are put off by leather would be too frightened to get in touch. (Oscar, London)

Since pictures are crucial for attracting clients, Garry from Toronto says he will "play with pictures. I've learned how to Photoshop. It's tedious and a bit soul destroying to alter your own pictures, but I'm good at it." Aligning their physical features with a "cyber-type" (Nakamura 2002), an innovative display of the online self, is an effective way for Internet escorts to signal what niche sexual market they cater to.

These narratives about self-appearance suggest the centrality of aesthetic labor to escorting. Warhurst and Nickson (2007) define aesthetic labor as the positioning of workers in the labor process based on bodily appearance. However, escorts engage in aesthetic labor not for the competitive advantage of an employer but to leverage competitive advantage as sexual entrepreneurs. Aesthetic labor requires plucking, trimming, waxing, and shaving. Rather than an employer choosing which bodily features to value, this aesthetic aspect of escort labor process is individuated. This work on self-appearance to fulfill clients' sexual demands demonstrates that escorts' appearances are crucial for obtaining and continuing work as an escort.

Escorts have no professional association through which they locate clients or work-related support. Nor do many escorts advocate such an association. Escorts rarely correspond with one another because of how clandestine escorting can be in some cities: "people I see, one's an admiral, one's a high-ranking judge, I could get in trouble if it ever came out. It's incredibly discreet" (Bob, Ottawa). Some activists and scholars consider the requirement of anonymity as a barrier to sex workers' activism.[15] Certainly, male sex workers can be stigmatized if they do not keep their work quiet,[16] but escorts can be more "out" in particular cities. The important point here is that successful escorts must be skilled at something other than keeping secrets. Escorts catering to the transnational capitalist class need to know how to operate in elite settings:

Escorting is not just about having a nice cock and a nice ass, it is about knowing what people want and marketing it well. If you are a traveling escort like I am, you need to know how to conduct yourself in a five-star hotel, how to eat at a restaurant with five forks. (Ben, London)

Some authors have claimed that the sex work skill set is similar to that of service economy jobs, including surface acting or "putting on" a face to engineer a feeling for customers.[17] But the specific skill set of escorts depends on their clientele. Rather than a labor process marked by routinization of various social competencies, as in service economy jobs, escorts' work tasks are "not unlike those of self-employed individuals or other small business owners" (Parsons et al. 2007:238). Similar to the stories that female sex workers shared with Jeffrey and MacDonald (2006), these men's narratives suggest that they prefer escorting because it differs from service-sector work. Frank's narrative earlier in this chapter, in which he talks about "regular work," suggests his valorization of this difference. Valenzuela (2000) also reports embarking on escorting out of boredom and frustration with the service industry. If commercial sex is a way of earning an income without participating in the minimum-wage service sector, then sex work may be thought of as a way of maximizing control over the labor process—another reason for LPT to focus on such sexual entrepreneurs' work.

Advertising

Escorts advertise on specialty websites, just as other self-employed workers do. Ads allude to which sexual services the escort offers. The wording of ads must be precise if escorts are targeting a niche market, such as bondage. Profiles include notes about penis size and body hair, which constitute sexualized features of the escort body. Commercial sex profiles must account for many details, including a description of the services offered:

> When I went on Gay.com in the summer of 2007 for the first time I placed a very nice ad. Age, weight, height, with details about what I do during my massage. When I go online, I put in my bio something like Magic Blacks Hands, commercial massage, for generous gents. (Sam, Ottawa)

Pictures of the body are important for alluring clients, and email correspondence between client and escort often pertains to this body. The displayed body and the sexualized body: these are what the client is keen to see and to touch. Body type influences the escort's sex work persona and marketing:

> If someone's skinny and they don't have muscle, they can't market themselves as a jock. The thing about escorting is it's a market where anybody could be an escort. A 90-year old grandmother could be. It's a matter of marketing yourself. (Steve, Toronto)

Placement of an ad is no guarantee that the escort will develop a clientele. Clients post reviews of escorts and rate them with a score, which determines where the escort's profile will be positioned in the hierarchy of profiles: "if you are not in the first 10 pages forget about it. People get bored, and they're going to find people before you. You move up through the pages based on reviews" (Gabe, Toronto). If one escort offers a talent that impresses the client and the client writes a glowing review, this difference can catapult the escort ahead in the rankings. Clients rank escorts on their sexual performance, overall charm, conversational skills, knowledge of a city, and the provision of temporary companionship.

If escorts do not receive strong reviews, their web profile plummets and is viewed by fewer potential clients. Escorts can lose repeat clients and work can become less steady:

I think bondage is a niche market. . . . it may have saturated. I have a few regulars that I still see, but I haven't gotten many phone calls from new clients. There may have been a bad review at one place. (Donald, New York)

The role of online client reviews in determining escort access to the client pool demonstrates how the escort labor process is tied to the Internet. Internet technology enables certain relations between escort and client but also constrains escorts in various ways. The websites allow clients to search easily and to contact escorts in any city, but the websites also sort escorts based on reviews, making it harder for some escorts to find clients because their profiles move down the list and get buried. Depending on the city, escorts may use print advertisements. Few escorts in Canada advertise in magazines or newspapers, but this type of advertising is more popular in the United States and England. In England, however, prices for advertising are higher in magazines than online:

The advertising is expensive. That is the area where we are exploited. To get a double print box in the major magazine Gaytimes monthly is 200 pounds. Gaydar.com the main site in the UK charges the escorts 45 pounds per month. (Oscar, London)

The costs of advertising, sex toys, and condoms add up. As Sean from Toronto puts it, "you have to spend some money to get some." Ads are a costly necessity for the sexual entrepreneur, whose sexualized bodily features must be known in order to be enticing.

Getting Paid

Some days are long and boring. I have taken clients where I did not feel like doing it but I knew it was going to be $120 or more, or I have taken an exhausting client, but it pays $100 a hour for ten hours because he likes to do ecstasy and jerk off to porn and all he wants you to do is jerk him off. There are times when I am like "not *tonight" but the client has called three times and he cums in 15 seconds and is out the door. Nobody makes that kind of money in so little time. (Tyler, Ottawa)*

Escorts develop informal strategies for getting paid and negotiating fees. There are no paychecks. There are no contracts. Some escorts maintain nonnegotiable set fees, while others exercise greater flexibility in pricing. Tyler from Ottawa charges repeat clients less, a common practice among the self-employed:

People who meet me once a week get discounted in a major way because in the long run after four weeks or five weeks I see the benefit of not charging them the same price I charge one-time customers. It makes business sense.

Being an independent sex worker can create certain "leverage points" (Gall 2006:34), since Internet escorts control pricing to a certain extent. But, because escorts are not subject to formal pricing regulations, there remains the possibility of undercutting other escorts. Escorts express animosity for other escorts who pull the prices down and create an expectation among clients that certain services can be had cheaply:

I do not give $20 blowjobs. I will judge you if you give a $20 blowjob. You are taking my business away selling it cheap. I hate people who undercut. If everyone were to ask for the same prices, it would raise the playing field. (Tyler, Ottawa)

Most Internet escorts set their prices high and feel that advertising higher prices makes them appear more professional: "You hire a lawyer that charges $500 an hour you're going to expect a lot more of them than a lawyer who charges $250. Escorting is the same" (Claude, Montréal). Prices are set to maximize the income earned per meeting with a client:

You can do five calls at $300 and get $1500 or five calls at $150 and get half that. It makes sense to get more every time you see someone because if you are good looking and have youth to yourself and have a nice body it is easy to get that amount. We call them professional tricks, they want to see everyone. So if you only see them once and then they see others, you might as well get as much as you can. (Byron, Houston)

Escorts treat what they do as a way of earning an income, and their pricing reflects this attitude. As Oscar from London remarks, "I try to keep it like any other business." Most escorts set prices high so that they can generate and retain surpluses for themselves.

Thinking of Calling It Quits

Some escorts feel pressure to abandon escorting. Their reasons include loss of repeat clients who provide a steady income but are hard to come by, desire for a secure job, lifestyle changes, and lack of sexual interest: "There is no victim here. It has never been an issue for me legalizing or not legalizing. This is not something I want to do for the rest of my life. I want to find a good man and move along" (Sam, Ottawa). Some escorts do not want to leave the trade but do want to enjoy upward mobility; they want to see fewer but "better quality clients" who are willing to pay more money per hour. Upward mobility in the industry requires a shift in persona to attract a new clientele:

I'm going to get more professional and higher end clients . . . shift more toward like business travelers basically who are the best ones who come to the city for a weekend and plan it ahead. They pay more money. (Conrad, Toronto)

One issue that differentiates male-for-male Internet escorts from other kinds of sex workers is that this work is often conducted as an extension of their sex life. Sometimes escorts feel like leaving escorting because other opportunities have come along or because they are frustrated with the demands escorting places upon them:

My career is almost over. I am establishing a training business here in London. I have been here for three months, and it is going really well. Once the personal trainer business picks up, escorting will drop off. (Mark, London)

For the most part, escorts express no overarching theme of exiting the industry because of violence, poverty, or drugs. Entrepreneurialism marks these men's orientation—a curious feature given their general reluctance to embrace the term "sex work" as a way of valorizing what they do. Most escorts narrate their exit from this work as a life course shift or a transition into other forms of work.

Discussion

The male-for-male Internet escorts that I interviewed consider their sex work to provide serious income despite the lack of a social context that would legitimize it as work. Male-for-male Internet escorting does not have ties to organizations, although the work is organized by parameters set out by the Internet (e.g., the ranking of escorts based on client reviews). Though the labor process of Internet escorting has more to do with self-management than the scientific management of Braverman's (1974) version of LPT, escorts still exchange labor power, occupying what Marx (1976:451) calls "a particular mode of existence of capital." Escorting work has many dimensions that intersect with LPT's concerns. Since the work of male-for-male Internet escorting is largely clerical, taking place in front of a computer, the labor process is individuated. Escorting involves the sexual entrepreneurialism of aesthetic labor, as escorts manage their bodily appearance to attract and maintain clients. Because escorting also concerns men's bodies touching together, it constitutes a form of body work that makes central the sexualization of men's bodies in the labor process.

Male-for-male escorting requires that sociologists assess how fundamental the sexualization of men's body is to their labor process. LPT accounts for emotions and aesthetics at work and how these are valued, but more research is required to understand how the sexualization of men's bodies has become significant to some forms of nonstandard work. Accounting for how sexualities are compelled through the labor processes of late capitalism not only supplements LPT but can help overcome the impasse between materialist LPT and poststructuralist sexuality studies.

The work of the entrepreneurial self-employed is situated in commercial networks, relocating the competitive logic of labor process in entrepreneurial settings. Though Internet escorting occurs outside organizations and beyond employer control, forms of self-management inhere in the aesthetic labor of sexual entrepreneurship. The sociology of entrepreneurship remains underdeveloped. LPT provides a path for developing future studies of entrepreneurs and understanding the relationship between self-employment and surplus value. Researchers might extend LPT by analyzing nonstandard forms of work, like the work of the entrepreneurial self-employed.

I end this chapter with the following question: what does the individuated labor process of male escorting mean for understanding the idea of "sex work"? Sex work literature has emerged out of the sex workers' rights movement to divorce commercial sex from its associations with sin and crime. Male-for-male Internet escorts make up only a small portion of a diverse sex industry, and scholars have not analyzed how well current conceptualizations of sex work are borne out by male sex workers. The commercial sex industry's diversity of labor processes makes it complicated for workers in different sectors to identify with one another. It is difficult to apply the label of sex work to male-for-male Internet escorting because such escorts lack explicit social context beyond online competition among escorts and clients' ranking of escorts on specialty websites. Co-worker interactions and formation of an occupational culture are largely absent among online escorts.

One purpose of this book is to understand how male-for-male Internet escorts make sense of the idea of sex work. Sex work discourse includes two fundamental ideas: first, that sex work should be decriminalized; and second, that sex workers should organize as a community because of their ostensibly shared labor process. However, few of those escorts I interviewed explicitly associated themselves with the idea of sex work. When I asked Byron from Houston, "do you wish your work was decriminalized?" he responded bluntly, "No, cause if it was everyone would be doing it and I would not make as much money." When I asked Josh from Toronto, "Do you feel like you have an escort community?" he responded, "I don't, nor do I want that." Some of the escorts felt connected to other escorts, but most felt entirely disconnected and were fine with that: "I do not know the market, cause everyone works for themselves. People do not talk about what they do with each other, workers do not know the other workers" (Sam, Ottawa). Escorts describe themselves as entrepreneurs or self-employed as opposed to service-economy workers, who are compelled to toil under management's thumbs. At the same time, many escorts use labor vocabulary to narrate their touching encounters with other men while disavowing the sex work discourse. Their narratives substantiate Gregor Gall's (2006) point that many escorts do not identify with sex work discourse. This remains a complicated issue, however. Since the decriminalization of sex work would mean greater regulation of their income, some male escorts reject the subject position "sex worker" and the sex work movement as a whole; other male escorts support the movement for political reasons; and some identify as "sex workers" despite differences in labor process. The "sex worker" subject position may fragment support among escorts, but this fragmentation has not necessarily damaged the movement. If movement organizers are interested in growing the movement's base and reaching out to sex workers with highly individuated labor processes, however, then other recruitment and promotional strategies may be necessary to increase solidarity.

Sex worker activists have been organizing for sex worker rights and providing a context to support the attribution of work to commercial sex, but their directive comes unevenly from different sex industry sectors. Not many male-for-male Internet escorts wholeheartedly support politicizing the activities of commercial sex as work. Some escorts feel that calling what they do "work" would make it more visible—an effect antithetical to their and their clients' desire for relative privacy. The shift toward Internet-based escorting has increased the individuated, careerist orientation of these men and discouraged the formation of solidarity with other people whose work approximates their own. Although escorting requires a great deal of escort interaction with clients, such an individuated labor process produces little interaction between these sexual entrepreneurs themselves.

At Work in Sexual Cities

In male-for-male Internet escorts' narratives of sex and work, place matters: particular parts of cities act as destinations for clients who travel and provide a market where escorts sell their services. The cities in this study, with the possible exception of Ottawa, share the traits of global cities: they are interconnected with and almost indistinguishable from other nodes in networks of global capitalism. Adam Green (2007b, 2005) argues that such major urban areas support a wide range of sexual communities as well as diverse enclaves within these sexual communities. Big cities with "gay villages" serve as important sites where sexual subcultures and practices depart from heteronormative conceptions of sexuality. Place also matters to male-for-male escorts because local cultures of gay masculinity in different cities emphasize some sexual practices more than others. For instance, Toronto is known as a "city of bottoms." The particularities of local sexual cultures within cities influence the kinds of services offered by male escorts in those cities.

Bernstein (2007a:16) argues that the cities where sex work happens are "nodal points of transnational economic and cultural processes." What does this mean for escorts in terms of finding and working with clients? Some escorts are dissatisfied with the cities they work in:

The clientele here sucks. The reason I say that is because Ottawa is still very much, even though it is a capital city, it is very conservative in nature, a lot of gays and lesbians here work for the civil service who are government officials who work in this sector which is huge. Listen, if you are over a certain age, 40 or 50 or older, 55 and up, chances are they are closeted, they live out in the burbs or they live with a partner they have been with for 20 years, it is not the same mentality as Montréal or Toronto. . . . the market for escorts and hustlers is really small, and because it is small it is very competitive. If I lived in Montréal right now, and I plan to move there, it would be much busier. . . . I can vouch for that cause I know people who are sex workers and when this town is dead, it is dead. Everyone has left town or is on vacation. Certain months are harder. (Tyler, Ottawa)

As Tyler's narrative makes clear, Ottawa is curious as a city when it comes to working as an escort. These specificities have to do with the clientele, as well as the acceptance of sex and of sex work. Some escorts say Ottawa offers low demand compared to Montréal, whereas others deem Montréal the most awful city to work in (see Mark's narrative below). Escorts' city of residence also impacts their standard of living: "my rent in London was over a 1000 pounds a month and an in-call rate was 100 pounds, so say 10 jobs to pay the rent. Here, my rent is 1000 dollars a month and my in-call rate is $180, so six jobs to pay the rent" (Garry, Toronto).

As another escort explains, place matters for the kinds of services one can offer, the prices one can set, and work's sustainability over the long term:

London is a lot like New York, you have all these people who have a lot of money and not a lot of time. London and New York are the best cities to be escorts. I travel to New York to see clients probably one week every three months. California is not a great place for escorting. You need a city that is condensed, people with no time, people with money, people who are working hard, no bullshit, they know what they want and they can pay for it. In Los Angeles, there are a lot of people pretending they are something they are not. In Berlin, there is so much emphasis on free sex—it is a wild sex frontier! You need people with serious busy lives, or people in repressed, Catholic cities. Toronto in Canada is a great city because everyone is so busy, it was fantastic working there. In Montréal, you won't make a dime because they think of sex differently. They think like Berlin. Boston is good because it is repressed. So you need upwardly mobile people who are working hard. I have been to Paris, Rome, Toronto, Berlin, Montréal, New York, Washington DC, Boston, Miami, Dallas, Houston, Chicago, Seattle, San Francisco, Las Vegas, and Los Angeles doing this work. (Mark, London)

The city where an escort works affects how the encounter between client and escort will occur. The difference between Montréal and other cities, according to Harvey, is that "it is accepted here. Massage is normal. Rub and tug. It is very accepted. Vancouver, Toronto, the USA, it is looked at as prostitution; here it is not looked upon as prostitution at all." Labor process in the US differs from that in Canada because of intense policing in the US:

I have been to Detroit. Made a trip to Chicago, I only broke even on that trip. I did not turn a profit, I was only going to learn how to escort in the USA. It is a different game. I have not made any other trips, because I had a boyfriend for a few months who would have been worried sick. Then we broke up. So I am free to go to the USA, but I am afraid of it. It is different because you have to dance around on the phone and in your emails, you have to pretend you are offering a massage, you cannot answer blocked numbers. The police will set traps, they will do stings, if someone calls and says "do you suck, do you fuck" you have to play dumb, assume that is a police officer trying to entrap you, so you do not talk about that over the phone. You can only see clients who know what they are doing. They ask about prices, they tell you a particular time and place, then you arrive, some are still not with it, they ask if touching is allowed, and of course touching is allowed, this is prostitution. But you do not bring that stuff up in the USA. Whereas in Canada you can say "I top, I bottom." When I work in Toronto I do not have to worry about arrest, being convicted. In the USA, it is frightening, it is hard to make money because you have to dance around talking about sex and you have to turn down a lot of clients you suspect might be police. The police are always out to get you. (Frank, Toronto)

American escorts confirm having to worry more about policing and regulation than escorts in Canada or the UK.

Although we commonly think of work as tied to larger national structures, while sex, emotions, and intimacy are relegated to the interpersonal realm, this binary is artificial. Sex work is situated in sexual cities that shape the touching encounters possible between clients and escorts. Some cities are more closeted than others, as in Ottawa, where clients want this activity to be kept secret at all costs:

It's a government town. . . . There's a lot of people just in for a day or two, or they're here for a couple of months with a different government or an agency . . . a transient population, temporary workers or whatever. And a lot of military people seems to be the other. . . . Most of them are pretty good: like higher ranks want to be dominated; tie them up and whip them and that sort of thing seems to be like the reverse of the role that they're in their regular everyday life. (Bob, Ottawa)

The sexual city forms part of a global city, connected by transportation and communication networks. Both escorts and clients use these networks to get what they want and to arrange encounters. Toronto's and Montréal's specificities also influence how escorting work is carried out:

Toronto is a hub. If you're leaving Canada to go to the States, if you're leaving Canada to go to Europe you know your chances are you're going to come to Toronto to get there. It's also a financial and tourist destination . . . and it's the business capital of Canada. So it attracts all of the, "Oh I'm going away on business to Toronto." So these guys are getting their rocks off while whoever is at home doing whatever. Montréal is a party town. People go there to party, you don't usually go to hire a ho. Like I mean a 60 year old man isn't going to go hire a ho in Montréal when he's from out of town unless he's there on business. (Eddy, Toronto)

Certainly the novel idea of a suburban escort (see Lawrence 1999) is closely tethered to the rise of satellite cities and urban sprawl. As transnational flows of people and capital reconfigure the intimate and the proximate, they also affect escorting work, which is networked with these global flows of capital and people.[1] Internet escorts often cater to the highly mobile transnational capitalist class, marked by what Connell (2002) calls transnational business masculinity; the services that escorts offer must accordingly appear high class and professional. Despite how extensive the network becomes—the fluidity of sex escorts mimics the liquidity of capital, flowing across borders—and despite extensive travel from place to place, the escort and client must ultimately come together and meet in the flesh, in the encounter.

Chapter 7

Touching Encounters

Male-for-Male Internet Escorts and the Feigning of Intimacy

This chapter wrestles with a key argument made by some sex work scholars: sex workers feign intimacy with clients. Debates about feigned intimacy began with Albert Reiss (1961:118), who wrote that male hustlers pursue "affective neutrality" and desexualize the blowjobs they give, rationalizing the exchange as economic. J. Boles and A. Garbin (1974:139) also present sex work interactions as superficial. Erotic dancers, they claim, are typified by "apathetic disengagement." In related literature, scholars claim that sex workers split the work self from the private self as a coping mechanism,[1] erecting a boundary between work sex and so-called real sex or home sex. Sex work follows a fixed script, according to researchers such as Teela Sanders (2008b): "the script is a set of shared conventions based on mutual dependency and sets out the boundaries and roles that determine control, power, initiation, pleasure . . . . sex workers who are in control of their work and surroundings often plan and 'act out' the sexual script to work in their favour to gain maximum profit and control" (pp. 401–2). Sarah Oerton and Jo Phoenix's (2001:402) comparison of sex work and massage work similarly posits that the encounter must become "not-sex" in order for workers to maintain self-worth. According to Oerton and Phoenix, erotic masseuses exclusively emphasize "the repudiation of sex in the context of sex work and bodywork." Yet key questions, such as the connection between sex and intimacy as well as the performative character of intimacy, remain unexplored because of this emphasis on surface acting.

Arguments about feigned intimacy during sex work encounters lead to the further claim that the sex between escorts and clients is bound by rules against touching intimacy zones on the body. But these claims about touching rules assume the sex worker to be involved in monogamous sexual intimacy beyond work, an assumption that does not necessarily apply to male Internet escorts. This heteronormative definition of intimacy stems from what Noah Zatz (1997:281) calls "the lingering influence of procreative teleology" in the sociology of sexuality and sex work. To make space for analysis of male-for-male Internet escorting and the sexualities it entails, I aim to undermine the lingering influence of procreative teleology in the sociology of sex work.

Taking a role in the Goffman sense undoubtedly constitutes "an essential lubricant for social interaction" (Takoland 2005:308). In this chapter, however, I want to examine the idea of counterfeit intimacy and its acute impact on sex work research. Men who enjoy sex with men have diverse senses of intimacy that are not easily categorized according to heteronormative understandings of human relations. As Tim Dean (2009:45) explains, "the term intimacy sometimes stands as a euphemism for fucking, but it also signals the emotional experiences that accompany sex." This definition can be expanded to include all the ways that bodies come together and the enigmatic "range of attachments" (Berlant 2000:3) that comprise sociality. Earlier I suggested that starting with identity in the sociology of sexuality may lead to essentialism; in this chapter, I argue that sociologists must begin with touching if we want to understand the way that discourse matters for (and materializes in) human interaction. In what follows, I emphasize that the "feigning of intimacy" is better described as part of sexual performativity. Although sexual performatives imply an intimacy script that may be followed during the encounter, there remains an open tendency to encounters, whereby dominant scripts about sexuality and intimacy are undone through creative touching.

Though some of the male-for-male Internet escorts I interviewed discussed scripted work rules, most narrated their encounters with clients in ways that complicate arguments about their work being akin to service-economy labor process and based on surface acting. Some escorts comment on how friendships emerge with clients, how work sex is an integral part of their sex life, how central the enjoyment of the encounter with clients is, and how they understand sexuality as more diverse than straight versus gay binaries would suggest. But beyond the closed tendency toward scripted sex, there is an open tendency between escort and client toward unanticipated relations.

To offset this focus on predetermined scripts and to conceptualize the diverse sexualities of male-for-male Internet escorting, I draw from Foucault's *Histoire de la Sexualité* (1978a). Foucault's project is to provide an

understanding of power beyond prohibition and sovereignty. His intervention is to conceive of sexuality not in terms of repression or law but in
terms of power, defined as "the multiplicity of force relations immanent in
the sphere in which they operate and which constitute their own organization" (p. 92). Foucault identifies the body as a nexus of power, conceptualizes power as local but nonlocalizable, and criticizes the privileging of a
universal theory of the human subject. I make use of Foucault's comments
about discourses of sexuality by beginning my analysis with people's narratives about sexual conduct.

My purpose here is to understand the connections among sex, sexuality, and power in escorting encounters. Male-for-male Internet escorts
represent a socioeconomically privileged sector of a varied industry. The
problems of violence experienced by on-street, female, and transgendered
workers were not reported by these men. Though I acknowledge that intimacy may well be performative when escorts capitalize on clients' confessions about sexual categorization, I de-emphasize male sex workers' feigning of intimacy as a matter of labor process.

This chapter is organized in four parts. First, I discuss the significance
of Foucault's writings on sexuality for thinking through sex work encounters. Next, I discuss some sex work scholars' claims about the feigning of
intimacy. I then discuss examples of the two tendencies in male-for-male
Internet escorting encounters: the closed tendency toward determinate,
scripted exchanges and the open tendency toward unanticipated interactions. These narratives present a picture of sexuality, work, and joint actions that cannot be reduced to feigned intimacy.

Foucault's *Histoire de la Sexualité*

To establish that sexuality is not simply about repression, Foucault (1978a)
identifies modern society's preoccupation with confessions of sexual identity, defining confession as "all those procedures by which the subject is
incited to produce a discourse of truth about his sexuality which is capable
of having effects on the subject himself" (Foucault 1980:215–16). The confession is a technique that calls forth all details of sex. It will "transform
your desire, your every desire, into discourse"; in this way, revealing everything possible about one's sex becomes akin to sharing a secret treasure
of self-identity (Foucault 1978a:21). Foucault claims that confession has
become our modality for producing truth: "Western man has become a
confessing animal" (p. 59).

Into his discussion of sexuality, Foucault introduces the distinction between *ars erotica* and *scientia sexualis*: in *ars erotica*, knowledge was transferred from body to body, and sex represented merely one among many forms of learning how to take pleasure; in *scientia sexualis*, "we demand that sex speak the truth. . . . we demand that it tell us our truth . . . the deeply buried truth of that truth about ourselves which we think we possess in our immediate consciousness" (Foucault 1978a:69). In *scientia sexualis*, sex moves to the center of truth, which must be extracted through confession.

Ars erotica does not disappear with the rise of *scientia sexualis*. Rather, Foucault suggests that *scientia sexualis* functions as a proxy for *ars erotica* in Western societies. We take pleasure in thinking we know the truth about others and ourselves. Foucault holds that discourses about sexuality proliferate through confessions and "telling the truth" about oneself; all one needs is "a little skill in urging it to speak" (Foucault 1978a:77). Indeed, Foucault writes, "homosexuality began to speak on its own behalf, to demand that its 'naturality' be acknowledged, often in the same vocabulary, using the same categories by which it was medically disqualified" (p. 101). People thus establish comfortable homes for themselves in identity categories.

Building on Foucault, my inclination here is to claim that today we see a sort of *sexualis ad infinitum*, a proliferation of discourses and practices with no limit. But such a claim would not reflect how the sexual encounter is socially ordered or how certain apertures open, providing opportunities for sexual conduct to be altered through touch and gesture. Instead I suggest that there are two coexisting tendencies in an encounter: the first, a tendency toward discourse and confessions about the self; the second, a tendency toward friendship and compassion. These tendencies are immanent to the encounter. The encounter between the escort and the client is not a simple economic exchange, nor is it an automatic exploitation of the sex worker by the client. Rather, the encounter is imbued with power as a game of truth. Escorts are not selling sex or bodies per se but broker "truths" about themselves and their clients. Confessional moments work their way into touching encounters as a search for stereotypes, roles, and scripts. The confession is oriented toward maximizing what can be made out of the truth of sex. But the second tendency veers toward a different economy of bodies and pleasures. This tendency does not depend on ruses of sexuality. It is unanticipated, and it parts from the deployment of sexuality by being located in the realm of friendship and compassion.[2] Foucault suggests that this different economy of bodies and pleasures could rally against the science of sexuality. The open tendency, for Foucault, is associated with friendship as a way of life.

Another way of putting this is that there are two tendencies in male-for-male Internet escorting, one that sexualizes the relation and one that potentially desexualizes the relation. But how can an erotic relation between two men be desexualized? This question returns us to the distinction between *ars erotica* and *scientia sexualis*. Relations between men often operate with reference to sexual categories. The diversity of queer masculinities within the "gay" identity category are many (e.g., the "twink," "bear," "daddy," "muscle mary," "studio gay," "gay-for-pay"). These self-fashioned identities are oriented toward what Foucault calls *scientia sexualis*, since they track "along the course laid out by the general deployment of sexuality" (Foucault 1978a:157). Yet relations between men are not without *ars erotica*. Those in the encounter need to feel their way through it. The second tendency, the open tendency, is toward erotic relationality.

These two tendencies—a power that plays on the truth and an erotic relationality for the sake of pleasure—exist in any sexual encounter. Given that sexuality is produced in the interactions of encounters, thinking about discourses of sexuality as abstract and fixed by history restricts our understanding. I want now to argue that in male-for-male Internet escorting, the use of pleasure mingles with identity and categorization insofar as clients select escorts based on fixed identity forms (e.g., the "daddy" or "twink") and associated sexual practices, thereby sexualizing the relation. Similarly, escorts select clients based on the latter's understandings of identity and sexual practices. Yet the encounter can spiral into unpredictable pleasures that border on friendship, desexualizing the encounter and challenging phallocentric and identity-based understandings of eroticism.

Feigning Intimacy?

The issue of feigned intimacy has a loose connection to sexual scripting theory. Gagnon (2004b:140) writes that sexual scripts function to make sure "an actor is meeting the expectations of other persons and guiding his or her conduct in terms of the conduct of others," indicating that the script provides meanings. But sexual scripting theory is limited insofar as it tends only to account for the closed tendency of any sexual encounter. The idea of a sexual script detaches sex from animal behavior and emphasizes conduct, yet researchers' propensity is to treat these scripts as fixed instead of involving an unforeseen element. Claims about surface acting and the feigning of intimacy during sex work encounters assume sexual scripts to be set and ignore the open tendency of interaction. In what follows, I provide an overview of this literature on the feigning of intimacy.

Browne and Minichiello

Jan Browne and Victor Minichiello (1995:598) explore how workers categorize clients, the meanings that workers attach to sex, and the "psychic contexts of male commercial sex." They claim that condom use "demarcates work from personal sex, and *symbolizes a false sex where real human contact is not possible, a mask is worn, and the true self is not shared.* Condoms are seen as an excellent physical and psychological barrier between the worker and clients, especially those they find dirty and repugnant" (p. 603, emphasis added). These comments about the "true self" not only assume much about sex workers' psychology but also suggest that when a worker puts on a condom without a client noticing, it is because the worker wishes to maintain this distinction between work self and private self. Here, work sex and so-called private sex are conceptualized as mutually exclusive. Browne and Minichiello uphold this distinction between feigned and real self in claims such as "after the sexual sale, sex workers need to switch off the work personality and go on with living their lives" (p. 614). They assume both client and worker enter the interaction with ready-made sexualities, yet sexual encounters can also produce meanings. To minimize such claims about the "true self," Browne and Minichiello could have argued instead that intimacy and friendliness with clients are performative in the context of work relations. Only recently have Minichiello and colleagues (2008:167) acknowledged, "both workers and clients may realize that what the transaction will look like is partly situational . . . unpredictable and negotiated as the event unfolds, sometimes over several encounters with the same client."

Sanders

The concept of feigned intimacy is similar to Arlie Hochschild's (2003/1983) influential distinction between emotional labor (a paid feigning of self to appease customers) and emotion work (experiencing so-called real emotions in private contexts). Some scholars have argued that Hochschild's approach assumes a dichotomy between the feigned and the real self, but Teela Sanders adopts Hochschild's concepts to understand indoor female sex work. Sanders (2005:319, emphasis added) argues that "sex workers create a *manufactured identity* specifically for the workplace as a self-protection mechanism to manage the stresses of selling sex as well as crafting the work image as a business strategy to attract and maintain clientele." She considers how a "certain kind of identity in the sex industry, borne out of the specific requirements of male desires that clash with female desires to separate sex as an economic unit from romantic relations in private, is intrinsic to how some sex workers perform the 'prostitute' role," assumed to be a feigned self (p. 323). Sanders also discusses bodily exclusion zones: "these parts of the body and specific sex acts are considered *too intimate* to be sold, or reserved for the worker's own sexual pleasure" (p. 327, emphasis added). This assumes that the escort's pleasure does not form part of power relations between escort and client. Discussing the condom as a psychological barrier, Sanders remarks, "Closely tied to the notions of creating a *non-intimate* experience for the sex provider during the commercial sex act, the condom is consistently used in commercial sexual transactions, not only as a health protection mechanism but as a psychological barrier" (p. 327, emphasis added). According to this claim, some sex acts are "too intimate" to share with a client, so the escort uses the condom to make the touching encounter "non-intimate."

But such a claim inscribes a romanticized distinction between "real" intimacy restricted to other relations and feigned intimacy offered to the client. Sanders claims that sex workers like to stay on top and remain dominant as a ploy to control the situation: "sex workers do not themselves engage in the sexual fantasies that the client requests but instead act out a set of prepared, *routine speeches and predictable interactions* that they repeat with other customers" (p. 327, emphasis added). Unlike Browne and Minichiello, Sanders is discussing a sample of female sex workers, and feigned intimacy with clients could be a major element of the labor process for them. But my point is that Sanders's account mostly represents the closed tendency of sexual encounters. Although these claims about feigned intimacy and labor process break down stereotypes of sex workers as disease vectors, they also establish new misconceptions of sex workers as anxiety-ridden and profit-motivated. Given the diversity of labor processes and sexualities across the commercial sex industry, this claim about feigned intimacy does not apply to all sex work equally.

Brewis and Linstead

As with the idea of feigned intimacy, scholars sometimes generalize specific claims about female sex work to all forms of sex work, casting the work relation as a façade while valorizing the home relation. In such a heteronormative claim, scholars imagine sexuality as ready-made. Joanna Brewis and Stephen Linstead (2000:86, emphasis added) likewise argue: "One requirement for the emotional management of one's self is the maintenance of *an appropriate degree of psychological distance from the encounter*, or at least from certain aspects of it. One means of achieving this distance and bolstering the work persona for some prostitutes is the use of drugs." Rather than construing sex workers as sexually compulsive, destitute, or exploited, Brewis and Linstead cast them as controlling the time of their encounters in order to assert that work sex does not bear on sex workers' nonwork sex or intimate relations. Yet Brewis and Linstead (2000:94) offer a proviso: "prostitutes do not necessarily, in every encounter, want or need to maintain these strict divides." Not all sex workers separate a work self from a private self: I build on this claim as I analyze the sexualities at play in male-for-male Internet escorting.

The Sexual Stories of Male-for-Male Internet Escorts

Some of the escorts I spoke with did try to separate their work and private lives. Sean from Toronto said that he had to go into character to go to work, and that "if you show emotion, you are fucked." But the bulk of escorts told different sexual stories about their work, stories that complicate the claim that intimacy is always feigned. The idea of intimacy is loaded with associations of monogamy, heterosexuality, and procreation. Although "a queer baby boom" and the rise in popularity of gay marriage have broken down "the orthodoxy of nonprocreative homosexuality" (Marcus 2005:206), this is not the case with male-for-male Internet escorts. Escorts have various understandings of intimacy, and sex is not always part of the picture. As one escort explained,

With some of my guests I have a lot of intimacy. Last Friday night there was a guy who booked me for the whole night. He took me out to a fancy restaurant, Italian. We went home after and he got a nice massage. It was very late. He wanted to have a shower. Spent a good time, playing around. Went to bed at two in the morning, did not wake up until 9am. It was a lot of intimacy. A lot of kissing and cuddling. (Sam, Ottawa)

This escort does not describe his encounter in terms of feigning a sense of self, though the "kissing and cuddling" the escort and client shared were performative and the sequence of events (dinner, massage, snuggling) follows a romantic script. Though it is difficult to tell from Sam's narrative whether this intimacy is an act or not, male-for-male escorts do talk about how "honest" their relations with clients are. One escort discussed the pleasure he experiences with clients:

the guy I've known for 15 years, that's always fun. It's always different, he lets me be creative and he'll give me parameters to work with him and then I take it from there. And he likes to be surprised, so that's always thrilling for me. We always have a good time together. (Ricky, Toronto)

Some escorts emphasize that they are not faking or acting with clients:

*it comes out of trust and honesty. The thing I hear the most often is, "Wow you resemble your picture, thanks, you didn't lie. You are what you say you are, you're not pretentious, you're not arrogant. You seem down to earth. You seem to honestly be having a good time with me. You're not just doing it and watching your watch."
... Because a lot of them have been with enough guys to know when a guy or the person is just faking it. I am what I say I am, how I look, I'm genuinely interested and I have fun too. (Ricky, Toronto)*

Escorts often have repeat interactions with a client; this repetition involves regular interactions in escorts' everyday lives, including their sexual lives. Over time, escorts' encounters with clients lead to a touching rapport or a "corporeal itinerary" (Diprose 2002:107): putting their bodies together becomes a habit. For the most part, escorts do not claim to be acting with clients any more than they would with any partner.

The issue of biography is central in male-for-male Internet escorting insofar as the logic of the lure (which male-for-male Internet escorts follow) is often based on anonymous sociality involving an itinerant element. For these men, the sociality of noncommercial sex and that of commercial sex can be very similar. Talking about the touching he shares with clients, one escort reported:

I do almost everything I would do with a boyfriend. I'm very limited sexually, but intimate-wise I have no problem, kissing, because for them you can get a blowjob anywhere, like I can get a blowjob in 90 seconds here, right now, but getting someone to snuggle for an hour is not the same thing and just to talk, watching TV with

somebody naked on the bed, for some people that's a bigger thrill. It works for me
too because I don't have a boyfriend. (Gabe, Toronto)

This sexual story is not simply about sex work but also touches on the escort's biography and how his biography connects to the relations he forms with clients. The issue of sexual biography cannot be separated from the escort's worker persona, which means the distinction between feigned intimacy and "real" intimacy is hard to sustain. Some escorts take pride in not faking:

I think they enjoy the way I am. They are attracted to me . . . I do not play. I have
to get something out of it more than the money. I have to have fun or otherwise
I will not put myself through it. The fact that I am not faking, because I choose
people I do not have to do that because I cannot really do that, fake it. (Chris,
Montréal)

The conventional idea of intimacy encodes subtle messages about appropriate sexuality. For men who have sex with men, intimacy is not governed by "the illusion of long-term commitment or the heteronormative construction of good, clean, and reproductive sex" (Green et al. 2010:20). In this sense, intimacy is detached from monogamy. These escorts express that they care about their clients enough to avoid insulting them or wasting their time:

I met somebody off of it who I've now seen . . . three times and all he wants to do
is rub your back and hold you and just chat. And you know what I said to him the
first night, I'm like, "You know what, honey," I said, "don't call me like for an hour;
you know what you don't live that far, just next time you call me, call me and I'll
come and spend the night." He's like, "You will and you won't charge me extra?"
"You don't want to have sex with me, all you want to do is just like sleep beside
somebody," and he's a friendly person and I got along with him . . . it's not so much
of a business transaction. (Eddy, Toronto)

As this example makes clear, not all escorts treat clients as income units. The biographies of these men interleave with escorting in queer ways, which means that anonymous and itinerant sexual encounters are prevalent, whether commercial or not. Judith Stacey (2005:1926) has claimed that "because many gay men can more readily separate physical sex from

romantic and domestic commitments, they enjoy greater latitude to negotiate diverse terms for meeting their sexual and emotional needs." But why
should we assume that sex is about romantic and domestic commitments
to begin with? Some of these men defy the trend toward containment sexuality and vanilla sex in queer communities.[3] The overlap between these
men's work sex and nonwork sex confounds scholarly claims about surface
acting and feigned intimacy with clients.

Enjoying Sex

The stories of male-for-male Internet escorts provide a counterpoint to the
claim that sex workers treat the sex of their work as a series of instrumental
tasks akin to those in the service economy. This is because many male-
for-male Internet escorts are not established in monogamous partnerships
beyond work. Even if they are, sex work, nevertheless, remains a crucial
part of their biographies. When male-for-male Internet escorts do have
partners, these partners are sometimes also escorts—or at least aware and
supportive of their partners' escorting work. Male sex workers understand
itinerant or nonmonogamous sex differently than do non–sex workers, and
perhaps differently than other sex workers too. Bolton (1995) discusses the
communitas fostered and extended by the logic of the lure and an emphasis
on nonexclusiveness when it comes to partners. Most escorts do not set
up so-called real sex as that which happens with their partners and work
sex as a technical set of operations on client bodies. Several escorts discuss
how much they enjoy the sex of their work—not because they are sexually
compulsive,[4] as some public health researchers suggest, but because work
sex constitutes their sex life:

*I do not have sex privately, so I am always ready. Even if the guy is not hot enough,
if I have not had sex for three or four days it is not tough to get hard when he
touches me. I do not really act. Unless I have two guests the same day. I have
to cum with one. I make sure all the guests cum. But I need to cum if I have two
guests. People who like to swallow, you have to provide. When the guest is my type,
I enjoy it more than when the guest is not my type. But I do not act. You have to
love it to do it. It has to be fun. I do not have a boyfriend, so this is partly my sex
life. (Sam, Ottawa)*

Sam's narrative suggests that he does not separate the sex of his work from
the sex of his life. The next narrative, from a sex worker who is 64 years old
and has been working for over two decades, demonstrates the same point:

"I had not had much of a sex life outside of the work for many years" (Gerald, Toronto). Scholars assume that sex workers feign intimacy because they have a so-called real sex life to return to when work is over. This is not always the case. The sex of the work is part of the sex of these workers' lives. The overlap between the sex and work lives of these men makes it hard to sustain the separation between feigned and real intimacy.

The work sex of male-for-male Internet escorts cannot be cut off from their sex life, and their work cannot be separated from their biography. Some escorts impress clients so much during encounters that clients begin asking the escort for sex outside the commercial context: "'Wow, you're great, can I bottom for you?' I actually get tops ask to bottom for me" (Ricky, Toronto). Ricky enjoys the sex of his work not because he has no sex life beyond work, but because he feels enjoying sex is an integral part of his job: "what I find I have to do is hold back a lot" (Ricky, Toronto). The sex of his work is not policed according to procreative and monogamous expectations of sexual conduct. Again, the encounter is described as an "honest" interaction by some escorts:

there is a guy that . . . lives in Chelsea, he's a very hot, got a great body, and has a great apartment and you spend all night having sex and it's a lot of fun . . . there is another guy you know and I have clients that they like to see me with other escorts so they tell me to pick the guys up so that happens a lot actually and you get paid for that, you know you cannot beat that. And a lot of times, I'm having fun, I'm really having fun and it's good because the more fun I have the more fun they have and the more money I get. I just feel good because I'm being honest. I'm not taking advantage of anybody. . . . I don't pretend that I'm not having a good time. I really let myself go. (Roberto, New York)

Escorts' sex work cannot be separated from their life histories; this inseparability is further affirmed by their talk about how intimacy in the encounter is performative as in any other sexual encounter. The following escort's narrative also describes a pleasurable situation in which a relation develops rather than manipulation by either client or escort:

Sometimes you think "I am being paid to do this?" I have had some gorgeous clients and cannot believe I am being paid to do it. There was a guy I had seen for a long time, he was part of a couple but he liked me too much so had to end it with me because the partner was jealous, but on one occasion, he booked me for the whole night, good money, but he said from now on we are not client-escort but we are just *friends, we went out to sex clubs, I could do what I wanted, we went back to his place, we ordered more and more escorts, wine, it was a huge sex party and I was being paid just to be there with him. (Oscar, London)*

These narratives about sexual pleasure suggest that there are specific sexualities at work in male-for-male Internet escorting that differ from those of other commercial sex sectors. The sociology of sex work must be attuned to this difference in order to appreciate the labor process and lives of male-for-male Internet escorts. While it is important to acknowledge the prevalence of sexual pleasure in male-for-male Internet escorting, the fact that male-for-male Internet escorts enjoy sex does not constitute the most interesting sociological finding of this study. The more important point here is that power operates in the most intimate relations and itinerant encounters. Sexual pleasure is connected to the deployment of sexuality and power in the capillary form that Foucault discusses.

What's "Gay" Got to Do with It?

Below I discuss how male-for-male Internet escorts categorize themselves and how categories of sexuality influence the way escorts arrange touching encounters with clients. The men I interviewed possess various understandings of what "gay" means. Some male-for-male Internet escorts fully embrace the gay identity category in their talk about themselves, while others resist binary understandings of sexuality. Some escorts felt pressure from clients and from their existing network of friends to perform a stereotypically "gay" identity: "Labeling myself as gay and hanging around only with gay people, it limits you. There is more to the world than being a man who likes to sleep with men and being in the gay bar. . . . is there such a thing as straighter gay sex?" (Leon, Ottawa). Though he enjoys having sex with men, Leon feels there are too many strings attached to fixed identity. Similarly, Bruce from Toronto reports:

I don't consider myself a part of the gay community; I don't like the gay community. . . . I find there's a lot of hypocrisy in the gay community because a lot of people in the gay community are constantly bitching and complaining that society discriminates against the gay community . . . then I don't really see much effort being made for them to break the myths of the stereotypes. I see them embracing these stereotypes. I used to live in the gay village for a few years, and I didn't like it because I found it to be a very promiscuous lifestyle. I found that even within the gay community there is a lot of discrimination. . . . I just found it ironic that you have this community of people who are bitching and complaining that there is a lot of discrimination and then right in the community there is discrimination against themselves.

Bruce felt that the gay community was as exclusionary and limited by stereotypes as other sexual communities, thus making it difficult for him to refer to "community" in relation to men who have sex with men. These stereotypes are fostered by commercial endeavors that capitalize on marketable images of gay identity. The "pink economy" refers to a now well-established market in global cities that caters to gay and lesbian consumers and bases its products on stereotypical images of gay and lesbian life. Some escorts criticized the pink economy identity that is prepackaged and consumable:

You can consume it, it's in the gay parade, everyone can consume it. . . . you won't get beaten on the street, oh it's marvelous. But that is very recent and it's not a good or bad thing in itself even if I think that the gay parade is, well, I really don't feel well about it at all, I don't like it. (Etienne, Montréal)

Other escorts expressed antagonism about stereotypical and commercial gay identity:

there are not a lot of gay people who I enjoy to be with, because everything is always about them, what they like, their interests, driven by this idea that everything behind who they are is gay, they always remind you they are gay, and at the end I do not give a shit because this is a person. I find it superficial. (Chris, Montréal)

"Gay" does not have a fixed meaning, even in the so-called gay community. For Chris, it did not make sense to limit his relations with others to an identity category that governed their lives, and this included his relations with clients. Although they all enjoy sex with men, these escorts live according to sometimes starkly different understandings of sexuality. The sociology of sex work must address how diverse sexualities operate in male-for-male Internet escorting.

The gay versus straight binary of sexuality does shape some male escorting encounters. Some escorts judge other men who have slept with women, an example of gay men's sexism.[5] Other clients enjoy finding men who are sexually expansive and do not limit their activities to those played out as part of a narrow identity category. One escort told a story about the way these identity practices matter to his work:

> *A lot of guys love the straight acting guy so a lot of guys get off on the fact that I also fuck women occasionally and am turned on by it and legitimately jerk off on porn sometimes. . . . some are grossed out by the fact that my cock has been in a vagina. . . . I get fewer and fewer of, "Oh that's gross" kind of thing, most of my friends are more questioning, "really, that's, did you like that, did you get off on it?" They're more like that than, "That's gross, fish" that kind of stupid bullshit which I hate. The gay misogyny bullshit. (Ricky, Toronto)*

In the words of Jonathan Dollimore (2001:371), "one of the most embarrassing aspects of gay history has been the overt misogyny of some gay men." While for some Internet escorts these sexual identity categories are malleable and permeable, others rely more on fixed understandings of gay versus straight in their work. Some escorts categorize clients according to perceived sexual orientation, which influences their comportment and talk during the encounter:

> *It depends if the guy is gay or not. If the guy is gay, he wants to kiss and he wants to cuddle. He wants that relationship feeling. If he's straight or if he's married, he wants to suck cock and he wants to get his dick sucked and he wants to maybe like get fucked or whatever. . . . I will fight tooth and nail to not do it just because I'm not a top anyways and to me, like it's just, it's too much bullshit. I don't need to shove my dick up some shitty ass. (Eddy, Toronto)*

For some escorts, "gay" was an identity they embraced when they were younger, though they had since engaged in a wider range of sexual activities and no longer felt "gay" represented who they were. For others, the idea of "gay" versus "straight" appeared in discussions of client sexuality but not of their own. In this way, diverse sex practices—but also diverse meanings of sexuality—exist among these men.

People "do" sexuality in economic contexts, though queer theories of sexuality and gender have failed to show how identity performatives are compelled through work imperatives. Queer theory has also failed to demonstrate how discourses that inform performativity are translated through touch. I now turn to a discussion of just how such performatives of sexuality operate in the encounter between client and escort.

Finding One's Spot on the Sexual Mosaic

Sex work literature has not considered how male escorts strategically arrange the joint action between themselves and clients according to discourses of sexuality. Focus on joint actions allows for a productive view of power, the view of power that Foucault provides, since joint action enables another action only insofar as that action meets certain criteria of intelligibility.

Sexual stereotypes and categories operate in the communication between escorts and clients. Discussing the city of Toronto, one Internet escort said, "people tend to advertise more here what they are, top or bottom. . . . you don't go home with someone unless you know. . . . I'll let you know this about Toronto, we call it a city of bottoms" (Ricky, Toronto). We might assume the escort's statement, "you don't go home with someone unless you know," refers to HIV/AIDS status, but this is not the case. Ricky refers instead to sexual preference, the kinds of kinks, fetishes, positions, and forms of play that people engage in as an imagined extension of their sexual identity. Pleasure and power are related here. Sex work encounters build in a confessional element so that clients are invited to comment on their own supposed sexual truths and preferred corresponding sexual activities. The confession is "an operation by which the self constitutes itself in discourse with the assistance of another's presence and body" (Butler 2004a:163). The clients reveal something of themselves so that the escort can undertake a corresponding action in the prescribed manner.

Foucault (1978a:47) suggests that discourses of sexuality are deployed strategically through positioning on a "sexual mosaic." While many male escorts have arrived at a more complex understanding of what sexuality means through their work, some do deploy discourses of sexuality strategically in relations with clients in order to align the services provided with the client's understandings of sex. Power permeates the relation—not as repression, but as a game of truth. For one escort, "I think conversation is important to get to know people to size them up and see what type of people they are. It's important to get into their head before you get into their bed" (Mike, New York). Male-for-male Internet escorts can capitalize on clients' confessions about where they place themselves on the sexual mosaic.

What escorts do sexually with clients does not express some predisposition. Instead, the range of sexual activities builds up over time as an outcome of previous encounters. Sexuality is not fixed but in flux. Escorts are generally comfortable with sexual conduct that includes a range of kinks and fetishes. For instance,

Piss play is fine with me. Because it is piss I will not swallow it, but you can piss in my mouth or piss on me, that is fine, I like water sports. Not into scat. On my profile I say this is what I do and this is what I don't do, and what I don't do is very minimal. (Tyler, Ottawa)

An important part of sexuality is signaling one's sexual persona, thus signaling a range of activities one will participate in. The process of signaling sexuality in escorting has a confessional dimension, since the escort often has to ask the client to confess what sorts of activities they want to pursue; similarly, the client sometimes asks the escort to confess something about their sense of identity:

I want them to be very clear about what they want. I want them to know what they want. Because they will get frustrated if they don't know what they want because I won't give them what they want because I don't know. I need them to think about it. I can help them, I think there's a big part of my job to help people try things and to know if they like it or if they don't like it, to discuss it. (Etienne, Montréal)

Dean (2009:33) describes "anonymous sex [as] frequently . . . punctuated by interesting conversation." This conversational element is central to escorting. By coaxing confessions from clients, the escort capitalizes on the client's sense of sexuality by moving the encounter in particular directions. This is the closed tendency of the sexual encounter, making conduct fit according to fixed categories of sexuality and scripts for sex:

It's not about having the best body in the world. It's not about having the biggest dick. It's about being able to relate to people and to make people feel comfortable and to figure out what people want from you sexually. It stills shocks me to this day, even when people are paying for sex they have difficulty articulating exactly what they want. (Claude, Montréal)

What clients want from escorts varies from city to city, and some escorts develop specific understandings of sexuality related to the cities they work in. Local sexual contexts develop that escorts can work to their advantage, and niche markets are always emerging:

Toronto is a city where people are incredibly stressed out all the time, more than any other city I've ever visited including New York. And I think for a lot of people the experience of being a bottom in a sexual situation, not even necessarily exclusively about getting fucked or getting penetrated but about that experience of letting somebody else use your body for their pleasure, I think it serves as a source of release for a lot of people from their stressed out every day lives of work. (Claude, Montréal)

The way that escorts position themselves sexually depends on the city they are working in. For instance, some cities demand more "bottom" services than others. Moreover, sexuality is irreducible to particular genital relations. Some escorts discuss how the diversity of sexualities draws attention away from the penis, which is usually thought to be the proverbial center of male sexuality:

With escorting it's all about my cock or their cock. I find sex in general too based on the cock. Escorting yes, definitely cock based, even guys who want to have their ass played with. A lot of these people paying for sex aren't as experienced and haven't honed in on or narrowed down what gets them off. Most guys I play with couldn't care less if I saw their cocks or touched it. Like the guy tonight, I think I've seen his cock once in a year or whatever, eight months, it's always covered and his ass is there and it's all we need. He doesn't care because he's into his ass. (Ricky, Toronto)

The client holds an image of the truth of sexuality that he is living out through the encounter and that the escort caters to by "doing" sexuality accordingly. The escort negotiates that demand in order to satisfy the client but also takes pleasure in, and capitalizes on, confessions.

The scenarios outlined here suggest a more distributed field of power relations, where both escort and client are capable of producing an effect that draws on pervasive sexual stereotypes. Identifying clients' wishes and identities before or at the beginning of the encounter makes it easier for escorts to play into the fantasy clients may have—in short, to capitalize on their sexuality. London, where Ben works, influences what kinds of niches and tropes of sexuality can be worked with in developing an escort persona:

People in London want a type of sex. I became interested in extreme sex, fetish sex, domination, master-slave scenes, leather play; I learned more and then I became more specialized. Not many escorts in London offer these kinds of services, know how to do them well. I was already getting interested in this stuff, but London pushed me more. In London, people are already experimenting with their sex, and you do not need to be an escort to be experimenting with sex in London, but I was in London and I was interested in experimenting and I was able to use this beneficially for my work. Looking at the profiles of escorts in London, I can see there are only a few escorts who had good knowledge of extreme sex and fetish sex. Then I started a profile on a site for people who play these games. (Ben, London)

These escorts must negotiate their sex relations with clients within the parameters established by discourses of sexuality. Gaining knowledge of the extreme sex scene exemplifies a gearing up for a game of truth. Discourses of sexuality make the encounter a game of truth "related to specific techniques that human beings use to understand themselves" (Foucault 1988:18). But the encounter is not reducible to this closed tendency. Although sexual stereotypes are sometimes pursued strategically within these contexts, the sexual encounter is not fully determined by gender or sex scripts. That sexuality is not dual, but multiple and multiplying, means that the outcomes of sex between people are open-ended rather than fully scripted.

Unanticipated Elements of the Encounter

The encounter between client and escort is not predetermined by some fixed notion of "gay" sexuality or queer masculinity, since what "gay" means is variable. The encounter between client and escort has an open tendency toward unanticipated relations. Claude found that escorting work had an unanticipated impact on his sex life:

I'm providing emotional intimacy to a lot of people as my job, and I find that it changes the way my sexuality plays out outside of that and then outside of sex trade work I'm actually looking for the hot and dirty fuck fest because I have all of those sort of emotional intimate touchy feely needs satisfied within the context of my work. So I don't need that with my other partners. . . . one of the kind of regular clients that I have in Montréal is a hard core S&M top so within the context of the

*work that I'm doing here, I'm actually finding I'm craving more emotional intimacy
from the other primary partner. (Claude, Montréal)*

The itinerant and anonymous sex often pursued by men who have sex with
men can generate unforeseen possibilities for relations with others. The
next escort also stresses how much this work changed the way he viewed
sex, intimacy, and relationships:

*There are times when gay men have a sexual imperative, but I do not have it to the
same extent or I do not have it as much anymore. All the messing around on the
Internet all night trying to get someone to come over and then when they arrive
they are not what you expect. When someone comes around and they are not what
I expect or they are not what I want, I do not go through with it. That is a good
thing. I do not take just anything at work, so why should I do it in my private life.
(Oscar, London)*

Encounters between escorts and clients produce unanticipated meanings and ways of bodies coming together. The claim that these encounters are scripted and made predictable by escorts to control the process is
misleading. Even when we try to control encounters, even when we script
everything, there are unanticipated elements.[6] The encounter undergoes
desexualization and resexualization, changing the meaning of the relation
for the people involved; these two tendencies are always at work in the encounter. Sometimes grids of intelligibility break down. Foucault (1990a:4)
recognized silence as "a specific form of experiencing a relationship with
others," one that he thought of as integral to friendship and pleasure.
Friendship is one outcome of the encounter related to Foucault's thoughts
about relations beyond the categorization regime imposed by sexuality.
According to Foucault (1997a:135), "the problem is not to discover in
oneself the truth of one's sex, but, rather, to use one's sexuality henceforth
to arrive at a multiplicity of relationships." People must invent a formless
relation, which is friendship, "the sum of everything through which they
can give each other pleasure" (p. 136). Affection, fidelity, camaraderie, and
companionship: Foucault associates these forms of intimacy with erotic
relationality. The goal is not to liberate desire but to lead a life relatively free
of classification and categorization. The aesthetics of existence Foucault
associates with desexualization and creation are not part of an individual
project but one that starts with the potential inventiveness of encounters.

Beyond sex workers' enjoying sex with clients and this being part of their sex life, beyond the impact sex work can have on escorts' understanding of self and their deployment of sexuality during work, clients and escorts can also develop friendships. Friendships often develop out of sex between men.[7] Sometimes the escort and client become activity partners. In the words of one Internet escort, "I've gone out of their age range type of thing, but we're still good friends" (Claude, Montréal). Boles and Elifson (1994) report that on-street male sex workers have trouble making friends with clients as well as each other; they are stereotypical loners. Not so with escorts. Of repeat clients, Jeff from New York said, "we probably know more about each other than our families or our spouses." Likewise, an escort describes that with repeat clients he feels

more relaxed. More open. More trust. They feel more comfortable, I feel more comfortable. . . . it is not business anymore. They talk about their lives, what is going on. I talk about my life. We are friends. It gets to the point where I do not even want to charge them money. Because we have fun together. (Harvey, Montréal)

Of repeat clients, Harvey adds that if he were to retire, "I would miss them." Friendship between men is key in Foucault's writing about the self; it not only challenges heteronormative understandings of masculinity but can be a form of desexualized intimacy that represents "perhaps the end of this dreary desert of sexuality, the end of the monarchy of sex" (Foucault 1990b:116).

Recent contributions in the sociology of sexuality argue that clients of sex workers prefer the honesty of sex workers to the "mind games" that people play in the dating scene.[8] Here it is escorts who prefer clients to potential dates outside escorting. Bruce discussed how his interest in intimacy is satisfied by clients and how clients can become more like lovers:

I get more honesty from a fucking escort client than I do from a guy that I meet, like it's ridiculous you know and you tell them that and they get upset but people just need to chill out. . . . I've been dating a guy recently, funny enough, after he called my ad. . . . sometimes you know you get some really great people who will as well just be so nice and say, "Hey, you want to go grab dinner?" I mean sometimes outside of getting together with these people and engaging in the sexual act, it's almost as if you're just sort of like going out and hanging out with a person and having fun and getting paid for it. (Bruce, Toronto)

Speaking about clients, another escort said, "I wouldn't go on a repeat with somebody if I didn't like them like as a person" (Eddy, Toronto). This same Internet escort told a story about one client whom he enjoyed his time with so much that eventually

> I said to him at some point, "OK don't give me any more money. This is ridiculous, you're either my friend or I'm one of your staff. . . . I don't want you thinking that I'm around you because of the money." . . . it doesn't get boring, because I've developed a connection. And then with the new ones it doesn't get boring, because you don't know what the fuck to expect. (Eddy, Toronto)

These relations can involve elements of friendship, enjoyed for the sake of pleasure. The issues of mutuality and honesty in sex between men were narrated again and again as a reason that friendships emerge: "I've become friends with a lot of my clients. . . . I can't lie, I can't just pretend so I can get money from them" (Roberto, New York).

Friendship represents an intimacy that is engaged in simply for the pleasure it affords: "a friendship of the future that calls us to come to a space beyond (hetero)sexuality, a space in which friendship as a work of art can be received and preserved" (Garlick 2002:571). Arriving at a position of friendship undoes the distinction between escort and client, desexualizes the relation, and creates a situation for particularly queer intimacy. Friendship between those who were once escort and client shows that sex work in this context is not fundamentally about a staged sexual performance. It is about power, in the strategic and capillary sense Foucault means it. Sometimes these power relations are absolved of their necessity in favor of friendship as a way of life, if only for an evening. Sex, then, may have little to do with the work required to subvert sexuality as a regime of categorization,[9] although such ethical relationships begin with and are extended through touching other bodies.

Discussion

In this chapter, I have tried to undo the binary between "real" and "feigned" intimacy by pointing to the performative character of both. I have explored how escorts make distinctions based on their understandings of sexuality, as well as on the confessions of clients, which some escorts capitalize on. "Intimacy" has many meanings in encounters between escort and client, from sexual intimacy to friendship. The sociology of sex work must recognize how diverse sexualities operate in male-for-male Internet escorting. Comprehending sexuality in male sex work requires a different set of theoretical tools. The narratives of male-for-male Internet escorts suggest that the sex of sex work greatly shapes their so-called private sex lives. In their private lives, some sought more kinks while some sought more closeness, depending on the kind of sex they performed at work. Sex lives were situationally linked to the kind of sex they were having at work, as well as the market they played to as an escort. The boundaries between working life and sex life are more porous and sometimes nonexistent when it comes to the sex and work lives of male-for-male Internet escorts. Sex work cannot be separated from biography, as the two are connected through touch.

There are two tendencies in sexual encounters: first, a tendency toward the strategic deployment of sexuality and the use of ready-made tropes; and second, a tendency toward the unanticipated, and friendship. Insofar as the encounter follows the tendency toward the deployment of sexuality, it relies on confessional moments whereby stereotypes, roles, and scripts configure the relation. Insofar as the encounter follows the tendency toward friendship as a way of life, the relation can challenge and convulse conventional understandings of masculinity, although this is not necessarily the intention. The open tendency in the encounter is not an organized resistance to sexual categorization; it is more of a surprise, an aperture for recomposing new relations on a minor scale.

Foucault was not operating at a level of analysis concerned with interaction. But his discussion of sexuality, confessions, and friendship can, nevertheless, be reconciled with interactionist sociology. Some scholars have argued that Foucault is only useful for discussing discourse and knowledge in abstraction and that he ignored specificities of sexuality and gender. By engaging with the sex and work narratives of male-for-male Internet escorts, I hope to have shown that Foucault's writings can be brought to bear on the most touching encounters of our lives.

Keeping Secrets and Feeling "Washed Up"

An Excursus

The social and economic position of these men is such that they do not often discuss issues of violence and criminalization that on-street female and transgendered workers face.[1] Yet, contrary to some stereotypical understandings of male sex workers that assume these men do not experience stigma, escorting can have all kinds of negative impacts on their lives. This excursus is about secret-keeping and stigma in the work of male escorting. In some cities, there is pressure to keep quiet since if the story gets out, stigmatization can result. Below I share some narratives about the more unfavorable aspects of these men's working sex lives, including stigma.

Sam

Sam moved to Ottawa from the Caribbean in the late 1990s. He has been working as an escort and masseur part-time for more than a decade. When he first started out in escorting, he felt unable to be honest with his partner. He harbored a secret:

My first boyfriend, when I was abroad, we had been four years together. I was doing it before I met him. I never told him I did it. I stopped advertising because I knew I could not be available as much. We were spending all of our nights together. We started living together. A couple of blocks apart. I could not then have guests in the evening, first of all, so all my guests would not come unless they could come before ten o'clock. I was not taking any new calls, I was only taking calls from old regulars who still had my number. When I lost customers I was not doing anything to look for new ones. When I was coming to Canada, he found I replied to one ad of a guy, because we knew when I was leaving it was the end of the relationship since he could not come to Canada with me. I used his computer to reply to this ad.[2] I asked the person to call on my cell phone not to reply to the message, but he

replied instead of calling. My partner saw it. I was screwed. His reaction was heavy.
"Escort, you want to be an escort, is that what you want to do when we split!"

For Sam, "trouble" refers to the association of escorting with drug use, health problems, and poverty. When the story gets out, the reaction can be "heavy" not only
because people associate sex work with depravity but because keeping secrets implies
keeping others out of one's life.[3] Internet escorts are good at keeping secrets because
there can be pressure for escorts to protect their clients' anonymity and confidentiality. Escorting can sometimes be tense: on the one hand, escorts must keep secrets;
on the other hand, they often feel a desire to confess and "come out" as a sex worker.
Managing the demands of a relationship can prove troublesome when the secret of
sex work stands between partners.

Tyler

Tyler has been escorting off and on since he moved to Ottawa in 1999. He escorted
full-time when he could not find other work. Recently, he found a full-time job, and
escorting became part-time work. Though he did not dislike escorting and perceived
it as somewhat enjoyable, Tyler did feel escorting was cutting him off from some contacts in Ottawa's gay community. He also had a complicated history with escorting
because he and an ex-boyfriend had started escorting together in order to make ends
meet and pay rent. Tyler continues to keep some secrets and manage these conflicting
feelings about his work:

I do not feel guilty about what I am doing, but I would feel terrible if my mother or
father or immediate family found out what I do. They would be very quick to judge.
I know they would judge me. But aside from being found out by family as most
escorts do not want that, I do not feel bad about it and I am fine. Ever since I was
19, I was in love with River Phoenix and I saw "My Own Private Idaho."[4] And even
though I did not want to be in the fringes like he was, I just thought, there is such a
mythology surrounding hustlers and their clients that I thought, "could I do that." I
am not a shrink so I do not know why I love it and why I do it, but I always thought
it would be cool to be paid to have sex. When you eliminate the money, you are
having sex with somebody. Most people do not think of it that way.

Tyler begins this narrative by talking about the secrets he keeps from his family. For
him, the shame involved in his family knowing would be unbearable. He is good at
keeping secrets and goes on to tell a romantic story about his work, situating his
affinity for sex work in relation to actor River Phoenix. Yet not all the narratives in Tyler's story fit the romantic genre: he started escorting with an ex-boyfriend to pay the

rent one month; escorting, casual drug use, and heavy drinking then ensued, and they split up. As Tyler explains, "we had a tumultuous two-year relationship, I had to go to jail, we had a violent relationship, all kinds of bad stuff." This "bad stuff" that Tyler talks about and the more pleasurable aspects of the work do not belong in the same genre, demonstrating the contrapuntal nature of narratives about sex and work.

Conrad

Conrad has been working as an escort for more than a decade. At age 42, he grew up at the height of the AIDS panic. Experiencing the death of friends shaped his perspective about sex work and safe sex politics. A contemporary slogan was "Silence = Death," part of a campaign against remaining closeted about sexual status and HIV/AIDS status insofar as such closeting often diminished access to the care necessary for preventing or managing the virus. Conrad consequently took a more "out" approach to his work compared to other escorts I interviewed. He was not ashamed of his work, and although he is no longer politically active he did talk a lot about the safe sex guidance he offers clients. Still, Conrad keeps a few secrets:

I don't hide it, well I don't really want my mother to know but I mean there's a few people that every once in a while cross my mind because I do have my face on the Internet and it's the same old thing. They have something to hide too and if they show it to a friend then anyone, like if I were to show that, a picture of somebody to a friend that would be a friend that wouldn't give a shit. Most of my friends know, I don't give too much information I just leave it out, but I might just say, "Got to go do a rub down" and everybody just laughs, other people want to know the details.

Male-for-male Internet escorts still have to manage public understandings of what they do in order to avoid stigma. As in most life history narratives, however, there is a lot going on here: Conrad shifts back and forth temporally; different people come in and out of the picture. Keeping secrets is not simply a matter of being careful about whom one tells stories to; it is also a matter of managing one's "virtual body." The specialty websites where escorts advertise require pictures—some even ask them to include face pictures—but such disclosure can compromise escorts' anonymity. Conrad has to manage his anonymity, striking a balance between being "out" and ensuring that his family and others do not learn how he funds his semesters in school.

Leon

Most male-for-male Internet escorts explicitly position themselves in their storytelling as different from hustlers and on-street workers, suggesting that they do not experience "troubles" like other sex workers. But some of the men I interviewed did start out working on the street, and some continued to be street-involved for many years. Leon describes hustling in and being shuffled around Toronto during the 1990s. This specific narrative is about one stint with an escort agency:

You always knew you were going to be relatively safe, you were not just picking up someone off the street, and someone always knew you were leaving and maybe even the person you were leaving with. The one thing about the agency I worked for in Toronto, I got fired. I met a person who was really cool, really generous, was lonely and wanted a companion. Outside of the business, I stayed in contact. I lost my job because of that. But that person provided so much for a year or two. That is what happens to me. I go back into to the business, somebody wants me and they pay for it, they end up taking a liking to me, and they become not a sugar daddy but a "I like this guy and I will help him out" kinda thing. I am very fortunate in that way. What I am doing at this point in my life most people are doing at 25. So I am living the life of a 25-year-old. For the last 15 years. That is the drawback. It stunts your growth.

Leon still hustles and uses drugs but is trying not to. He reflects on his sex work and suggests it "stunts" his life chances. For him, sex is tied to drugs, though he tries not to mix them anymore.

Bruce

Bruce does not paint the rosiest picture of sex work either. Though many escorts narrate their entry into escorting as a choice they made when looking for work, some other escorts feel pressured into it, as Bruce from Toronto explains:

The reason why I decided to do it was because I wanted some extra money. I can only work part time because in my early teens I suffered from depression and anxiety attacks so I used to work full time. I have a low threshold for stress so I actually started to get sick, I started to develop some serious gastrointestinal problems. I was having bad panic attacks and having bad bouts of fatigue. So I saw my physician and was jumping from specialist to specialist and he recommended that I only work part time. I actually had to go on disability so I've gotten myself really struggling financially. I remember I was talking to a friend and my friend actually made a casual joke and said, "Why don't you just do some escort work?"

Bruce took on escorting work because he was unable to do other work that required long shifts or extended periods of time away from his home. Escorting provided a form of work that paid well and could be completed in an hour or two. Even though he cannot escort full-time, Bruce's biography and his sex work have become interwoven in many ways:

I had grown up in foster homes, and the last foster home that I had lived in my foster parents had died. I had just broken up with my last partner, so I had this appointment to go to, just an erotic massage for this gentleman who was staying in a hotel. It was hard because at that time of my life I was crying a lot. I was depressed, there was a lot of stuff that was going on in my personal life and I was tempted to call this person and cancel the appointment but I went through with it anyway because I needed the money. And when I showed up the client could tell that I was upset about something and said, "Oh if you want to talk about it we can talk about it." So as I was giving him the massage, I was kind of crying and everything, it was hard for me to kind of hold it together and so forth. You know we had a good time, the client and I, after the massage we just sort of sat around talking and so forth and he was actually a nice guy and he was giving me advice.

Bruce's and Leon's narratives show how the "choice" to enter sex work may be complicated for some men. Bruce's narrative also demonstrates the difficulty of keeping one's private and work lives separate. Work life and private life loop into one another.[5] His narrative also suggests how a passing pleasure can metamorphose into a touching encounter full of affection, in this case with the client supporting the escort. As these narratives suggest, male-for-male Internet escorting has more to do with the diversity of sexualities among men who have sex with men than criminological or public health research agendas can account for.

Some Internet escorts experience stigma, but because Internet escorting is less visible due to an individualized labor process (anonymity being the name of the game), they talk less about discrimination and more about managing stereotypes. For instance, Byron from Houston describes how he negotiates stigma: "There is stigma. I close myself off more from those who are not in the business. I do not feel it as much and I do not see it as much but I know it is there. I know prostitutes and call girls experience worse." Although Byron says he can sense stigma almost as if it is stuck to him, he does not mention any status loss or discrimination. His management of stigma, his closing himself off from those not involved in escorting, represents his attempt to avoid the character blemishes that could accompany his outing as someone who sells sex to other men.

Because the world of male-for-male Internet escorting is clandestine, stigma might seem to be less relevant for these men since it rarely involves public disgrace. This work is "under the radar because most people don't want people to know what they do" (Steve, Toronto). Keeping secrets implies management of stigmatization in the making: "I don't put out the neon lights to everybody. . . . you don't know how people are going to react. I have never gotten a real negative reaction, but I think it's also . . . because I've been careful about who I told" (Donald, New York). Escorts may report not experiencing stigma as much as other men who have sex with men because they are skilled at keeping encounters with clients a secret. Yet self-identified gay escorts do experience stereotyping by other gay men. Tyler from Ottawa notes:

I have been very good at keeping that part of life a secret to most of the people in the community. . . . I outted myself as a sex worker to a few friends of mine and these are people that I trust. . . . I think if you are too open about what you do as a sex worker you get labeled as a hustler and you are put in the category, you are pegged as this and whatever prejudices that come along with that. Gays can be just as discriminatory as other people, if not worse.

Similarly, Sam from Ottawa feels that when other men in Internet chat rooms find out he sells sex, they sometimes hold it against him: "he read [my ad] and then he called me a 'prostitute'; it was not a compliment, it was an insult." Labeling and stereotyping occur within the gay community itself. As Mark from London put it, "sometimes you hear or read snide comments, like he is 'commercial.' So there is some stigma. There is no pressure from the outside, it is all from the gay community." Other escorts describe being rejected by men in the dating scene because of their work. These examples hint at how men who have sex with men also engage in the labeling and stereotyping basic to stigmatization, even against men who hold similar ideas about pleasure and sexuality.

Some escorts talk about what they consider to be the dark side of the industry, as Steve from Toronto remarks: "you start to go down. It's very enticing with the money but then you start to realize how hard it is to stay on top. You get washed up." Keeping secrets for years on end can lead to a sense of isolation. But not all escorts dwell on the dark side. Eddy from Toronto, age 29, suggests there is no dark side to the industry itself: "I feel like I'm 100 percent alone in this, but that's what I want. I don't want a support network. I don't need that. I do not need an HR department. . . . I just want to do it when I need it and I don't do it when I don't need it."

Chapter 8 | **Aging and Escorting**

Playing Young, Getting Old, and Overcoming the "Best By" Date

The aim of this chapter is to discuss aging and male-with-male sexuality. Queer theory has tended to neglect the aging body. Even critical gerontology has not fully theorized how aging bodies delimit agency.[1] Brian Heaphy (2007) contends that the issue of aging in communities of men who have sex with men remains understudied by sociologists. This chapter draws from literature concerning aging and male sexuality[2] to understand how male-for-male Internet escorts navigate aging and deal with their bodies' failings.

I am primarily interested in what male escorts say about aging because talk about age is often talk about the body. Aging marks a temporal shift in the way people understand their life story and their bodies in relation to others. Because aging bodies are often associated with illness and frailty, most of us understand sex and old age to be incompatible. The escorts I interviewed tell stories about aging—about what their bodies can do and how their bodies often fail them when it comes time to touch. C. González (2007) suggests that older men become sorted and stigmatized according to "age-graded sexualities" and age-related tropes in gay communities. Exclusion between men who have sex with men on the basis of aging points to one of the contradictions of sexuality studies: scholars call for inclusion and flag sexuality as a site of struggle, but they have neglected aging men who have sex with men when it comes to research. Beyond emphasizing how aging and the body intersect for male escorts, this chapter reflects on this issue of aging men's sense of sexuality and how younger men who sell sex to men treat the issue of aging.

Age-Graded Sexualities and Male-for-Male Internet Escorting

Discussion of aging and male sexuality corrects queer theory's inattention to age as an axis of social exclusion. As we age, sexuality becomes stratified; we fall out of sex relations with younger people and those we once shared a sense of belonging with. This tendency results in what González (2007) refers to as "age-graded sexualities." There are many age-related tropes in gay communities concerning men's bodies (e.g., "chicken," "chicken hawk," "daddy"),[3] and these tropes come to shape life histories, figuring in the stories people tell about themselves and their encounters with others. The work narratives of male-for-male Internet escorts make clear that aging is important for both clients and escorts.

Escorts explain that clients generally look for something new and something young in an escort. There remain only limited possibilities for older escorts to open up niche markets, thereby remaining in the trade. Age proves pivotal in relations between these men. Most escorts lie about their age on their website to attract more customers. As Frederico from Toronto says, "it is a kind of unwritten rule, everybody shaves a couple of years off." The narratives of male-for-male escorts evince the high degree of inclusion and exclusion around age, as Tyler suggests:

I am 34 years old. Most clients think I am 24 or 26. They say I look that age. On my websites I put my date of birth as 1980, so I say I am 27 and that works for me. If they wanted younger they will go for a twink 19 or 20. That is fine. There are certain men who only want someone over 25. I say I am 27. And because of the way I look it works fabulously, because they see me and they say oh god you look good, how old did you say you were? I never tell them by the way I am actually 34 years old. It is about keeping the fantasy. If I did post my real age and told people I was 34 years old, I would not get as many calls. Because people still discriminate based on age. And the fantasy is that they want some young twenty something kind of guy. Even if you look good at 34, they will shoot for a lower age. I have never had someone tell me they thought I was lying about my age, even though I am. No one has ever said I am too old. I know I will not be able to keep that up forever. I think I look about 10 years younger. As long as I am able to look that way without any help, I will do it.

Aging is important in the lives of men who have sex with men, especially for escorts who feel pressure to provide a youthful appearance and virility during interactions with clients. This bind is akin to the agonized tale Oscar Wilde weaves in *The Picture of Dorian Gray* (1890, 1891). Wilde narrates an account of how far people will reach for beauty and adoration. As one character in the novel says to another, "you only have a few years in which to live really, perfectly, and fully." Many escorts abide by this impossible vision of the young, tender body, a vision one escort calls "illusionary perfection" (see Lawrence 1999:x).

As escorts advance in the life course, however, they position themselves differently regarding sexuality and their web persona. An escort who has worked in Toronto and Montréal describes how aging influences his escorting work:

I'm not really a boy anymore. I kind of was when I started, I was only 25. Now I'm almost 30 and I have a man's body and there's been a part of me that has had some trouble embracing that. I think partially because when I first started sex trade work my view was that all sex trade workers were young. All sex trade workers were hairless, they were sort of twinky, which I sort of never was although when I first started working, I always think I shaved my face really close, sometimes I would shave twice a day. I was always really hairless for my clients. I shaved my chest. And I was trying to kind of present this vision, it wasn't even a matter necessarily of being masculine or unmasculine but a version of boyishness or youth. And as I aged a little bit, I have grey hair coming in. I don't shave my chest at all anymore. I don't shave my face every day. And I actually found that since I've become a bit more masculine looking, first of all my existing clients were really into it. They like it, it turns them on. And I find that new clients find me more attractive because I look like a man, not a boy. (Claude, Montréal)

The facts of our body change as we age. Bodies become incapable of certain feats that once provided pleasure. Escorts' bodies provide resources they can draw on in advertising to clients and pleasing them during their encounters. Another way of saying this is that the body is an "open materiality" (Grosz 1994:191) insofar as it manifests a set of potentialities to be worked on and through. There is a market for mature escorts, but escorts must remarket at various points in the life course and make different uses of their aging bodies in order to be accepted.

Certainly a market exists for older escorts, but it is a niche market. Some men will always want other men who are older than them. Aging means the clientele one caters to must change:

there's quite a few I get who said they don't want a kid, they want someone they know who's going to show up on time, who isn't going to bang on my door at three in the morning or call me to borrow money, you know that sort of thing. And so I have gotten a lot like that, if I want a kid, I'll hire a kid you know . . . they don't want the games. They don't want the chat and all the bullshit, you know some of them might want drinks all night just to have them fuck off on them, that sort of thing so they view it as they would rather pay the same amount of money and get a guarantee. (Bob, Ottawa)

The aging body provides a different set of resources for escorts to draw on in marketing themselves. Aging allows an escort to self-position as responsible and trustworthy. These and other profile differences, such as pictures and client reviews, inevitably create a basis for comparison with escorts who are much younger. Oscar is 56 years old and started escorting when he was 48 because he could not secure work as an actor in London. He spends many hours a day in the gym pumping up his aging body. He talks about how age mediates his escorting encounters:

We all are, at the moment, with the credit crunch, people are dropping to lower rates. So far I have not brought mine down, and I am trying not to, because I want to remain at the top end of the market and be attracting wealthier clients. At the lower end of the market, there are lots of kids out there who will do anything for anything. And these younger kids probably can because they can do it for next to nothing because they can cum four or five times a day. But I cannot do that. I am too old for that. Once a day. Sometimes I can do three in a day still, but I am quite happy if I get one good client and spend time with them. (Oscar, London)

Oscar positions himself against younger escorts who are keen to do anything for any amount of money. Oscar has created a niche market because, as he says, "there are not many older guys doing it and not many guys with my kind of body." The focus on his body indicates that his sense of virility remains at the center of his sexual persona, yet he admits that the facts of his body have changed and he can now only be sexually active once a day. Being an older escort influences the labor process in other ways, too. Part of being an older escort comprises the ability to screen clients better and take only those clients one is interested in having an encounter with:

With age, I am in a much better position to control who I see and what I do. If I am not comfortable on the phone with someone I will not agree to see them. I get a lot more respect from clients, the guys who come to see me, the sex is sex, but they are

looking for something more, and I have to say that in the main I have been treated
with absolute respect, I have never had a problem, I have met some really nice
people. There has not been a bad experience. (Oscar, London)

Oscar's buff body mixed with the charm of his gentleman's persona is rare
in escorting markets, allowing him to capitalize on the presentation of a
particular age-graded sexuality at the age of 56. Harvey from Montréal likewise adds that clients "trust me because of my experience," which only
comes with age. Not all escorts can transition into a niche market: as escorts get older or sense they have reached an age limit, some leave the
industry in search of other work.

Aging does not necessitate an end to escorting, but it does present the
escort with several challenges requiring renewed attention to the work
they do on their own bodies, their advertisements, and their potential clientele. As Michel Dorais (2005:35) puts it, mobility in sex work "tends
to be downward with age." Staying in escorting past a certain age proves
difficult, though some escorts successfully transition into a "daddy" role,
which is easier to assume in leather and bondage communities where aging is less negatively perceived. Escorting while aging involves remarketing
oneself as a sexual subject.

As evidence of how age-graded sexualities shape the way escorts fashion
a sense of self, older escorts position themselves against younger men in
their talk about aging. For instance, in our conversation Sam (44 years old)
from Ottawa persistently reminded me that he did not consider himself an
"escort" because of the association of all sex work with poverty. Sam also
told many stories about how being an older man made him a more responsible worker, a professional, and that he would not engage in the activities
that younger escorts often undertook:

I am no longer in my twenties, you can see. Maybe that has something to do with
why I do not call myself an escort. Things like that may not be so appealing for
people my age, and I am offering more of a service than just sex. I found out maybe
I am making more money than the younger guys, some people say you are too
expensive, some say it is fair. Some say, what do I get for $60? I say you get a great
massage, including your crotch and everything, a good orgasm at the end. He said
"is that all?" He said I go to a guy and I get a blow job for $50. I told him to go
back to that person. That is a good deal. Stick to it! Another guy told me once that
it is good that I am a bit older because I know what I want, know what I am doing

and they can trust me more than those younger guys. People realize that what I do is different from what those younger guys do. (Sam, Ottawa)

In this narrative, Sam composes a sense of self and differentiates himself from younger escorts. Aging men must successfully reposition themselves in the sex industry, like Sam, yet they also have fewer opportunities for other forms of so-called legitimate work, especially other forms of work that pay as well as escorting. They need to align themselves with the acceptable age-graded sexualities that can work as an escorting persona:

I'd like to get out, but where else am I making 100–150 bucks an hour. It's so hard to go back to work for even 15 or 20 bucks an hour, or even salaries suck. It's hard to go from making that kind of money tax free to working full eight-hour days. I can pass for 25–26 most of the time, but in a few years I'm not going to be able to. (Bob, Ottawa)

Advancing through the life course can generate age-related worries for the escort, especially regarding the ability to achieve economic security. Some of these men worry about aging itself, but this concern is often tied to financial worries:

You basically have to stop it at a certain point because, I know the market, guys generally want younger guys. It's a very small niche market that want someone openly say 40 and up. And I'm not trying to be vain or arrogant, I got ID-ed on Pride Day and I know I can't pass for that, that's really pushing it. I probably wouldn't try to do this work if I actually thought I looked almost 40. I probably wouldn't even bother but I know I can get away with at least five years younger. So yeah, there's definitely a cutoff point for it. There is a "best by" date. (Ricky, Toronto)

Numerous authors commenting on aging and male sexuality describe new pressures on men in the "Viagra Era" to remain virile throughout the life course.[4] Viagra and other treatments aim to produce "posthuman" bodies that continue to be sexually active into old age, creating sexual senior citizens. I discuss Viagra and escorting in the next chapter. The point here is that in gay communities, stereotypes circulate about older men, sometimes construing older men as less touchable.

Men who have sex with men do not all use the same language to refer to themselves and sexuality. This variability of the "gay" signifier intersects with how men of different ages make sense of sex as well. The term "queer" was reappropriated by the New York City Aids Coalition to Unleash Power (ACT UP) in 1990. But the "queer" label might fail to account for the histories of older gay men, since their strategies of passing were based on assimilation to heterosexual norms of masculinity. Some of these stereotypes are explicitly callous toward older gay men. An interviewee who had just turned 50 at the time of our meeting said:

I think there's this huge stereotype that people over 40 are trolls. . . . there's this certain attitude with you know once you hit 35 or 40 you're just, you're not interesting, you're just put out to pasture and that's it. But that there's definitely a sense among older men themselves of being with somebody that has some experience, they have something to relate to, some common experience that they share and some life that they can reflect on together. Especially in terms of S&M, you want somebody that at least looks like they have the experience and can be trusted and that they know what they are doing and part of the whole daddy image depends on that. There's one thing I noticed about older clients too that they, like they're not so focused on ejaculation. If it happens it's great, but it doesn't have to and . . . sometimes no matter how much they wanted to it just doesn't, and they don't hold you responsible for that whereas sometimes a younger client might say, "it's your fault I didn't cum." You weren't good enough. Some older guys, Mother Nature, you know that's the way it is sometimes. But there's a lot more realism on the part of older men and they appreciate somebody that they can share that with . . . it's a maturity that comes with experience. (Donald, New York)

This narrative ties back to what Crossley (2007) calls the facts of the body. As Donald points out, the relation between client and escort can be desexualized insofar as it focuses on touching that is not genital-centric. Older men are said to be more comfortable with what their bodies cannot do. Barbara Marshall and Stephen Katz (2002:44) write that "relatively little attention has been paid to male bodies *qua* male bodies," and the functionality of the penis has always been defined by its ability to penetrate. Certainly heterosexual touching and focus on vaginal intercourse reflect a dominant sexual script that is penis-centric, yet the touching encounters of older men who have sex with men do not necessarily focus on the erect penis. Masculinity is often associated with being hard, strong, competitive, and in control, but the fallible penis is a fact of the body that can lead to desexualized touching among older men. The penis loses its functionality and it fails; as a result, the aging body can be desexualized. Although many men valorize the erect penis, the aging gay community is more likely to recognize the limits of the body and what the escort and the client can still do.[5]

Discussion

Jackson and Scott (2010:163) suggest that little scholarly work has addressed the issue of older men's sexual lives. This statement becomes doubly true when the issue is older men's commercial sex lives. I have focused on aging as a corrective to the tendency in queer theory to overlook aging bodies; I have also mapped out the implications of aging for understanding how male bodies come together. The queer project of undoing the universal male subject might well start by looking at aging as a major source of difference and distinction among men. Aging constitutes a prominent axis through which men who have sex with men can become marginal. For Julie Jones and Stephen Pugh (2005:258), "the emphasis in gay spaces has always been and continues to be on youth, and therefore older gay men are excluded from a world in which being old equates to being unattractive and being attractive is a precondition for entry." Yet we may also find solidarity among aging men who recognize the limits of their bodies and find other dimensions of their selves to share with one another. While there are older personas available in gay communities (such as the "daddy"), not all escorts can provide these services, so most slowly leave the industry, hanging on to repeat clients until the clients let go.

Ragan Fox (2007) claims that younger men who have sex with men tend to neglect their aging counterparts. I likewise suggest that men who have sex with men hold varying understandings of sexuality depending on their age and biography. Some of the narratives shared here suggest that age-based stereotypes operate among men who have sex with men and that these stereotypes influence the ability of male-for-male Internet escorts to continue doing this work as the facts of their bodies change. This sample of male Internet escorts is slightly older than comparative samples, which allows me to provide insight into how age-graded sexualities influence work and sex lives. Some of these escorts' narratives suggest that older men who have sex with men are more comfortable with touching encounters not completely organized around an erect penis. By demonstrating how older escorts become entrepreneurial in finding clientele despite their aging bodies, I have shown how aging does not necessarily lead to a decline in social position for older men who have sex with men, although it presents certain hurdles to men who sell sex to men.

| **How Bodies Matter in Male-for-Male Internet Escorting**

Body Work, Body Capital, and Body Trouble

Two meanings of "touch" run through this book: the first refers to imbrications of bodies, and the second refers to mutuality and camaraderie. My conception of "touching encounters" highlights the role of interaction in relations between escort and client, while pointing to how participants translate discourses of sexuality in joint actions. In this chapter, I explore the dual meaning of touching encounters by analyzing escorts' talk about and work on their bodies, as well as the bodies of other men.

Carol Wolkowitz (2002) blames the lack of scholarly attention to working bodies on feminist cultural writings that emphasize constitution of the body by discourse. Indeed, critics accuse poststructuralist theorists of positing the body as a form of text inscribed by discourse and thereby neglecting its materiality. Butler (2004a:198) herself admits this material neglect, writing, "I am not a very good materialist. Every time I try to write about the body, the writing ends up being about language." Even in the sociology of sexuality, we find few humping and pumping bodies.[1] Ironically, scholarship concerning male sex work has not fully investigated issues of touch and corporeality. Here, I offer a corrective to this inattention to the material body, focusing specifically on how male-for-male Internet escorts talk about touch and bodies.

Discourses of sexuality and gender provide the parameters for understanding bodies. Yet sometimes discourse falters upon, and scripts are shaken off by, the moving body. The use of the body need not always be pinned to a sexed or gendered meaning. For instance, O'Connell Davidson (1995) discusses the way female sex workers "milk" clients with their vaginas to bring the men to orgasm quicker. Female respondents in Prus and Irini's (1980) study like men to be on top because if clients move the way they want, then they cum faster. Josh from Toronto similarly reports, "I'm kinda like a power bottom, you just give into it for a minute and they're usually done. Lots of times I can make 300 bucks in fifteen minutes." Being a "power bottom" is about the materiality of the body and what it can do. To develop a corporeal understanding of sex work, sociologists must start with what bodies are capable of and not with an abstract notion of discourse. An interactionist approach to the body is attuned to how bodies mean through movement in specific contexts. I start from escorts' body work in theorizing the relation between work, their bodies, and the bodies of other men.

This chapter unpacks three concepts—body work, body capital, and body trouble—connected to male-for-male Internet escorting, with an emphasis on how each of these concepts enlivens a discussion of touching. Body work refers to what we do with our bodies and the bodies of others. The literature on body work examines how people work on or with other bodies and body fluids. When scholars have studied working bodies, they have assumed that these bodies are heterosexual male bodies, so they have neglected queer bodies and women's bodies at work.[2] Male-for-male Internet escorting represents a form of body work that requires body reflexive practices generated out of concern for and touching with other men's bodies. As an example of the touching involved in body work, consider Sam's narrative:

> With my body, I have power because they so enjoy being with me they are ready to pay for it. This changed the way I think about my body and myself. They realize that if they do not pay for it they will not get it. . . . many of the guests, they turn around at the end, and they say thank you, you are giving a real massage. . . . a guy told me, . . . "I am sore when I come here and I want the massage. The erotic part is good, but I am not taking the erotic part without the massage," so he said, "you're good. The last guy I went to see he was giving a superficial rub, next five minutes he was all over my cock." (Sam, Ottawa)

Part of these men's work is to touch others: they are professional touchers. Body work is not reducible to "sex" or to "work" in a conventional sense, however, so my analysis supplements understandings of sex work by focusing on its corporeal elements.

Loïc Wacquant argues that body work can be conceptualized as an accumulated and ossified form of "body capital."[3] Body capital refers to how what we do with our bodies becomes valued. Certainly particular body stereotypes and racialized bodies become valorized in male-for-male Internet escorting. But I suggest that the idea of body capital remains only partially helpful for conceptualizing how bodies are valued in escorting, since there is no ideal body that all escorts or clients seek. Nor do escorts adhere to a strict regime of discipline or training. Additionally, escorting can be oriented more toward caring about clients instead of competing against other escorts. In these cases, escorts and clients value compassion shared through bodies' coming together in ways the idea of body capital cannot account for.

Body trouble refers to how what we do with our bodies becomes problematized and regulated. Talking about escorts' bodies also means talking about HIV/AIDS and sexually transmitted infections, not because male sex workers are disease vectors as the public health literature has assumed,[4] but because escorts are proactive in protecting their sexual health and educating clients about safe sex. In attempting to mitigate body trouble, male escorts negotiate health risks through touching, even with men who have HIV/AIDS or sexually transmitted infections.

This chapter is organized in four parts. First, I consider male-for-male Internet escorts' stories about their bodies in relation to the idea of body work. I then examine the idea of body capital and consider its usefulness for thinking about the touching encounters and masculinities that escorting requires. Next, I consider escorts' narratives about body trouble, sexually transmitted infections, and HIV/AIDS. In conclusion, I reassess what the ideas of body work, body capital, and body trouble contribute to thinking through the corporeality of sex work.

Body Work

The idea of "work" often evokes a hard, male, and dirty body: this is the worker's body under industrial capitalism; these are workers' bodies in factories or mines. Wolkowitz (2006) argues that bodies have been largely ignored in the sociology of work. Scholars have singled out the bodies of manual laborers instead of the bodies of other kinds of workers, including those who work on other bodies. Male-for-male Internet escorts' bodies are central to their work, as are the bodies of clients. All the touching that happens during escort encounters can be conceptualized as body work.

Researchers have used the idea of "body work" to refer to work on one's own body, work on the bodies of others, the management of bodily gestures, and the modification of bodies through working. Sometimes body work is dirty work, where less appealing parts of others' bodies are managed. (Miliann Kang's [2003] research on work in nail salons is one example.) Escorting can be conceptualized as body work since escorts work on their own bodies to attract clients and to keep the clients they already have. Male escorts work on clients' bodies, manage clients' bodily fluids, and use their own bodies to provide pleasure. These men provide diverse services to clients, and the kind of body work they undertake depends on the kinds of clients the escort aims to attract:

When someone is paying for something they want to have something good. When you go to the grocery store you do not want to buy rotten bananas. I have the power in this job. I have the power because my body is demanded. . . . I have the body he is looking for. I make sure it stays that way. I do my push ups, I make sure I do my sit ups. I carry weights. I play tennis and I play badminton. I keep in shape so I have the body that people want to pay for. (Sam, Ottawa)

Male-for-male Internet escorts are not only concerned with maintaining the body's exterior appearance. Our bodies are more than semiotic surfaces. Senses rise to the fore. The inside of the body must also be kept smelling and feeling aesthetically pleasing:

I always douche. If I am with a client who wants to fuck me I will douche at least three times and make sure I'm really clean. The clients do not want to have shit stains on their sheets or their dick. Like any good escort, you douche properly, you are clean, shaved, your balls are shaved, you trim where you are supposed to be, unless a client has requested a punk hustler look from the street, because some people like rough trade fantasies. . . . I do not wear cologne. You should never wear cologne with a client. You do not know if they are married or if they have a girlfriend. You do not want your scent on the client. I learned that from female escorts who told me they do not wear perfume. (Tyler, Ottawa)

Ricky: I have a douche device if they need it. Most guys come over clean.
K: Do you ever recommend maybe take a minute and . . . ?
Ricky: Yeah, in both private and sex work. Sometimes it's not their fault, you're human. They think they're clean, they may have cleaned up an hour ago but something's moved down, and I don't give a shit, you're human, I'm human. We'll "touch up" as we say.

Senses of smell and touch are central in these narratives about what Tyler and Ricky do with male bodies. Tyler mentions that most clients (and most escorts) do not appreciate the sight and smell of excrement, so it is preventively removed. The escort fashions his body depending on what kind of aesthetic the client is hoping for. There are numerous stereotypes in queer communities that compel sexual performatives. Sometimes men attempt to embody these stereotypes. Embodiment of a "rough trade" persona, as Tyler indicates, is one example. Body work thus implies more than merely working on the body's surface appearance; it also implies managing the body's odors and fluids.

For these escorts, a sense of self is created through working on other bodies, which results in reflexive management of one's own body.[5] These body reflexive practices involve plucking, cutting, trimming, preening, waxing, pumping, and shaving:

I shave my chest. I shave all of my upper body. I shave every part I don't want hair on. . . . I didn't do it before, I used to trim my hair before, but I didn't take a lot of care on some parts. I didn't shave my chest before, I didn't shave my back and all of these kinds of things. Now I do it. (Frederico, Toronto)

All parts of the body are subject to reflexive self-management practices. The materiality of the escort's own body changes as he shapes it toward certain ends: escorting "made me a lot more conscious of the way I look. I constantly prep myself up. If there's something that I think is a flaw I'm going to find it and obsess over it" (Gabe, Toronto). These reflexive stylizations of the body are what Foucault calls technologies of the self. Technologies of the self allow individuals "to effect by their own means or with the help of others a certain number of operations on their own bodies and souls, thoughts, conduct, and way of being, so as to transform themselves in order to attain a certain state of happiness, purity, wisdom, perfection, or immortality" (Foucault 1988:18).

This stylization of the body requires time and effort:

It's a pain in the ass sometimes getting ready to go and having to look good and be "on." That's the worst, the phone rings and it's 10 o'clock, and I'm in my sweat pants watching "Friends" and I don't feel like doing this or I just masturbated an hour ago or I'm hungry and feel fat. That's the hardest thing, is getting yourself together. (Conrad, Toronto)

Such body reflexive practices are also situated in larger networks of relations. Instead of bodies being passive objects of symbolism and power, the concept of body reflexive practice suggests that bodies are at once constituents of regulation and push-back. Such body work is socialized by one's network of relations; this means that body work is never idiosyncratic. People work on themselves over time to meet the demands of gender and sexuality that are thrust upon them as part of their work. Gill and colleagues (2005:58) argue that "the body is a site not only for the performance or enactment of masculinity, but also for its profound and intimate regulation," so that body reflexive practices are pivotal in presentations of self during work.

Male-for-male Internet escorting is not all about sex, and some of these excerpted interviews describe how many parts of the body are subjected to body reflexive practices. Yet the penis often figures centrally in escorts' narratives about touching encounters. Talk about sex tends to emphasize the genital zone. At 64 years of age, after seeing hundreds of penises a year for over 20 years as a sex worker, one respondent mentioned that he uses "condoms on guys who I thought had ugly cocks" (Gerald, Toronto). Certain penises become "ugly" in comparison with others and then are correspondingly touched (or not) as part of the work. Frank from Toronto states that the primary task involved in escorting for him is "learning to tolerate disgusting things." In the words of Jonathan Dollimore (2001:374), "there's a long tradition of people of the same—the very same—sexual orientation being disgusted with each other." However, disgust does not translate into intolerance, partly because the escort depends on the client for income. Rather than forming the center of sex work, the penis becomes simply another body part to be managed. An escort may charge more money if the client's body puts him off or if the client asks him to do something with his body that he prefers not to do.

Much of the work occurs before escorts meet clients, as in the case of escorts' work on their own bodies. The escort must reflexively work on his body before the encounter (and also during the encounter) in order to make it serviceable. Part of this work on the body intersects with the use of supplements to enhance sexual performance:

I've never taken Viagra in the context of sex trade work. I've used it recreationally with other sexual partners, and I've had times in the context of sex trade work where I wished I had taken a Viagra because for whatever reason I'm not able to maintain a full enough erection for the client. But the thing about Viagra is it takes an hour to kick in, your session is only an hour so if you get half an hour into your session and you realize you're not getting it up, taking a Viagra doesn't do any good because you're not going to be hard until after the session is over. . . . maybe as I

get older it will become more important to me. But I do always try to be as genu-
inely turned on by a client as possible. (Claude, Montréal)

Because the escort needs to create some immediate sense of arousal to make the sexual component of the encounter happen, he may take various performance-enhancing substances, such as Viagra. Annie Potts (2004) argues that Viagra operates to sexualize bodily relations, restoring penetrative sex to the center of relations. Viagra certainly aids escorts in preparing and presenting the sexualized body:

I take Viagra and Cyalis fairly regularly. If I know I am going to have several tricks in quick succession I will take a Cyalis, or if I have a client who is difficult to work with because he is hideous, I will take a Viagra or Cyalis. And I always make sure not to masturbate before so I can have an erection, because you are expected to have an erection and there is no way out of it. The other guy is paying a lot of money. There is only one guy with whom that is a problem because he is so spectacularly ugly. Every time I see him I have this problem. I need to make sure that I do not masturbate for a couple days to get off. And I make sure to take Cyalis ahead of time to maintain an erection. For the clients who want to get fucked, I need to be hard. There is another guy who is a very intense bottom and he wants to be fucked for hours, so we do two hours of the same thing, I have to be hard for hours, even after I cum he wants me to keep going, so Cyalis is needed. (Frank, Toronto)

Some clients demand particular performances from the escort body. Because escorts must usually fit a certain stereotype and their bodies need to be prepped for performance, escorts can become preoccupied with constantly trying to manage their bodies. Body reflexive practices lead to self-surveillance and supplementation of the body's facts in order to meet client demands.

It is important not to overstate the case about body regulation. Sex workers take their bodies as fields of action, but the process is negotiated. Bodies need to be made sense of.[6] Sexual encounters can produce unanticipated meanings as well as new ways of putting men's bodies together. For example, body work can change the way escorts think of their bodies and the bodies of other men:

There's definitely guys that turn me on more than others, but I'm way more open to a variety of body types and all that, ages, which also has opened me to women funny enough. . . . One time I walked into a dark room and there's a guy on the bed with no arms and no legs and the money is there and he wants me to do this, and I just said, "No" and I said, "It's not because you have, you know, things for legs, but it's because you lied to me and it freaked me out." The odd time if somebody is a little too old, it's not their age, but it reminds me of my father and it freaks me out. If they have physical attributes or if they remind me of my dad, my dad and I never did anything, my dad is dead now, but it's weird. (Conrad, Toronto)

I used to have issues with people if they were not in shape, I would feel like it's weird. I felt almost disgusted by touching them. Now I see people of all shapes. I can see their hearts. I see guys that are skinny, flabby or fat or chubby whatever, I mean I see, you know, the totality, the body is not that important anymore for me. Now I can have sex with anybody, pretty much. But I know how in the gay community that's not likely, gay people are very judgmental. (Roberto, New York)

Working on other men's bodies has challenged Conrad's and Roberto's perceptions about what bodies are acceptable as bodies to be near. In a sense, this work thus challenges the valorization of particular body types in the gay community. Here, there is a looping effect between the encounter and the escort's understandings of bodies and self. Hacking (2004) discusses the looping that occurs among classifications, people's reception of the classification, and the attendant redrawing of the classification. Not only does the materiality of the escort body change because of the work; the meanings of men's bodies can also change such that escorts will be more or less accepting of different body shapes and sizes:

Having to give a massage to a 90-year-old man that is 400 lbs, yeah, you know. . . . I'm going to go to the gym for the rest of my life. I had a guy in a wheelchair, a hot guy too. He was really built from the waist up, he was stabbed in the back in high school and he lost all the feeling in his legs. I had never been naked with a guy in a wheelchair before. And you know what, it wasn't bad. I've had a lot of different experiences and seen a lot of body types now. I would say it just makes me see what I don't want for myself. They might be perfectly content, but I don't want to be 300 lbs when I'm 60 years old. (Steve, Toronto)

In this looping effect, the escort's body reflexive practices are shaped in relation to bodies he encounters during work. Hacking (2004) suggests that his idea of looping at the level of discourse works because it has an analog at the level of interaction. The consequence is that the body is not a fixed object; its meaning is fluid. Touching the bodies of other men has unanticipated consequences for how escorts attribute meaning to their own and other bodies.

As I discussed earlier, some scholars have claimed that sex workers create a firm distinction between their work life and personal life. This distinction is hard to maintain with male-for-male Internet escorts because their sex work and their sexual biographies overlap.[7] Similarly, the body work of escorting builds up in a set of habits influencing the escort's daily life:

When I am preparing before a client, I am turning the lights down, turning a porno on, getting the lube ready, on a normal date you would not do this but escorts find themselves doing this stuff, I do it. For instance, the idea of washing down. Escorts wash down before they see a client. But when you are escorting for two or three years, it becomes a part of you, you find yourself worried about washing down before a date. (Ben, London)

Escorts cannot separate their work sex from their sex life. The habits of their work sex life can reflexively become the habits of their whole sex life, demonstrating again how sex work and biography overlap for these men. Sex work cannot be separated from the biography of the escort since the bodies of workers and clients become entwined. The touch of body work can thus collapse the professional and private spheres.

Encounters between escort and client are touching encounters based on bodies coming together and senses engaging. These encounters are also "touching" in a second way as the imbrications of clients' and escorts' bodies can be tender and poignant:

There was one guy who would come to see me, spoke to him on the phone, I thought he was young, in college, early twenties. You get a mental picture. He arrived, he was the ugliest human being I have ever seen, hook nose, humpback, covered in hair. But very sweet, appreciative, probably never had sex before, it was all over quickly. Then he held me. I let him stay the whole time. I felt that someone like that very rarely is touched, never has a chance for human contact, it was all about holding another human. That was a satisfying experience. We never think about people like that. We take for granted being touched. It is sad. I felt sorry for him. (Oscar, London)

Oscar's narrative exemplifies the sort of mutuality that can characterize commercial sex between men. More than a simple display of affection, this kind of touching by the escort provides validation for the client. In a similar example, Jeff from New York met a client who had lost both legs to diabetes at age twelve. The client stated that he never was able to meet men for companionship because of his body's appearance. Jeff commented, "it is sad that people, not just gay men, are so childish about the human body." Men who have sex with men sometimes live their lives in lonely silence because of stigmatization.[8] This lonely silence can be amplified for men who cannot match up to body stereotypes. Many clients of male sex workers are unable to engage in sexual encounters outside of this context because of the ways their bodies or faces look. Touching encounters provide contact for men who might otherwise remain untouched. In this way, men's bodies are not simply disciplined and dominating (see Morgan 1993); they are also sites of emotion and fraternity.

To reinforce the dual meaning of touching encounter, consider the increasing confluence of disability rights and sex worker advocates. Disability rights advocates argue that touch is highly remedial, as do sex worker groups. The Tender Loving Care Trust in the United Kingdom and the Touching Base Collective[9] in Australia both facilitate links between persons with disabilities, their advocacy groups, and the commercial sex industry. While not all escorts think of their work as providing the poignancy of touch, some do.

Sociologists are not used to thinking of the work that people do on their own bodies and on the bodies of others as complicated or valuable work. The way that body work is carried out, the way that touching becomes the basis of encounters, is influenced by the stereotypical bodies sought by clients and escorts' stylizations of their bodies. Over time, the work that escorts perform on client bodies and their own bodies can become more valued. Nick Crossley (2005:9) discusses body reflexive practices that "modify, maintain or thematize" the body. The body stylization that escorts engage in to lure customers can be conceptualized as a body reflexive practice; it constitutes work done on the body according to the unwritten requisites of a relational network that fosters particular forms of the male figure.

Touch is central to body work since it involves the worker touching himself or others. But male-for-male Internet escorts undertake this work on themselves and others not only for fun; they get paid for it and it becomes imbued with value. How, then, should sociologists conceptualize the value of escorts' bodies and the body work escorts conduct in encounters?

Body Capital

Body capital represents an alluring concept in the sociology of the body. The body capital concept is attractive because it draws together a conceptualization of the body with a theorization of economy. This concept has become widely used to explain how bodies are valued and judged in consumer and competitive contexts. Wacquant (1995) describes body capital as a form of accumulated body work that is highly valued. The body is conceptualized as both the means of production and that which is produced. Since capital by its very nature accumulates, the "body is capable of producing more value than was 'sunk' into it" (Wacquant, p. 67). Judgments of body capital refer to body parts (e.g., the penis and ass) that are integral to the involved bodily practices.

Like body work, body capital involves work on and with bodies. The difference between the two concepts is the claim that body capital can be accumulated and ossified. This accumulation and ossification result from training and discipline. A training regime varies depending on the bodily practice it is designed to facilitate. Body capital cannot simply be equated with the boxing example Wacquant provides, but there remain interesting parallels between boxers and escorts. According to Wacquant (1995), male boxers often refrain from sexual intercourse for weeks before a fight. Escorts must also manage their sexual output and refrain from ejaculating in preparation for the encounter:

Most of the times with clients I do not ejaculate. That is extra. That is the highest. That and anal are the highest. Because if I ejaculate and have an orgasm, what if I got a call and I cannot do nothing. That ruins the next call. (Harvey, Montréal)

Escorts must reflexively manage their body fluids. I want to suggest, however, that these body reflexive practices do not necessarily end up in an ossified and transferable form of body capital.

For Wacquant (2004), the body has somatic potentialities that can be capitalized on. For the boxer, these potentialities are the strengths and weaknesses of their anatomy. For the escort, these are penis size and build, skin color, muscularity, and so on. Whether the escort's penis is circumcised matters for the kinds of clientele that will be attracted on that basis (cut or uncut foreskin is usually the first item listed on most escort websites). The body capital concept assumes that there is a build-up of body work that materializes in a body when it performs optimally. In an activity like boxing, the efficient and lean body is the ideal body that all boxers aim for, whereas in escorting there are multiple ideal bodies. Some clients refer to themselves and are referred to as "size queens," preferring and seeking out men with "larger than average" penises. Each escort body can be valorized depending on what the client is looking for:

I used to think you needed to be the all American or all Canadian boy next door with the abs and the pecs and the tan to be a successful male escort. A flawless body. Guess what? After reviewing all the escorts who advertise on the site and on other sites, escorts come in all shapes and sizes. They are not all muscular. Some of the most popular ones on the first page of my site are twinks, not muscular. I do not feel great about my body, I know I should work out and try to look a little bit better, but I have been told that my body looks great, and I have a natural physique, I am not overweight, I have a few curves. I have never had a client from the site or otherwise say "you know what, you are so not what I wanted." (Tyler, Ottawa)

There is no singular ideal body in Internet escorting, so there is no one stylized body that body work could aim toward. When Wacquant (2004) discusses accrual of body capital, he means it almost literally since the trick is to build body capital without burning it up through training and performing. The goal is to peak with body capital during a performance to maximize attainment of symbolic capital, which then converts body capital into economic capital. With Internet escorting, however, the proliferating sexual mosaic means that there is no one ideal body that is honored across the industry. Instead, there are multiple valorized bodies for each different market.

Computer work is part of the labor process of male-for-male Internet escorts. While part of escorting requires the mingling of bodies, the seemingly disembodied way that escorts recruit clients is through online sites. While escorts once attracted clients through print ads and phonebooks, a majority of escorts advertise on specialty sites dedicated to male-for-male commercial sex. I think of this computer work as part of body work rather than in terms of fantasy as online communication about bodies aims to generate a corporeal encounter. My interest lies in the physical effort that goes into touching and being touched by a client.

Most of the correspondence that occurs between escort and client before the encounter concerns the escort's body. Despite the stereotype that all men who have sex with men spend most of their days in the gym pumping up, escorts spend almost as much time as office workers on computers, challenging the association of computers with "nerdy" bodies.[10] The escort's virtual body must match up with the encountered body or else the client will be suspicious. Clients contact escorts on specialty websites and then select escorts based on pictures posted at these sites:

Anybody I am online with, say in a chat room, where I advertise my stats and I have a few pictures, where my face is not showing, it is basically my ass or my cock. Or a part of my body from my neck to my torso. I am not wanting to show my face. People message me and ask for a face pic. I say no. . . . there are half a dozen on a nightly basis. None of them show a picture of their face, just the body. (Tyler, Ottawa)

In escorting, the body initially becomes known through online pictures (escorts also "select" clients based on photo-swapping before setting up a session). Semiotic display of the body in picture form is thus the first moment of valorization and translation of body capital. The materiality of offline bodies relates to the virtuality of the online body: clients will be dissatisfied with escorts if the image offered in the profile does not match the body that shows up for the encounter. Some websites demand a face picture, whereas on other websites and in other cities it is customary to show only pictures of the penis and ass. Certain particularities of the body matter and attract a certain clientele: "the hairless chest is the biggest thing, that's like the huge demand is the lack of body hair. . . . I didn't have a photo for years and it really hurt the amount of business that I got" (Bob, Ottawa). Even when men who have sex with men do chat online, the chatting focuses on various body parts.[11] These online text-based performances of gender and sexuality remain coupled to the actual body of the escort because misrepresentation can lead to a bad review and a decrease in clientele. Online performances offer possibilities for challenging gender and sexuality stereotypes, although Niels van Doorn and colleagues (2008) claim that stereotypes are usually affirmed.

Online pictures are not oriented toward one ideal type body that ostensibly represents the pinnacle of body capital for male escorts. Instead, there exist multiple ideal body types, which influence the way escorts stylize their bodies, groom, pluck, shave, and wax: "if I stopped doing sex trade work tomorrow, I wouldn't stop going to the gym because I still want to get laid and anyway I want my body to be attractive to a wide variety of people" (Claude, Montréal). Body stereotypes can influence these men's escorting work, but they do not orient their body work toward a single ideal form; instead this work is highly contingent on what the client wants.

Wacquant (1995) assumes that the body worker needs to build up capital through convoluted and repetitive episodes of training. If we adapt the idea of body capital in conceptualizing male-for-male escorting, then we must acknowledge that the bodies being produced for escorting are far less disciplined. One example of this relates to clients' hair fetishes. Hairy men or "bears" represent a highly valorized subtype of queer masculinity in some cities and age groups.[12] Some escorts accentuate these body features to attract clients:

---

there are not a lot of hairy guys in the industry and I'm sure that of course they don't call only me, I get sort of like people that like a certain type because they like hairy. People who like hairy definitely call me eventually. I have a little niche. Plus the fact that I'm Latin and I'm uncut, some people like that. (Roberto, New York)

Roberto describes the features of his body that he reflexively accentuates; yet such emphasis is not the same as disciplining the body to achieve a pinnacle of body capital. Hair growth does not constitute dutiful discipline. Because the same features of this body may or may not be useful and may or may not attract other clients, they do not exactly constitute "body capital": whatever body the escort has produced through body work remains relevant only to a specific niche market and not to all potential clients.

As escorts age and gain weight, they must position and advertise their bodies differently. Just as hair can be a sought after body feature for men who enjoy sex with men, an aged body can also be sought after in the form of the "daddy" figure: "I'm absolutely not an Arnold Schwarzenegger but you cannot become totally obese, especially for a daddy figure. A little weight is OK but you need to keep it within limits" (Donald, New York). The daddy figure can be hirsute, challenging the idea that the escort must be taut, young, and stereotypically sexy. The daddy figure represents a valorized age-graded sexuality in male-for-male Internet escorting. There are body reflexive practices in male-for-male Internet escorting that require self-surveillance, but there is no pinnacle body. Nor does all the body work transform the self for the self, as in the body capital concept. In escorting, much body work is oriented toward clients, which complicates the valuing of bodies.

Despite multiple valorized body types in male-for-male Internet escorting, this multiplicity is not infinite: some bodies are much more valorized, as in the racialized body, for instance. Should the racialized body be conceptualized as a form of "body capital"? I can only sketch out the contours of a response here. Certainly skin color matters in escorting. Some clients are not looking for particular sexual favors but wish to touch a body that is different from their own:

People ask how can I have such a good body for my age, they touch me, and they say things like "what a gorgeous butt." You feel a lot of respect from those people, which gives you another look at your own body. I feel younger. I feel I can still do it. Maybe there is some curiosity too. People look and say he is black, I want to see a black, I want to touch a black. My difference is my advantage. (Sam, Ottawa)

Sometimes the desire for an exoticized, cultured body can reinforce preexisting inequalities, though we should not presume what those inequalities are in advance.[13] Some of the escorts I interviewed self-identified as black, Latino, and Lebanese. Green (2005) argues that these skin color and ethnic status characteristics are subtle yet influential in separating some of these men from others and in making it harder for some men to feel a sense of belonging. Queer theory has touched on issues of ethnicity but tends to focus more on sexuality instead of other differences, with age-graded sexualities being an obvious lacuna.

The work narratives of these men sometimes include talk about the way clients value their skin differently because of its color or value other parts of their body for their exoticism. One escort told a story about how clients valorized his penis more because of skin color:

They always ask, how big is it. I do not like to answer this question. I tell them what the rates are and what they get. But then they say again, how big is it. I won't tell them. I say take what you get, and don't come if you do not like it. . . . it is stuff like "I would love to be massaged by a black, how big is it," and what is funny is . . . my youngest guest who came last week is 26, he said how big is your cock, and I said I am naked, I am going to turn you around at the end and you are going to see it [laughing]. You better play with it when I am giving you an orgasm. That was cute . . . but whites also ask whites how big is it, it is an obsession amongst gays basically. As a black, when I get that question it has another connotation. (Sam, Ottawa)

Encounters with male Internet escorts can approximate a quest for authenticity for clients, who both wish to locate a desired ethnic type and to achieve gay identity.[14] Yet how racialized men fit into the "gay community" is less well known. Some authors have pointed out that gay men from Afro-Caribbean countries who live in Canada and the United States must keep secrets about sexuality from their ethnic communities (this argument is made by Green 2007b as well as Crichlow 2004). For these men, "the village" is the only place to feel accepted concerning their sexuality even as these spaces are "often, though not always, white dominated" (Green 2007b:770). This tension raises questions about power relations and inequalities within communities of men who have sex with men.

Skin color is often associated with stereotypes about sexual performance. While blackness is associated with penis size, the stereotype about Latino men is that they are amorous and hirsute:

When I moved to New York everybody was shaved. I don't mean to say I started a trend but I, maybe I had. I went to Brazil in '91 and I met this guy in New York before going and he's like, "Why do you need to shave?" And I was like, "When I was younger I wanted to be like everybody else." And he said, "No man, let it grow, it's much hotter." So I started letting it grow. And I really liked it because I started getting more attention from the guys that I liked. . . . That's how I met my lover . . . when I came back from Brazil, I came back hairy and he noticed me. . . . since then little by little I started seeing a lot more people that are hairy and sexier. But in New York when I got here everybody shaved. I remember I went to a club with the hairy chest and everybody was surprised and my friends were all against it, "Oh why don't you shave, shave it." And they saw me with the hot guys later. . . . I think the taste now is the more mature looking. (Roberto, New York)

Skin color can be exoticized in male-for-male Internet escorting, with corresponding assumptions about penis size, shape, body smell, and hair color. Whiteness is also valorized in this work. Jeff from New York served time in the American military and positions himself online as offering a WASP masculinity to clients. White, Anglo-Saxon, Protestant (WASP) masculinity refers to an emotionless, macho whiteness, which he claimed is popular among Latino and black clientele. Jeff's marketing technique involves posting profile pictures that present an intimidating figure as part of the sexual persona he is trying to build up. In certain American cities, "tops" and "bottoms" "bear racial connotations whose significance may be exploited to heighten a sense of transgressiveness" (Dean 2009:41); this distinction plays out in other cities in other ways. Whiteness also appears in this array of racialized bodies. Escorts accentuate skin color in their ads and play on it during the encounter, rendering blackness and whiteness just as performative as sexuality itself.

The concept of "body capital" is only partially helpful for thinking through how bodies matter in male-for-male Internet escorting because "body capital" invokes a pinnacle formation of the body that is transferable between contexts. A hard, hot body is not needed in escorting. Rather, successful escorting depends on how escorts position themselves in the sexual mosaic. Not all escort bodies can approach the stereotypes concerning attractiveness. Yet stereotypes do exist, especially about racialized bodies.

Body Trouble

K: Has doing this work changed the way you think about sexual health?

Donald, New York: Well, it has made me much safer. I mentioned that I would be willing to take more risks in a nonprofessional context, but once you put it into a professional situation everybody is more cautious. It has made me play much safer than I might otherwise. I did have one experience a year ago with a broken condom, and the guy that I had been fucking said, "You know, I'm HIV positive, you should go see the doctor." I took the postexposure anaphylaxis for a month. Who knows whether I would have gotten anything, but that took care of it. I haven't had any troubles since and I have continued to test negative. People are generally pretty up-front when they need to be. I haven't had any experience with people deliberately trying to jeopardize anybody.

It is difficult to shift into a discussion of HIV/AIDS because of the trauma it has exacted in so many people's lives, especially those of men who have sex with men. HIV/AIDS and sexually transmitted infections are tethered to the body because they are transferred through bodies coming together. The term "body trouble" suggests how bodies can be problematized by public health agencies, the law, our sexual partners, and other regulatory agents.[15] Bodies can be regulated if they are designated as unruly by organizations with different ideas about what our bodies should be doing. Men who engage in nonmonogamous sex or unsafe sex can thus be stigmatized as "dangerous queers" (Smith 1997). For this reason, very few escorts dis-

CHAPTER 9

close their status as commercial sex workers to public health officials or even to their general practitioners. As an example, one escort describes a conversation he had with a doctor about sex:

he asks "Oh, how many?" and I'm like I don't know a hundred just this year . . . but at the same time when you have someone like my father that will sleep with two or three women in a year but won't wear any condoms, will go see a prostitute . . . who is more dangerous? I want the public health system to exist for everyone and to have any sex worker that is doing thousands of clients a year to still have a doctor that won't get out the red marker and say like, "Oh, shit. Maybe you should stop." And thinking you're just like a disease. (Etienne, Montréal)

Because HIV/AIDS is linked to pollution, contagion, and blame, public health researchers focus on escorts' bodies and bodily fluids in claiming that escorts are sexually compulsive and risky individuals.[16] Some escorts face stigma because male-with-male and nonmonogamous sex are associated with disease, especially in the United States.

Public health agencies' primary concern in relation to men who have sex with men today is "barebacking" or anal sex without a condom. The literature on barebacking tries to comprehend why gay men continue to have sex without condoms in a world pervaded by awareness of HIV/AIDS. Whereas men who have sex with men were pioneers in establishing condom culture, today many men engage in anonymous sex without a condom and even in purposeful HIV transmission. Some scholars argue that some men who have sex with men engage in risky behavior because they associate riskiness with subversive transgression.[17] It is true that a new vocabulary has emerged around barebacking: doing it can be viewed as "more real" by some men who have sex with men.

Rather than demonizing men who enjoy sex with men without a condom, Tim Dean (2009) suggests that "uncloseting HIV" requires in-depth analysis of bodily contact "organized around the giving and receiving of semen" (p. 10). Barebacking is what Dean calls "antihomonormative" sex (p. 9); he claims it is too often characterized as "extreme acting out or freakish behavior" rather than "sociability or intimacy" (p. 20). Like Dean, I do not endorse one form of sex as more ethical than others. Instead, I aim to understand how sexually transmitted infections and HIV/AIDS are made sense of by the touching encounters of men who sell sex to other men and how they factor into those encounters.

Public health officers rarely understand how sexual health is negotiated through touching and sensing during the encounter. Public health agencies also fail to recognize that men who have sex with men do not always or often think of anal sex, even without a condom, in terms of risk prevention.[18]

Safe sex is not as safe as it is made out to be. . . . any time I try to research information about sexual health I get a party line. Useless advice. I tried to read about sexual health on the Internet and basically it says "do not do it." Useless advice. Talk about it with your partner. As if people who have sex anonymously, with an escort, are going to talk about it. Not realistic. "Do not sleep around. Avoid anal sex." Who do they think they are talking to? (Frank, Toronto)

HIV/AIDS prevention campaigns impose a public health party line on men who have sex with men and may actually facilitate so-called risky health practices in unanticipated ways.[19] There remains a gap between public health discourse and the practice of sexual health during encounters.

How do we reconcile what male-for-male Internet escorts say about their work and public health claims about barebacking? Stories about HIV/AIDS and health do not figure centrally in male-for-male escorts' talk about work or sexuality. This lack of emphasis on stories about HIV/AIDS among these men may result from certain medical advances in treatment (there may no longer be a palpable sense that silence equals death) or from escorts' limited contact with outreach agencies or even public health agencies beyond tests for sexually transmitted infections. As Heaphy (1996) points out, people have diverse understandings of HIV/AIDS. When escorts do talk about it, ideas about prevention of body trouble feature prominently in these understandings: "you only have one body and you want to protect it, you want to be careful with your body" (Sam, Ottawa). Byron from Houston insists that "if someone wants to touch me in a way that puts me at risk, I will tell them no. I will get out of it, keep myself safe." Almost all of the escorts suggest they practice safe sex at work: "I always sleep with everybody as though they have HIV" (Steve, Toronto). Others express the same sentiment:

I assume everyone is positive. I would say the doctor knows more about how to take care of the disease than the patient, so if you're accusing me because I'm a hooker then you don't know, we are the ones that worry about it and think about it. I think

it was probably in the 1980s the last time I had consciously unsafe unprotected sex.
I had a condom break one time like ten years ago, which scared the hell out of me.
(Conrad, Toronto)

This response about "treating everyone as if they are positive" remains consistent across the various cities in which I interviewed escorts.

Sex, however, is biographical. Men who did not live through the 1980s, who did not see their friends dying, may not experience the same visceral defensive response. For these men, talk about HIV/AIDS and sexually transmitted infections relates to their age and biography:

I'm at an age where I caught the AIDS scare from 1983 on, so condoms have been
part of my life all my life. I don't ever fuck clients without condoms. I occasion-
ally do in my private life as a top only and that's what I call an educated risk that
I'm taking. . . . occasionally with guys I know and trust, I've looked at their ass if
they're bleeding or not, I'll occasionally bareback, but never with clients. What hap-
pened one night though, I was with a client and we had used a condom to fuck, he
was blowing me and I looked down and my dick is covered in blood. He had dental
work that day. I looked down and said, "Is it me? Did you pull my dick? Is it you?"
"Shit, I had dental work done today." And my dick is covered in blood. You try all
you can to be safe, and then shit still happens. (Ricky, Toronto)

Ricky treats unprotected sex as a top with someone he trusts as an educated risk but would not bareback with clients for fear of HIV/AIDS. As Ricky suggests, bodies are unruly and can exceed our capacity to control them. Nevertheless, escorts who have grown up without their friends dying from HIV/AIDS may have a different outlook:

It's a disease that doesn't kill you anymore, it's just a disease that is a pain in the
ass. I also don't go down on a guy without looking at his cock and feeling it first. . . .
you're obviously not going to cut it when it's in there, and you know when you have
a cut in your mouth because you feel it. Anal sex, absolutely 100%, yes, I wear a
condom. I don't know where he's been, and I don't know where I've been. (Eddy,
Toronto)

These men's numerous understandings of body fluids and body parts related to HIV/AIDS and sexually transmitted infections are shaped through touching men's bodies. In sum, these men report engaging in serosorting, "the tendency to pursue unprotected sex only with those who share one's HIV status" (Dean 2009:12). Negotiating sexual risks in this way is a "supremely safe version of barebacking," which Dean writes "hardly qualifies as barebacking at all" (p. 15).

It takes at least two bodies to make a touching encounter. Clients play an important part in moving the interaction one way or another. Often escorts do not police their bodies or the bodies of clients because clients are so afraid of disease that they ensure safe sex themselves:

Most guys I find are really protective of themselves because they think you're a diseased whore. . . . if you're fucking in the doggie style position, they're forward and you're behind they'll spend the whole time being fucked looking back to make sure you haven't slipped the condom off. . . . I had one guy he wouldn't even let me blow him without a condom because he had a fear of getting something. I talked him into it because I didn't want to blow him with a condom on but he wouldn't blow me. He needed condoms. He should have come over in a body bag frankly, with some holes cut out. (Ricky, Toronto)

These examples show how escorts negotiate the prominent sexual script of "risky sex": they negotiate risk not in an abstract or calculated way but more through the sensing and touching that occurs during the encounter. Escorts and clients achieve safe sex not through strict adherence to public health discourse, but by meandering through what makes sense to do in an encounter. Voon Phua and colleagues (2009) found that only a quarter of online escorts mention safe sex in their ads, taking this as an indication that the other three quarters prefer and promote sex without condoms. This assumption glosses over the point that escorts do not facilitate sexual health according to a preset formula but negotiate it during the encounter. Touching, feeling it out, thus becomes a strategy for getting to know others' sexual health. Despite public health literature's claims about barebacking, male-for-male Internet escorts do not seek transcendence through unsafe sex, partly because they want to continue with their work and partly because they are well educated about HIV/AIDS. Consider the absurdity of promoting safe sex by advocating the termination of touch. A clinical approach does not foster condom culture. Safe sex must be hands on.

Touching encounters refer to the mingling of bodies but also to the caring and camaraderie between men who have sex with men. Living with HIV/AIDS can be desolate since "the ageing or diseased body is considered non-sexual, a horror of degeneration" (Lupton et al. 1995b:105). Disclosing HIV/AIDS status almost automatically leads to rejection in the dating scene except in groups of men who actively engage in "barebacking." But some escorts refuse the pervasive fear of HIV/AIDS and, in a sense, break the touching barrier. This next escort describes how being with a man with HIV may be remedial and caring:

There was one of the clients that I used to see regularly, he was an HIV patient. All he wanted to do is cuddle with someone and have that human touch. He was pretty emaciated, he was pretty sick. I think he passed away now, but he used to have me come over. I would put my arms around him and watch a movie, and that's all that he wanted was that human touch. Unfortunately, a lot of people like that are forgotten about and cast aside. . . . I don't think he had a lot of people visiting. It is rewarding, like healers. . . . my friends used to joke, I'm the healing hooker. (Steve, Toronto)

Beyond working as healers, sex workers sometimes act as sex educators in teaching clients about safe sex practices.[20] Escorts report that safe sex is harder to practice in personal relationships compared to work sex because condoms can always be introduced into work encounters as part of the labor process. The next escort agrees that escorting sex is safer than dating sex:

Some of the safer sex or HIV prevention materials assume that if you engage in sex for money, then you're going to be engaging in more dangerous behavior. But I found that it resulted in more safe behavior because the clients were nervous and didn't want to catch anything and I certainly do not want to catch anything from them. So it sort of reversed the stereotype. (Donald, New York)

The escorts I interviewed do not fit the picture of risky sex painted by public health agencies. Escorts' narratives about HIV/AIDS and sexually transmitted infections suggest their ability to orient touching toward safer forms of sex without relinquishing attention to play and pleasure. Another escort suggests that starting to work at the same time he entered into a serious relationship changed the way he practiced sex:

Americans are very safety conscious. I was going to whack someone off and I was going to spit on it to lube it up and he would not have it. No spit. I do not use condoms with my partner. I use condoms in every other situation, which makes it easier. It is not just my own safety, but now it is [someone else's] safety I must account for, so that makes it simple. (Jake, London)

Prior to the HIV/AIDS panic, male sex work was criminalized. In the late 1980s, however, male sex workers became objects of epidemiology; in addition to being criminalized, they were said to be "reservoirs of disease and transmitters of infection from the gay population" (Scott 2003:194). Public health discourse characterizes men who have sex with men as "irrational, dangerous citizens" (Gastaldo et al. 2009:413) who will trigger the next epidemic of contagion. But the narratives of escorts I interviewed suggest that escorts who advertise as professionals on specialty sites usually avoid barebacking and practice safe sex. Their infrequent engagements in unprotected sex result from high trust levels with the client and a negotiation of sexual scripts about "risky sex." Male-for-male Internet escorts negotiate health risks through touching and sensing in encounters, even with other men who have HIV/AIDS or sexually transmitted infections, in a way that demonstrates the often caring or empathetic orientation of such encounters.

How Bodies Matter in Male-for-Male Internet Escorting

The bodies of men who have sex with other men have not received due attention in the sociology of the body or the sociology of sex work. Scholars have claimed that men having sex with men undergo pressures similar to those experienced by women regarding body image, slimness, and youthfulness. Although giving specificity to homoerotic bodies should be vital to sociologists, we must also take care to avoid homogenizing these bodies. What can we hold constant about queer bodies besides a set of sexual ins and outs that differ from heterosexual repertoires on the surface? It is essentialist to assume that the bodies of men who have sex with men have a lot in common, just as it is essentialist to assume, as Michael Warner (1993:xxi) does, that all the sex in "het culture" is the same. The deployment of a hetero versus homo binary renders homogeneous the bodies of men who have sex with men and their sex practices. Gay men manifest important differences along class, age, and ethnic lines, and these embodied differences matter in sexual encounters.

My study builds on Wolkowitz's (2006) claim that scholars tend to caricature the sex worker's body. In my examination of how bodies matter in male-for-male Internet escorting, divisions and differences between men who have sex with men operate through touching and being touched. The literature on body work shows that the work people undertake with their bodies or on other bodies may be the central activity of some work. The literature concerning body capital, however, assumes the existence of a pinnacle body that must be achieved for success in the field. Male-for-male Internet escorting confounds this idea of the pinnacle body because, in escorting, all body sizes and specificities can be valorized depending on the client's desire. Finally, body trouble concerning HIV/AIDS and sexually transmitted infections appears in escort narratives. These men generally orient touching toward safe sex. Public health agencies assume men involved in commercial sex spread body troubles, but escorts repudiate this argument in their work narratives and practices.

Touch is crucial to the meaning of sexual conduct. Dowsett (2000) asks why scholars focus on identity categories and discourses of gay liberation instead of the way people touch one another as a basis for understanding sexuality. This question remains central to my analysis. The men I interviewed engage in commercial and noncommercial sex marked by an itinerant way of coming together that differs from monogamous, procreative sex scripts. Male-with-male sex, even commercial sex, is often based on a "meandering through" (p. 33) rather than adherence to scripted rules. My study suggests that body-based practices must therefore become central to scholarly understandings of sex work.

Sexual encounters are not only inscribed by discourse but are also productive and creative. How male escorts think of the sex of their work, how they position their work in relation to other work, and how they think of their bodies and other bodies: each of these issues is mediated by the touching of encounters. Discourses of sexuality and gender do not fully inscribe bodies, as if a role is waiting for individuals to inhabit before they meet. Instead, touching encounters produce new meanings and produce new ways for bodies to come together.

Chapter 10 | Conclusion

I began this book with a short narrative by Conrad from Toronto. His client, a soldier, paid to kill, could only feel alive and healthy again when touched by an escort. Both Conrad and the client had everything to lose if the story got out: they could end up stigmatized or in jail. I begin the end of this book with another escort's narrative. It is partially an account of what can happen when these men's work is publicly revalorized. In 1995, Gerald was released from Ryerson University in Toronto and his job as a contract journalism instructor when it became known that he sold sex to men. Gerald commented that there "was sensation in the papers with much mockery and nasty calls. . . . people yelled at me in the street, it was bad for a while." The union eventually won a settlement for Gerald, signifying some recognition of discrimination. Gerald now manages his relations strategically: "mostly I do not feel stigmatized, but I only hang around with people who knew me before or got to know me because of this. . . . [The university incident] is not something I would want to go through again." Still, Gerald feels his work is valuable:

> This is what I am: 49 years old (though I'll claim 38 if there are dimmer switches), with a plain face that can look alternately dopey and intelligent.
>
> I have a better body than most 49-year-olds, though it is far from magazine material. It's quite a hairy body—a real turn-on for many men—though I shave my shoulders, back, and balls in the belief that the overall look is more pleasing.
>
> I have a great ass and a small-ish cock. Excellent social skills—I know how to make men feel comfortable from the moment they arrive. I take pride in my work.

I think a lot about what I do, and try to do a good job. I'm also a frequently published journalist who has won two National Magazine Awards.

I feel part of a new social phenomenon: whores with attitude, men and women who choose this profession, men and women who have perfected that most ingratiating of personality traits—shamelessness. But it is a shamelessness untarnished by insolence, by the bravado of those who suspect they are in fact quite as trashy as everyone thinks they are. It is a sunny shamelessness. I think you'll like it. I think you'll like us.

Enough about me (for just a moment). A bit about you. You're fascinated by whores. You see us along the streets at night, wide awake, authoritative, lithe. You imagine we know everything there is to know about dark and the city. You see our ads and find something funny about their calculated lubriciousness. You've been to the movies so you know our lives are a little empty, a little sad, a little loveless.

We have hearts of gold sometimes—you know that too. Perhaps you don't know that your marriages depend on us. Or—and here I'm becoming just a little grand—that the proper business of any prostitute is to become a saint.

I sold my body for the first time at five o'clock in the afternoon on August 29, 1987.

I did it for that most mundane of reasons—I was out of work, and I was broke.

The decision did not strike me as the first step in a spiral of degradation. I had never had any theoretical objections to the selling of sex. It seemed not much different from selling my editorial skills. I just never thought that anyone would pay good money to have sex with me. I thought hustlers had to be young, hung, and full of cum—or at least one of the three. But a friend who is young-ish and hung-ish—and was the one real live whore I actually knew—explained that, in the skin trade as anywhere else, there is such a thing as niche marketing. "Sell your muscles," he told me. "Sell the fact that you're hairy. Sell your age. Not everybody's attracted to young guys."[1]

This narrative evokes many themes of *Touching Encounters*. A major theme here is that the stories people tell, whether sexual stories or work stories, emanate from encounters. Men enter escorting for many reasons. They come to escorting at various times in their life course. They may hold other jobs. They do not need to have buff figures that meet stereotypical body ideals. These men market themselves according to what their bodies give them to work with. Ultimately, what these escorts' narratives communicate is the sense that encounters with clients are about bodies coming together and men caring for other men.

Social scientists, activists, and journalists increasingly invoke the idea of "sex work" to talk about commercial sex, yet they understand few of the intricate meanings of sex and work across the commercial sex industry, particularly in commercial sex between men. I have attempted to tell a story about how male-for-male Internet escorts, who constitute but one discrete sector of the commercial sex industry, make sense of sex and work. I have located my project in relation not only to sociological literature on sex work but also literature on sexuality in order to show that the sex of sex work is neither predetermined by innate drives nor fully scripted according to cultural tropes. Neither escort, client, nor researcher can assume in advance what will occur during the encounter, the shifts in meaning about sex and work that may arise, or the swerves in life course that may result.

Sex Work Revisited

"The whole business is misrepresented by the press, by the government, all you ever hear about is the seedy side of it, people trafficking and using it to support drug habits," according to Oscar, of London. And Dan Healey (2001:236) argues that social scientists who study commercial sex must go "beyond received definitions of prostitution as a sex-for-cash trade-off." Tropes abound. I have suggested that male-for-male Internet escorting is at once transitory and intense: encounters are itinerant and anonymous but also corporeal and full of meaning. The work is at once intimate and impersonal: some escorts and clients may develop friendships and trust, but other escorts may wish to curtail their engagement. The work is at once physical and social: the thrust of the encounter may be to touch and be near another body, even though the encounter may be arranged through frequent virtual communications. At the heart of the encounter, confessions remain central to the joint action of escort and client.

The idea of "sex work" retains political salience as an organizing metaphor for the labor struggles of commercial sex workers. I would never argue that sex workers and their allies should abandon struggles for safer working conditions and basic respect. Indeed, the recent legal challenges in Canada are particularly inspiring. A constitutional challenge against prostitution laws is working its way through the Canadian courts.[2] Yet the idea of "sex work" becomes increasingly blurry the more I speak with these men and think about the sex and work lives of male-for-male Internet escorts. Much of what escorts do is not exactly work, yet it is not simply sex either. I have tried to emphasize where these boundaries blur and how these imbrications of sex and work might matter to sociological conceptualizations of sex and work. Instead of locating the meaning of sexuality outside the encounter in an ultimately sexological or psychoanalytical referent, I have been taken in by the sexual stories that escorts share after coming together with others. In exploring the sex and work of escorts, I have not only been trying to describe their relations, but I have also sought to demonstrate that sex and work are integral to biographies. Escorts narrate the sex of sex work as part of their sex lives. There are a few reasons for this. First, anonymous sex between men, commercial or not, leads to sociality. The encounter is not simply an economic exchange. Second, the escorts I interviewed tend to be older than most male sex workers, a fact that influences how these men narrate their sense of self and how they engage with clients.[3] Yet we cannot assume that the sex of sex work is the sole goal of either client or escort. Sometimes what escorts and clients do concerns not sex but camaraderie, the idea of friendship as a way of life that Foucault leaves us with.

Instead of locating the meaning of work in the lexicon of political economy (e.g., exchange value), I have investigated escorts' work narratives about what they do. One interesting finding is that male-for-male Internet escorts use a labor vocabulary to describe what they do while simultaneously manifesting little interest in sex work activism or advocacy. For a long time, working in the sex trade meant being present, on-street or in a bar or hotel, with other sex workers. But today most sex work begins online or is mediated through Internet communication, a configuration that creates a different sort of workspace. The Internet makes possible work that is no longer tied to a particular locale, spreading work out across conventional boundaries and borders. The labor process of male-for-male Internet escorting is individuated because the Internet allows encounters to be arranged from a distance. Notably, these escorts do not seem to use the Internet to create e-communities among themselves.

The highly individuated labor process of male-for-male Internet escorting is part of the reason why there appears to be less solidarity among these men and less solidarity between them and other sex workers. This individuated labor process detaches escorts from conventional settings of sex work (e.g., the stroll, the agency), making interaction with other escorts uncommon and inhibiting any shared notion of collective labor. At the same time, the labor process of male-for-male Internet escorting differs greatly from the ill-treatment common among on-street sex trade and even bar hustling: Internet escorts deal with a clientele that more or less represents the transnational capitalist class, a clientele that often seeks camaraderie and temporary companionship.

Some male escorts reject the label "sex worker" and reject the sex work movement, while other male escorts support the movement. Some escorts identify as "sex workers" and express solidarity with other people who sell sexual services despite differences in labor process. Frank, from Toronto, declares that "the anti–human trafficking movement is a front for antiprostitution. Escorting is a service, not evil"; he criticizes the inclination of prohibitionist feminists and other moral entrepreneurs to lump all kinds of commercial sex together in an effort to outlaw them. My point echoes Frank's: because there are substantial differences in labor process across the commercial sex industry, the messaging and recruitment that sex work activists use to build the movement must be situational, strategic, and as diverse as the industry itself.

Expanding Understandings of Sex and Work

Grounding this book in the narratives of male-for-male Internet escorts, I have purposefully complicated ideas about sex and work instead of folding these men into particular social scientific categories. Butler (1993:240) argues that "the thought of sexual difference within homosexuality has yet to be theorized in its complexity." By demonstrating how the body's facts matter in these touching encounters, I hope to have contributed to the project that Butler calls for. Studying one kind of sex work in depth brings to light the significant differences between forms of commercial sex. Below I want briefly to revisit the book's overarching argument and to highlight some of these significant differences.

Part of what this book inadvertently does is to assess the adaptability of claims about female sex workers to male-for-male sex work. Some female sex workers, especially on-street workers, suffer systemic abuse at the hands of male pimps and punters. Yet few male-for-male Internet escorts report violence at work. All sex work can prove precarious as it is not associated with guaranteed income, contract salary, or employment. As with female sex work, some men turn to escorting because salaried or wage-based work becomes difficult to locate or because they wish to avoid the labor process of customer service work.[4] Yet in the chapter concerning vocabularies of work and labor process, these men do not always express solidarity with other sex workers. Male-for male Internet escorts do not often know who their competition and allies are. And they do not regularly share information about clients. For these reasons, male-for-male Internet escorting seems to have its own unique rhythm; it is itinerant, intermittent, anonymous, and, in some cases, it involves elements of friendship with clients.

The way that academics often talk about men who have sex with men assumes hedonistic, selfish sex is the basis of their relations, an assumption that O'Byrne and colleagues (2008) call the promiscuity paradigm. Moreover, people often assume that men who like sex with men operate with a stable sexual identity, one that is "gay." What escorts say about sexuality, however, troubles any fixed meaning of "gay." Escorts' talk about coming together with others also undoes conventional gendered stereotypes about effeminacy. Diverse sexualities operate in male-for-male Internet escorting, complicating the comparison of female sex work with male sex work. Queer theory positions itself as deconstructing identity categories such as gay and lesbian, but I have suggested that queer theory remains unable to break fully from reifying sexual identities. By emphasizing the varied life histories of men who sell sex to men, I have also demonstrated that escorts do not all share the same understanding of the terms "gay," "sex worker," and "escort."

In addition, the conversation of gestures occurring during the interview in part creates the sense of sexual self for both participants. I could assume no shared vocabulary or definition of the situation in advance of meeting and chatting with the escort. For instance, toward the end of our interview I asked Harvey, from Montréal, "Has escorting changed the way you think about your own sexuality?" He responded bluntly, "nope, still gay." Other escorts, however, did not view themselves, their bodies, or their relations with others, and other bodies, according to the gay versus straight grid of intelligibility.

My purpose in this book has not been to reinstate the privileged masculine subject of classical sociological theory but instead to show how conventional categories of "men" as gendered and sexual beings can break down through touching. I have tried to undo the privileged masculine subject, with its supposedly sturdy and impermeable body, by showing how touching between men may reproduce gender and sexual roles but may also offer moments when those forms of subjectification unravel. There is a specific logic of the lure in male-for-male Internet escorting that is itinerant and anonymous; such escorting is not quite the same as park or bathhouse cruising but is, nevertheless, aleatory in some ways. Following from this logic, I have tried to demonstrate the unpredictability of escorts' understandings of sexuality leading up to and during the corporeal encounter with the client.

All these details about male sex work can feed back into sociological theorizations of sex and work. Because male-for-male Internet escorting involves the male body's sexualization, its analysis requires that labor process theory be supplemented to account for the aesthetic labor of the self-employed. The final few chapters of the book explore touching's centrality to escorting and how this touching comes to be valued, though not exactly according to the "body capital" logic of valorization. The facts of our bodies change over time as we find new ways to put our bodies together with others. Some sex work scholars suggest that sex workers feign intimacy with clients. They claim that sex workers enforce rules about what body parts can be put into play. These arguments may work well for some sectors of the commercial sex industry. But these claims about feigned intimacy reduce the sexual encounter to set scripts and fail to explore how a sense of sexuality is produced through the encounter. Sexual scripting theory places too much emphasis on the predictability of sexual encounters, thus detaching it from the interactionist tradition in sociology.

I believe that the itinerant character of commercial sex between men shares commonalities with other kinds of encounters, which is why I dedicate many pages to discussing interactionist sociology and sexuality at a general level.[5] I modify interactionist sociology by putting Blumer and Goffman into conversation with Foucault; I critique interactionist sociology for naturalizing subjective sense-making; and I emphasize the encounter (the dyad) rather than the individual as the starting point for inquiry. Scholars have criticized interactionist sociology for merely offering a succession of nows, a criticism I have tried to overcome by emphasizing the closed tendency as a mechanism of social reproduction. I resist qualitative realism by maintaining that it is difficult to know participants since my awareness of their lives is mediated by narrative elaboration and interpretation, what I refer to as storied encounters.

In male-for-male Internet escorting, the sex of the work is often the sex of escorts' lives. Of course, the intensity of this overlap changes over time. Age-grading of sexuality also influences how escorts work on their bodies to create a certain appeal, attract new clients, and retain old ones. I have considered how age-graded sexualities influence escorts' work and sometimes lead to desexualized touching. For many of these men, the end of escorting comes when they are unable to transition into a market that reflects their new persona related to age-graded sexuality. Even if the penis is removed from the center of their relations with clients, however, some older escorts are entrepreneurial in finding novel ways to please clients with other parts of their bodies. Finally, I have considered how escorts talk about what they do in ways that are not fully explained with reference to sexuality since bodily touching is not always sexualized. HIV/AIDS and sexually transmitted infections matter for how escorts make sense of their work and how certain bodies get made into problems, but this understanding does not prevent escorts from temporarily breaking the touching barrier that has come to enclose many men with HIV/AIDS and bar them from intimacy and compassion.

The "touching" of touching encounters refers to the mingling of bodies and the gestures of sexual conduct but also to the caring and mutuality that exists between men who have sex with men. Touching implies bodies coming together. The specificity of how men touch and what they touch together in sexual encounters matters for how escorting work happens. Even when the encounter moves away from sexuality and bends more toward friendship, a shift that does happen, bodies are still together though they may be desexualized. "Friendship is perhaps the most important site where virile heterosexual masculinities are endangered by the specter of homosexuality" (Garlick 2002:560), such that encounters may produce a hitherto unknown erotic relationality and may generate friendships. These encounters often happen with male clients who are on the road, alone, and unable to live up to stereotypes of male beauty. While not all male-for-male escorts care about their work and their clients in this sense, for some escorts intimacy and compassion form part of their encounters with clients, especially repeat clients.

By introducing the idea of "touching encounters," I have tried to create an understanding of how sex relations are continually ordered according to discourses of sexuality and gender at the same time that there are moments of emergence immanent to the interaction when pervasive cultural scripts are broken down and recomposed. I have shifted from treating sex work as an economic exchange to understanding it as a relational encounter. The body is not simply a discursive effect as in some versions of queer theory, but instead translates discourses of sexuality and gender through touching during interaction. The two tendencies of the encounter, the closed tendency toward following sexual scripts and the open tendency toward creativity and unanticipated outcomes, are immanent to a sequence of interactions, produced by and modified through the ongoing conversation of gestures and confessions that make up sexual encounters.

Stories, Sex, and Social Science

This book emphasizes the importance of the encounter as a concept to inform research in the sociology of sexuality and sex work. I also highlight the stories men share about their escorting encounters with other men. Narratives form part of the longer story they tell about their lives. The sharing and writing of narratives are actions performed by people together; indeed, narrative necessitates some joint action. Narrative analysis provides an epistemological and methodological approach to inform analysis of encounters post hoc. Yet I have emphasized the limits of narrative research for trying to understand issues of corporeality and so have introduced the idea of storied encounters as a way of conceptualizing how people talk about and make sense of their relations after coming together with others.

The kinds of stories it is possible for us to tell are constrained by historical and social processes; one cannot tell a "gay liberation" story before the 1960s, for example (Plummer 1995). Similarly, one cannot tell the kinds of stories these men told me before the advent of the Internet because the Internet has facilitated forms of sex work that are highly individuated. The men I interviewed sometimes do not even think of what they do as work or think of what they have in common with other people who lead similar working and sex lives.

My discussion of discourse in relation to touching encounters has been motivated by numerous calls to reconcile the writings of Foucault with interactionist sociology.[6] Foucault avoids a discussion of actual sex practices and instead focuses on the historical emergence of an apparatus of sexuality. I have been interested in how one element of that apparatus—discourse—is translated through touching during sexual conduct. Instead of a sexed body, I view the body in the encounter as a sexing body that translates discourse through its imbrications with others, a sexing body that is the nodal point for mutating and proliferating discourses insofar as its gestures are reflexive and create unforeseen effects. My approach holds together an account of the constitutive force of discourse with an account of postencounter storytelling. Focusing on the storied encounter provides a useful way to understand the touching encounters we have with others and how these encounters and subsequent talk about touch are shaped by discourses of sexuality.

A story always represents a particular telling. Narrators can use stylistic devices to accentuate certain features, and respondents can tell stories they think the researcher wants to hear. I have been telling a story that does not rely on longstanding tropes about selling sex but that situates the sex and the work of male-for-male Internet escorts closer to generic social processes and the touching encounters that create intimacy with others. The sexological and psychoanalytic genres used to depict homoeroticism serve a normalizing function: "The pervasive narrative logic that inscribes AIDS as the life story of gay male sexuality, per se" (Ricco 2002:34), is but one example. As scholars, we still need to overcome stereotypes that misrepresent men who have sex with men and who sell sex. In this book, I hope to have shown that the "young, dumb, hung, and full of cum" stereotype misses the mark.

For Roland Barthes (1975), the point of writing is to evade language that is ready-made. The bliss one feels upon reading a text may "come only with the absolutely new" (p. 40). Inspired by the stylistic twists and turns of these men's stories about sex and work, I hope to have provided enough that is new in this text to create for the reader if not bliss then at least the recognition that the lives of male-for-male Internet escorts are touching in significant ways.

A p p e n d i x

Postscript on Methodological Issues

A Note on Interview Questions

- Can you tell me how you first got involved in this work?
- Can you tell me a bit more about what the work entails?
- Can you say a bit about the industry as a whole and how it is organized?
- What kinds of skills do you need to do this work?
- How important is the body and appearance to this work?
- What sorts of stuff do you have to do to take care of your body for this work?
- Can you tell me about a time you were working and something funny happened?
- Can you tell me about a time you were working and you felt afraid?
- Can you tell me about a time you were working and you felt sad?
- Can you tell me about a time you were working and you felt pleasure, like it was fun?
- Can you tell me about a time you were working and you felt embarrassed?
- Can you tell me about a time you were working and you felt bored?
- Can you say a bit about the ways you advertise?
- Do you ever feel like you are competing against other workers?
- Did you ever worry about making enough money?
- Have you ever worried about your health because of this work?
- Do you always feel you have access to the services you need to do the work?
- Was there anything else about this work that caused you worry at any time?

- Do you ever get burnt out or worn out from it?
- So what do you think is the riskiest part of the work?
- Can you say a bit more about the clientele you work with?
- How are relations with repeat clients different from those with first time clients?
- How has doing this work changed the way you feel about yourself?
- How has doing this work changed the way you think about masculinity?
- Can you say a bit more about how you think of your body in relation to this work?
- Do you ever feel you have to act or manage emotions with clients?
- Has it been tough to keep up personal and familial relations because of this work?
- How has this work changed the way you think about what is risky?
- How has this work changed the way you think about sexuality?

This list of questions appears in my ethics application for the research project. As you can see, a lot of the questions are general. Most of the questions could be asked of almost anyone doing any kind of work involving the body. This set of questions was developed for an ethics review board because ethics applications require a set list of questions, assuming that all interviews are highly structured. Although structured and semistructured interviewing techniques are appropriate for some research, I followed a narrative-based interviewing strategy.[1]

Narrative interviewing allows respondents to provide significant stories about past relations with others. During a narrative interview, the researcher makes interjections only if the dialogue veers completely off topic. The next question I pose as a researcher must resonate with the last narrative fragment offered by the respondent. If I had asked about emotions and relations with clients and the respondent had mentioned something about intimacy, the next question I pose would likely follow from the theme of intimacy. The next question I pose in the interview could be any from the list above or could even stray from the list, depending on the previous response. Narrative interviewing requires an interviewer who listens to what the respondent says and builds a dialogue within the parameters established by the research design. If, however, the dialogue strays from the established questions into a different set of issues, this is not a problem according to a narrative-based interviewing strategy and may actually generate new themes that become salient in future interviews and in the overall analysis. I did not ask these interview questions in any particular order, and I often rephrased them during interviews, depending on the language that the escort seemed comfortable with (see chap. 5 for this discussion).

Issues of Narrative and Biography in Working with Sexual Stories

The point of this research project is to provide a narrative account of the working and sex lives of male-for-male Internet escorts. Since I have engaged in narrative interviewing and narrative analysis, how narrative is defined becomes crucial.

Narrative is a smaller part of a bigger story people tell about their past interactions and relations. My approach to narrative, however, holds that the smaller part of the overall story one tells about one's relations is not a pure route to some unmediated self (for limitations, see Doucet and Mauthner 2008a, 2008b). The stories we tell about our relations with others are unevenly narrated because the way we interpret the past is always shifting on us. Narratives are not often presented as linear, but instead are reordered according to interpretive acts of remembering. In telling a story, one is re-presenting, interpreting, and elaborating (Squire 2008 and Mattley 2002). In re-presenting, one is also fashioning one's sense of self in relation to discourses that provide a grid of intelligibility for understanding our place in the world; this is how narratives link up with broader discourses, of sexuality, for instance (see Tamboukou 2008 and Polkinghorne 1988 on narrative and discourse). Though discourses shape the stories we share with others, interpretation means the story can shift or have a contrapuntal character.

Although some varieties of narrative analysis emphasize the personal, I focus on narratives produced out of encounters. When analyzing narratives, one needs to strike a balance between biography, with its emphasis on the personal, and broader discourses that shape the way we tell stories. To focus solely on the personal would create an account bereft of context; to focus only on discourse would create an account empty of biography. Biography is important to social science since the researcher tells a story using the stories others have told in remembering some encounters they have had. But in this book I place less emphasis on biography per se and more on the discourses of sexuality and labor apparent in escorts' talk.

"Biography" is therefore not what really happened to a person but a story generated out of a research encounter pertaining to some previous encounter. A sense of self is generated out of storytelling: the self that the story alludes to is not the "real" self but a self whose representation is facilitated through the process of telling the story.[2] In other words, "the interviewer and the subject conspire to construct a version of the self—and the strategies they employ in that conspiracy will probably derive from the shared, unspoken regularities of interaction expectations in their culture" (Angrosino 1989:104). The researcher thus deals not with real life but with the told life.[3] This approach to narrative operates in a conceptual space "between subjects who structure their lives and subjects who are overly structured" (Doucet and Mauthner 2008a:401). With narrative, the social scientific impetus to generalize meets a "gossamer wall" where the researcher is confronted with her or his own past, with the reflexivity of respondents, and with readers who perform their own interpretations of the account (see Doucet 2008, 2006 for her unique ideas on narrative, reflexivity, and writing).

My use of narrative must be understood as part of the recent rise of narrative analysis across the social sciences. This shift toward narrative as a central focus in social science represents a move away from authoritative truth seeking toward interpretation; it repositions the researcher as an interpreter and storyteller instead of an expert. This move toward narrative also means that traditional formats for coding interview transcripts must be reconsidered in light of dilemmas about authorship and reflexivity across disciplines. Traditionally, the coding of transcripts used preconceived codes purportedly representing universal knowledge or abstracting a category from a set of transcripts that would be applied to the entire sample. Here is the difference: a respondent's narrative need not be assimilated to a universal category or themes from other transcripts. Large parts of a respondent's narrative telling may be kept intact for the way the words evince the force of context on that narrative (see Mello 2002 for more on the use of narrative excerpts). Just as narrative interviewing is fluid in how it moves from question to question, narrative analysis is reflexive in the relationship established between the transcripts, text, and author. In certain chapters of this book, I let the narratives speak more for themselves, meaning that I draw from narrative analysis variably depending on the particular theoretical and empirical questions that each chapter addresses.

Turning to narrative is not a solution for addressing the problems of authority faced by social scientists. Even since the narrative turn, according to Carl Rhodes (2000:519), the problem remains that "the power of the researcher to shape and construct meaning out of interviews is hidden through the sanitized output of the interview transcript." Narrative analysts too often offer an infatuation with the "self" instead of emphasizing how the big stories of culture shape the little stories we share with others, especially when it comes to sexuality (a point also made by Tomso 2009, Tanggaard 2009, and Crossley 2004). Paul Atkinson and Sara Delamont (2006) suggest that recent qualitative research celebrates the biographical aspects of narrative too much and fails to link these accounts to cultural genres in which narratives are elicited.[4]

Some scholars have raised questions about narrative approaches to understanding corporeality. Alan Radley (1997) contends that claims about the body being made and unmade by discourse need to be qualified. Radley's point is that "there is an embodiment beyond that which is captured within speech . . . the body in its material aspect" (p. 98). The body is elusive: while narrative-based research is not useless for understanding corporeal processes, "it does not follow that narrative is in itself the royal road to an understanding of embodiment" (p. 99). Because I think that Radley's critique applies equally to this book, I am careful only to make claims about escorts' *narratives* or claims or accounts concerning bodies, touching, intimacy, and so on. These stories are confessions but cannot be treated as truths. For this reason, I differentiate between the touching encounter and the storied encounter, the latter being a narrativized version of previous interactions.

I have elicited the narratives of male-for-male Internet escorts to tell a story about the intersections of their sex and their work. Yet there still remains the issue of how to make sense of the stories that escorts share. Narrative analysis tends to focus too little on how theory and context matter for the account that is produced (on the scope of narrative analysis in qualitative research, see Atkinson and Delamont 2006 as well as Honan et al. 2000). I have drawn from what is referred to as listening guide analysis (Mauthner and Doucet 1998) to address this issue. Listening guide data analysis stresses the importance of narrative in constructing the self and attends to how the narrated subject is constituted by structural and cultural forces. By emphasizing the role of the researcher who interprets the narrative and focusing on the way narratives are shaped by broader discourses, listening guide analysis strikes a balance between letting the narrative tell the story and asking theoretically informed questions of the data.

A Note on Data Analysis

This section discusses some issues pertaining to qualitative data analysis. Research encounters are what Dorothy Smith (2005:135–39) calls "data dialogues." The primary data dialogue occurs between the interviewer or participant observer and one or more persons the researcher talks with or watches during interactions. A secondary data dialogue occurs between the researcher and the transcript of the audio-recorded interview or the field notes. This language of primary and secondary dialogues is misleading, however: it implies that data analysis is a minor concern compared with data production. Data analysis might well be a more theoretically demanding practice than interviewing or observing, and it is integrally tied to one's method of exposition and writing up the research.

Also referred to as the "voice-centered relational method," the listening guide was first developed in social psychology. At the core of the listening guide is a relational social ontology, which posits that selves always exist in relation to others rather than in isolation or separation. There is no single way to conduct listening guide data analysis, but there are several steps held in common by those who use it. These typically involve four steps.[5] The first step is to listen for the general plot, including protagonists being described by respondents. This step involves reading for plot and actors, as well as for researchers' reactions to the plot. This is a relational reading. Here I must be aware of my role as a researcher, of how I am reading the transcript in the second data dialogue, and of how I produced the transcript. This first reading also involves reading myself in the story. The researcher's decisions in mediating respondents' talk through interpretive frames will focalize the story in particular ways.

There was a time earlier in my life when I worked as an interviewer on a research project about sex work. I interviewed male and female on-street sex workers. Those interviews do not form part of the data for this project but the encounters I had years ago as a research assistant have influenced this project and continue to animate my interest in the topic. As the teller of this story, I should say that my own approach to sexuality aims to subvert rather than confess fixed and singular senses of identity. As much as it makes sense to refer to straight, gay, and lesbian identities, the corresponding communities can express hostility toward those not considered sexuality insiders. These details about my politics and my biography influence the way I work with texts.

In the second step of listening guide analysis, the interview transcript is listened to for the "voice of the I," or how the respondent narrates his or her sense of self. "I" refers to the sense of self constructed through narrative, or what Somers (1994) calls "ontological narrative." This reading amplifies the way the subject narrativizes him or herself and thus evinces the power of narratives in forming conceptions of self. Carol Gilligan and colleagues (2005) use "I Poems" to construct flows of text that reflect the voice of the "I." There are two rules in constructing such poems. The first rule is to pull out every first-person "I" in a given excerpt, along with the verb and important information that follows. The second rule is to maintain the sequence in which the narrative fragments originally occurred in the story. Narrative fragments are arranged on separate lines. The "I Poem" brings one's talk about one's self to the fore, thus illuminating aspects of the story not visible when the narrative fragments remain as parts of the whole transcript. This element of the analysis shows up particularly in the excursus on biographies and the excursus on stigma but also in chapter 8.

Conrad's "I Poem"

I hired a male escort
I enjoy it 99% of the time
I would say it's a little more professional on the Internet
I don't do any of that stuff
I'm not a pro and you know I'm not a scam artist
I do it for extra money here and there
I used to be an architect, believe it or not
I basically tell them you're not going to get what you want
I'm always reading them
I avoid sex at all costs
I do everything I would do with a boyfriend
I tell them on the phone
I don't like bringing them to my place
I don't really want my mother to know
I don't give too much information
I go on this other site too
I market myself as sort of like a real person
I don't have pedicures
I assume everyone is positive
I had a condom break one time
I don't like being around drunks
I just treat it very kind of casual

I get more honesty from a fucking client than I do from a guy that I meet
I've been sort of dating
I can find something that arouses me
I want a repeat customer, so I'm not going to screw them over
I tracked every ad, printed them and put them in order time-wise and I
figured out who did it
I just can't fake

The "I Poem" provides a foray into understanding how the respondent narrates their sense of self within the overall context of the interview. Creating an "I Poem" for every transcript allows me to hear elements of the respondent's story that may be lost in the transcript; this helps me select narratives to work with in analysis.[6]

Donald's "I Poem"

I've been doing it now I guess for close to three years
I contacted them and I ended up getting paid to do a couple of massage
sessions
I started advertising on Craigslist
I was also looking to find some kind of part time work
I've sort of targeted that niche
I flogged his back and his backside
I was about to take him down, he fainted into my arms
I saw him several more times
I finally dropped a couple of ads on the websites that charged too much
I would engage in sex without condoms with people unprofessionally, but
professionally I always use a condom
I certainly do not want to catch anything
I read a lot about the theory of escorting before I even got started[7]
I kind of cut corners and I start to rush through things
I'm not getting any feedback
I got hard, I figured, well, just jerk us both off
I found that just even privately I needed a little extra boost
I was able to carry on for a full session
I have to travel
I mention it on the phone, if they want to meet at a hotel I can arrange it
I just sort of round things off to a figure, you know, it will work itself out in
the end
I might feel jealous that, you know, I think they look better

I used escort services
I also have a very supportive partner
I hear stories of the old days when guys would line up on street corners
I read in an article recently that as far as the suburban escort has just
become a whole new phenomenon that didn't exist before
I advertised on Rentboy
I grew up on the West Coast and came to the East Coast for college and
then stayed here
I noticed about older clients too that they're not so focused on ejaculation

Gilligan and colleagues (2005) write that the first two steps in the listening guide provide an interpretive base for the next two stages. In Gilligan's version of the listening guide, researchers next listen for "contrapuntal voices" or multiple voices within one story that reflect the broader relations the subject is enmeshed in. Each contrapuntal voice is underlined with a different colored pen. In Natasha Mauthner and Andrea Doucet's (1998) version of the listening guide, the third step—listening for contrapuntal voices—is broken into two separate phases, prefacing the theoretical frameworks of the researcher (which for me are a Foucaultian understanding of sexuality and a Goffmanian-Blumerian understanding of interaction). These readings attempt to offer an analysis of power in respondents' everyday lives; they involve listening for relations or broader social networks the respondent is enmeshed in as these constitute the voice of the "I" and general plot to some degree (although the general plot and voice of the "I" cannot be reduced to the relations the respondent participates in). This third reading is a reading for social networks, informed by feminist critiques of the autonomous individual. Here I would like to introduce the idea of the "We Poem" as an additional means of locating narrative fragments. These poems are forays into understanding the ways respondents narrate their relations with others.

Conrad's "We Poem"

we can make money doing this
we both kind of started together
we are the ones that worry about it and think about it
we were major shit disturbers, like sex-positive and all that stuff
we went out to dinner in public
we just went to a resort in Long Island
we would have lunch, and we were together

Donald's "We Poem"

we arranged to meet for a session at the dungeon
we'll do this, next time we'll do that
we talked about it and thought, you know, it could be an interesting
experiment

Using the "We Poem" as a foray into understanding how respondents narrate their relations with others is a complement to the "I Poem": it can help the researcher hone in on how respondents talk about their sense of self compared with how they talk about their relations with others. It can also help the researcher identify when these key shifts in narration occur in the dialogue. This element of the analysis shows up particularly in chapters 5, 7, and 9.

Fourth, the transcript is analyzed for the cultural contexts and structural forces that traverse the respondent and limit her or his capacity for action. Put another way, this fourth dimension of analysis listens for how self-narration connects with broader discourses of sexuality, gender, ethnicity, ability, age, and so on. Such a reading considers the way the subject is structured. This element of the analysis shows up particularly in chapters 6, 7, and 9. The listening guide is not a grounded theory approach but is, instead, explicitly concerned with how the researcher's theoretical interests intersect with respondents' stories. The listening guide also makes explicit the researcher's presence, emphasizing the crucial roles of reflexivity and power in the social relations of research. It is important for researchers to note that, in using listening guide analysis, they are dealing with respondents' narratives, not respondents' experiences. Illuminating respondents' sense of self and relations with others, escorts' words represent elaborations and interpretations, hence my emphasis on storied encounters.

........................N..o..t..e..s..

Chapter 1

1. Here I make a distinction between compensated sex and commercial sex. Compensated sex involves exchange of sex for any material item, such as food, clothing, or drugs. With "commercial sex" I mean payment of money for sexual services.

2. Research regarding male sex work has focused on street workers (e.g., Kaye 2007; Aggleton 1999; Allman 1999; McNamara 1994; Simon et al. 1994; Boles and Elifson 1994; Visano 1987; Luckenbill 1986, 1985); has conflated sexual conduct with sexual orientation assumed to be "homosexual" (Hall 2007; Blumstein and Schwartz 1977; Freyhan 1947); and, since the 1980s, has used epidemiological data to draw a correlation between sex work and HIV/AIDS transmission (see Boles and Elifson 1994; Morse et al. 1992, 1991; Elifson et al. 1991). Weitzer (2000) and Poel (1992) make the case for more diverse sociological research on male sex work.

3. For more on the rights of sex workers, see Bruckert et al. 2003 and Chapkis 1997.

4. For prohibitionist arguments, see Barnard 1993 and Pateman 1988.

5. For more on sex radical arguments, see Bell 1995 and Delacoste and Alexander 1987.

6. See Weitzer 2007, 1999. Numerous scholars in Canada (such as Benoit and Shaver 2006; Benoit and Millar 2001; Lowman 1992, 1990; Gemme and Payment 1992) have made similar contributions to understanding on-street sex work. Yet on-street sex workers are a decided minority in Canada: almost 80 percent of sex workers work indoors. This figure is worthy of note because, as Sanders (2008a) argues, the sociology of sex work has been characterized by a focus on female, street-involved sex workers.

7. This claim echoes Foucault (1980:220), who writes that those who fight for "sexual liberation" are "caught at the level of demands for the right to their sexuality, the dimension of the sexological," so their work runs alongside discourses of sexuality as opposed to subverting them.

8. See Diaz et al. 2004, Hart and Boulton 1995, Hickson et al. 1991, McKeganey

et al. 1990. Bimbi (2007) argues the literature on male sex work has gone through four paradigms. The first paradigm framed males selling sex as mentally and physically pathological. The second paradigm categorized males selling sex according to fixed tropes of sexuality. With the HIV/AIDS panic in the 1980s and 1990s, males selling sex were thought of as vectors of disease. The sex as work paradigm is the newest.

9. Focus on sex work labor processes in Canada mirrors international developments in the sociology of sex work toward a focus on issues such as emotions. On the labor processes of sex work in Canada, see Jeffrey and MacDonald 2006 as well as Bruckert 2002. On the labor processes of sex work in the United States and the United Kingdom, see Bernstein 2007a, Sanders 2004, Frank 2002, West and Austrin 2002, Brewis and Linstead 2000, as well as Scambler and Scambler 1997.

10. On mutuality, care and sex between men, see Ball 2003.

11. For useful critiques of interactionist sociology, see Schubert 2006, Atkinson and Housley 2003, and Denzin 2001.

12. For some sympathetic critiques of queer theory, see Green 2002, Martin 1997 as well as Halperin 1995. Epps (2001:413) points to the irony of writings on identity in queer theory: queer "is consolidated as an identity, perhaps even as an identity to end all identities."

13. For more on the impact that information and communication technologies have had on the organizations of queer communities, see Castle and Lee 2008 as well as Ashford 2006.

14. For variations of this argument concerning feigned intimacy, see Sanders 2005, Oerton and Phoenix 2001, as well as Browne and Minichiello 1995. My critique of this idea concerning feigned intimacy is guided by the contributions of Frank 2002 as well as Delacoste and Alexander 1987, who both raise questions about the idea of "faking it." In addition, my focus on the encounter is part of an attempt to move beyond the notion of exchange value as a way of thinking through work. As Althusser (2006) argues, whereas the exchange is based on what is known will be given, the encounter is organized around the unforeseen.

Chapter 2

1. For similar critical commentaries on the work of Krafft-Ebing, Ellis and Freud, see Brickell 2006 and Irvine 2003.

2. For further discussion of gay and lesbian studies and identity, see Dean and Lane 2001, Wilkerson 2007, Glick 2000, as well as Butler 1997. Seidman (1993) notes that gay and lesbian theory was not a coherent project until after groups like Gay Liberation Front and Queer Nation had lost their effectiveness on the social movement scene. Many women had already left the groups because of the "malestreaming" of organizing efforts.

3. On queer theory as well as gay and lesbian studies, see Talburt and Rasmussen 2010, Gammon and Isgro 2006, Valocchi 2005, and Jagose 1996.

4. Jagose (2009), Noble (2006), and O'Driscoll (1996) have pointed to the limits of queer theory. Several authors (Jackson and Scott 2007; Stein and Plummer 1996) contend that queer theory must be supplemented through attending to the interaction-

ist elements of sexual encounters. However, none of these authors have suggested that conjoining Blumer and Goffman is necessary to provide a more complete interactionist approach; see chap. 3.

5. Numerous authors have assessed the impact of sexology on understandings of sexuality, including Brooks (2006), Kaye (2003), Green (2002), Dowsett (1996), and Stein (1989).

6. Krafft-Ebing used the name of Masoch to designate perversion. That perversion has now been has been linked with another perversion, sadism, in what is thought of commonly as a super perversion, sado-masochism. Sadism is said to be "the experience of sexual pleasurable sensations (including orgasm) produced by acts of cruelty, bodily punishment afflicted on one's own person or when witnessed in others, be they animals or human beings" (Krafft-Ebing 1886:53). Masochism, on the other hand, is the "wish to suffer pain and be subjected to force" (p. 86). Masochism is described as "being completely and unconditionally subject to the will of a person of the opposite sex" (p. 86). Krafft-Ebing borrows the names of de Sade and Masoch to invent these pathologies, yet "sadism and masochism exhibit totally different forms of desexualization and resexualization" (Deleuze 2006/1967:134), meaning Krafft-Ebing's designations of perversion are misleading.

7. Narcissism becomes Freud's major explanation for inversion. See the compelling works of Dean and Lane (2001), Dean (2001) as well as Bersani (2001) for a more developed discussion.

8. Likewise, Grosz (1994:198) argues that "the specificities of the masculine have always been hidden under the generality of the universal."

9. There is a call in the sociology of sexuality to focus on touch, such as the works of Wilson (2010), Berlant (2009), Parker (2009), and Green (2008). In addition to bringing touch back in, sociology needs an interactionist approach to sexuality capable of theorizing the unanticipated elements of the encounter. My approach to touch is indebted to interactionist thinking, which is quite different from phenomenological understandings of touch in the tradition of Merleau-Ponty and Jean-Luc Nancy elaborated by Manning (2007). Most development of the concept of "encounter" stems from phenomenology; my aim is to wrestle it back into interactionist sociology. For this reason, although touch is a core theme here, I do not enter into discussion of the haptic, which is the proper domain of phenomenology. Another set of literature on the encounter comes from Althusser (2006), who is not a phenomenologist either.

10. Blackman (2009) and Kirsch (2001) make this argument about style and sexuality.

11. Materialist feminists point out that acknowledging gender domination does not automatically deuniversalize masculinity or recognize inequality between gays and between lesbians. This argument has been made by Jackson and Scott (2004) as well as Jackson (1999).

12. In *Bodies That Matter* (1993), Butler reconceptualizes performativity as citationality to show that the reiteration of gender norms is always incomplete. If performatives succeed, it is because the "action echoes prior actions, and accumulates the force

of authority through the repetition or citation of a prior, authoritative set of practices" (p. 227).

13. For these critiques, see Cover (2004b), McNay (2004, 1999), and Stein and Plummer (1996). Lloyd (1999:210) similarly contends "one of the weaknesses of the concept of performativity . . . is that it is comprehensible primarily as an account of individuation," which ignores the context of interaction. West and Zimmerman (1987) have also been critiqued for ignoring bodies in their account of doing gender. Butler's comment on "doing gender" differs from the work of West and Zimmerman. The latter emerge from the ethnomethodological tradition and do not fully account for the intersection of gender and sexuality.

14. On the topic of conformity to stereotypes in gay and lesbian communities, see Cover (2004a).

15. Sender (2004) has studied this trend toward the "pink economy." Also see Hennessy 1995.

16. Cover (2004b) makes this argument. *Touching Encounters* is likewise an attempt to align queer theory with a materialist focus on work as well as an interactionist focus on touch.

17. See Green 2007a and Dunn 1997 on interactionism, sexuality, and the body.

18. Slavin (2009) also makes this argument about pervasive sexual scripts.

Chapter 3

1. Green (2007a), Gamson (2000), and Valverde (1989) make this point about how identity categories are taken up in everyday life.

2. Power has been reduced to "the procedure of the law in interdiction" (Foucault 1978a:86), which emanates from an association of power with the monarchy and then the state apparatuses or juridico-political system. On the topic of putting Foucault into conversation with interactionist sociology, see Denis and Martin 2005, Hacking 2004, Castellani 1999, and Cahill 1998.

3. Stories are not always confessional—there needs to be affirmation of a particular kind of self in order for the story to be a confession (Valverde and White-Mair 1999). Valverde (2004) also points out that confessional practice today does not always aim toward a single, coherent gendered or sexual identity claim, which is consistent with the focus on contrapuntal narratives that numerous authors interested in storytelling and social science have developed; see Doucet and Mauthner 2008a; Doucet 2008; Plummer 1995.

4. Foucault's later interviews put more emphasis on friendship. My rationale for including Foucault's interviews as part of his corpus is that, as Deleuze (1998:115) suggests, Foucault's interviews "extend the historical problematization of each of his books into the construction of the present problem, be it madness, punishment or sexuality." Conducted when at work on the uncompleted *Confessions of the Flesh*, his interviews come closest to talking about touch.

5. Foucault continues (1997c) that the gay rights movement needs the art of life more than the science of sexuality, and this art is built out of pleasure. In this sense,

"pleasures open bodies to worlds through an opening up of the body to others . . . queer pleasures put bodies into contact that have been kept apart by the scripts of compulsory heterosexuality" (Ahmed 2004:164–65).

6. Blumer could be accused of individualizing and subjectivizing Mead insofar as he fails to treat the individual as an abstraction from the group; see McPhail and Rexroat 1979.

7. Mead (2008/1902) is critical of Cooley since Cooley reduces interaction to "an affair of consciousness" (p. xxiii). The difficulty with Cooley's approach, according to Mead, is that "the action of the others upon the self and of the self upon others becomes simply the interaction of ideas upon each other within the mind" (p. xxx). Influenced by early psychoanalysis, Cooley (2008/1902) also tends to pathologize interaction, arguing that "the human mind is indeed a cave swarming with strange forms of life" (p. 263) leading to maladies.

8. There are no individual selves for Mead (1967/1934), only selves in conduct together. Mead's interactionism is not a form of subjectivism. He explicitly argues he wants to "avoid the implication that the individual is taking something that is objective and making it subjective" (p. 188). Jackson and Scott (2010) also make this point clear in their interactionist theorizing of sex and sexuality.

9. On these potential troubles with interactionist sociology, see Bastalich 2009.

10. The call for bodies to reenter discussion with Foucault has also come from prominent feminists. There is said to be a productive tension between Foucault's understanding of power and that of feminists since both identify the body as a nexus of power, both view power as local but nonlocalizable, both emphasize discourse, and both criticize privileging a universal theory of the subject (McLaren 1997). Munro (2003) argues that thinking of sexuality as infused with power is what Foucault and feminists share. Thinking about power and homoeroticism should be a concern for feminists: at stake is a critique of the universal male subject (Stephens 2007, 2004, 1999).

11. For Merleau-Ponty (2008/1945), touching aims to connect bodies in space. Foucault rejects phenomenology because of its focus on consciousness and intentionality. Likewise, I am troubled by the idea of intentionality and am more interested in touch as the basis of productive power. The ontology that Mead provides to interactionism is not the same as the phenomenological starting point, and while the former can be reconciled epistemologically with Foucault to a certain degree I do not believe the latter can. One possibility, however, for attempting to read these theoretical positions together if one were so inclined would be to consider what Merleau-Ponty says about the body as a work of art with what Foucault writes regarding the art of life. Oksala (2005) attempts to create an uneasy alliance of this kind between Foucault and Merleau-Ponty. Rosenthal and Bourgeois (1991) try to create an uneasy alliance between Mead and Merleau-Ponty.

12. Prus could perhaps be accused of subjectivism. Part of the reason Prus overemphasizes the tactical is that he is interested in the subject of gambling and dice hustling, which demands tactics.

13. How does institutional power exert control over sexuality? Numerous scholars (see Butler 2004a; Rubin 1993) have discussed issues of sexuality in relation to violence.

Sedgwick (2003) points out there is still a great deal of censorship and domination going on with sex. Brickell (2009) uses the example of female sex workers in impoverished areas who are not in a position to use condoms, otherwise the clients would not pay for sex. There is no question that power operates differently in survival sex trade. I am not arguing that the sociology of sex work should abandon this focus. Part of the reason I focus on power as productive is that male-for-male Internet escorting is largely without regulatory or institutional intervention (for reasons explained in chap. 4, which deals with the social and economic position of the male-for-male Internet escorts I have interviewed). There are few reported interactions with law enforcement agents, for instance. There are little to no interactions with public health agencies. The rationale for focusing on productive power is that the case demands it; other cases necessitate drawing upon a different conceptual model.

14. Nearly half of the 660 men whom Koken and colleagues (2005) surveyed about casual sex had been paid by other men for sexual services.

15. Gove (2000) calls these encounters "passing pleasures." Berlant and Warner (1998) have used the similar idea of "border intimacies." Chauncey (1994) points to how these encounters lead to opportunities for men who have sex with men to fraternize.

16. Grosz (1994:201) also argues that this logic of the lure produces a body open to otherness.

Chapter 4

1. Phone interviews still allow respondents to share stories, and might be more appropriate with some respondent groups.

2. For a comparative sample, see Minichiello et al. 2008.

3. For examples of the new sociology of sex work, see Bernstein 2007a and Sanders 2005.

4. On this point about how far sexual stories can extend, see Rickard 2001.

Excursus [2]

1. Seidman (2002) has developed this argument about life histories.

2. On surface acting and sex work, see Sanders 2008b, 2005, 2004 as well as Browne and Minichiello 1995. My critique of this idea concerning the surface acting of sex work is guided by Frank 2002 as well as Delacoste and Alexander 1987.

Chapter 5

1. On identity during interviews, see Atkinson and Delamont 2006 as well as Plummer 1995.

2. I am thinking of the work of La Pastina (2006), Carrier (1999), Fitzgerald (1999), Bolton (1995), Seizer (1995), and Newton (1993).

3. On reflexivity, see Riach 2009 as well as Mauthner and Doucet 2003.

4. On interviewing and roles, see Hoffman 2007, Coffey 1999, and Holstein and Gubrium 1995.

5. This argument about Goffman can be found in Manning 2005, Katz 2004, and Collins 1986.

6. For these critiques of Blumer, see Baugh 1990 as well as Hammersley 1989.

7. On the topic of hegemonic masculinity, see Connell 2001.

8. Although they are discussing a slightly different context, see Warren and Rasmussen 1977.

9. See Seymour 2007 and Coffey 1999 on the body and interviewing.

10. See Plummer 1995 on this interactionist approach to interviewing.

11. On interviewing and impressions, see Aléx and Hammarström 2008.

12. Lambevski (1999:400) asserts: "one cannot observe someone else's sexual desire from a safe, detached, distance. One has to experience it in order to understand it." But there is a flipside. La Pastina (2006) describes the repercussions that can come from sharing one's self during research.

13. On interviewing and gender, see Presser 2005 and Grenz 2005.

14. This point about masculinity is made by Jefferson 2002.

Chapter 6

1. On the role of labor in contemporary societies, see Bauman 1998a.

2. On commercial sex, new technologies, and e-business, see Phua and Caras 2008 as well as Pruitt 2005. Internet escorting is hard to define as an occupation: it lacks the features associated with occupations such as organizations, unions, contracts, taxes, and licensing.

3. See Bruckert and Parent 2006 and Jeffrey and MacDonald 2006 on labor process and sex work.

4. The works of Theodosius (2008) as well as Bolton and Boyd (2003) are important contributions to the literature on emotional labor.

5. The concept of aesthetic labor comes from Warhurst and Nickson 2009, 2007.

6. On the boundaries of LPT, see Doherty 2009 and Thompson and Newsome 2004.

7. For this argument about capitalism and sex work, see Gall 2006.

8. On "self-employment" and "dependent self-employment," see Muehlberger 2007.

9. The body work concept is developed by Wolkowitz (2006).

10. On emotional labor, see Theodosius 2008 as well as Bolton and Boyd 2003. On the sexualization of women at work, see Pringle 1989.

11. On men doing "women's work," see Sayce et al. 2007, Simpson 2004, and Lupton 2000.

12. See Smith and colleagues 2008 for an argument that some escort agencies with bosses who are former sex workers can create better working conditions.

13. See Bauman 1998a for this argument about work.

14. Mallon (2001) argues that labor scholars as well as sociologists of sexuality have ignored the experiences of working class gay men, especially gay men in the manufacturing industry.

15. For this argument concerning sex work activism, see Lopes 2006.

16. For a competing account, consider the prose piece written by Josh Kilmer-Purcell (2008), who argues that today, in the United States, several male-for-male Internet escorts have celebrity status. From having dated a male escort, Kilmer-Purcell learned that a

golden rule of escorting is "don't bite the dick that feeds you." Yet more escorts are outing their clients to gain celebrity status. The high-profile case in the United States involving Mike Jones and the Reverend Ted Haggard is one.

17. On this topic of surface acting, see the important work of Hochschild 2003/ 1983.

Excursus [3]

1. Povinelli and Chauncey (1999) make this argument about transnational spaces of sexual conduct.

Chapter 7

1. For this argument about surface acting and coping, see Weinberg et al. 1999, O'Connell Davidson 1995, as well as Høigård and Finstad 1992. Edwards (1993:103) also argued "prostitute women develop distancing strategies" that allow them to sell their bodies while saving their souls. My contention is that this viewpoint, which holds that sex work involves surface acting and a split between the real and the feigned self, does not apply to all kinds of sex work equally. The contributions of Frank (2002) as well as Delacoste and Alexander (1987) guide my critique of this literature on surface acting and sex work. Bernstein (2007a) is also critical of arguments that conflate sex work and surface acting with her notion of bounded authenticity.

2. Eribon (2001) provides this interpretation of Foucault.

3. On the politics of sexuality, see Sender 2003.

4. On this topic of sexual compulsivity, see Parsons et al. 2001.

5. For an essay on this issue, see Ward 2000.

6. Mead (1967/1934:177) argues: if a person "knows what he is going to do, even there he may be mistaken . . . the resulting action is always a little different from anything which he could anticipate."

7. See especially the work of Nardi (2007) and Adam (2007) on friendship.

8. See the contributions of Moon (2008), Bernstein (2001), and Prasad (1999).

9. Sawicki (2004) makes this argument about ethics, sex, and categorization.

Excursus [4]

1. West (1992) found that male sex workers, especially young and on-street workers, faced high levels of violence. Compared with other sex workers, especially on-street female and transgendered workers, male-for-male escorts face little risk of violence. Harvey from Montréal says, "I have never been screwed, I have been lucky that way," meaning he has never faced violence at work or been stiffed for his fee. In the few instances when violence was mentioned during the interviews, the escorts themselves were the aggressors: "I was with a guy and we got to his place, he had dogs on me, two dogs and I'm not an animal person . . . I was like, 'Yo get these dogs like yo I'm not playing with you. Like get these dogs.' I was like yelling about the dogs but I was just like saying it in a joking manner, like 'I'm about to hurt these dogs if you don't get them off.' So he was like, 'Oh you're not going to hurt nobody.' He was like 'as a matter of fact, you can just have a little

bit of money and get out.' And I didn't like that because I traveled far to see him . . . he lived in Staten Island and you know we called a taxi there and I was just like upset for him to want to just give me like $20 to get out you know so it got pretty ugly and you know we got into a fight because I wanted more money" (Mike, New York).

2. Commenting on the connection between internet use and anonymity, Sean from Toronto says "I had a client once who had a thing for jeans, loved jeans and he was calling me and wanted to know if I was available on Saturday. I didn't know that he was on my Facebook, so I saw he made a comment on my Facebook, on my wall. And I was like 'ooh, fuck, DELETE!'" For more on the impact that computer technologies are having on queer communities, see Campbell 2007.

3. Not all escorts feel they have to keep what they do secret from their partners. As Donald from New York puts it: "I have a very supportive partner who was a little cautious at first about my trying this, but we talked about it and thought, you know, it could be an interesting experiment just to see how it worked and to see how much I was able to make and then to also hear about it afterwards and that was a real turn on for him to hear about, to hear the description of each session afterwards. Not everybody is in a position like that, where they have a partner that's actively interested and supportive of exploring something like this and being part of it but not in the sense of going along on a session but not having to hide it."

4. *My Own Private Idaho* is a movie about street hustlers in Portland working with male clients. River Phoenix plays a narcoleptic street hustler in search of self-discovery and his estranged mother.

5. On the work and private lives of sex workers looping into one another, also see Calhoun and Weaver 2000 as well as Davies and Feldman 1999.

Chapter 8

1. For a sample of this work, see Tulle 2008 as well as Gilleard and Higgs 2000.

2. This chapter is informed by research on age and sexuality written by Vares (2009), Jones and Pugh (2005), Katz and Marshall (2003), and Marshall and Katz (2002).

3. "Chickens" refer to younger, clean-cut men, similar to "twinks" (without body hair, slender, permissive, and androgynous). "Chickenhawks" refer to older gay men cruising for younger, boyish-looking sex partners. "Daddy" also refers to the kind of older role that can be taken on as part of age play in male-with-male sexual communities.

4. On this point about the pressures and discourses that accompany new sex-enhancement pills, see Potts et al. 2006, Drummond 2005, as well as Katz and Marshall 2003.

5. On this argument about the failures of men's bodies, see Stephens 2007, Heaphy 2007, as well as Calasanti and King 2005.

Chapter 9

1. Plummer (2007) makes this point about humping bodies.

2. On body work, see Gimlin 2007 and Wolkowitz 2006.

3. See Wacquant 1995 on body capital.

4. See Morse et al. 1991 on men who have sex with men and AIDS.

5. The work of Crossley (2006a, 2006b) about the reflexive management of one's own body is crucial in drawing out this point.

6. Jackson and Scott (2007, 2001) have developed this argument about bodies making sense.

7. I have argued that men who have sex with men socialize over anonymous sex, and for this reason there is a specific logic of the lure with male-for-male Internet escorting that can lend itself to friendships and relationships beyond the one-off commercial affair. This might be true too for some female and trans workers. However, generalizing to the female and trans sectors of the commercial sex industry is not my objective.

8. On stigma and loneliness, see the work of Ward (2008).

9. To visit the Tender Loving Care Trust website, see: www.tlc-trust.org.uk; for the Touching Base Collective website, see: www.touchingbase.org.

10. For more on body stereotypes, see Lupton 1995.

11. See Jones 2005 for more on how men chat about and display their bodies online.

12. See the works of Hennen (2008) as well as Monaghan (2005) on bear communities and body hair.

13. Escoffier (2007), Wise (2001), and Dollimore (1997) make this argument about inequality in communities of men who have sex with men.

14. On desire and ethnic identity, see Padilla 2007.

15. See the research of O'Byrne and Holmes (2009) on public health agencies.

16. This is the argument of Lupton et al. (1995a).

17. For this literature on barebacking, see Martin 2006, Ridge 2004, Suarez and Miller 2001, as well as Kippax and Smith 2001.

18. On the social meanings of anal sex, see Gastaldo et al. 2009 and Holmes and Warner 2005.

19. Also see Ridge 2004, Crossley 2002, and Dowsett 1996 on sexual health.

20. See Smith and Seal 2008 as well as Browne and Minichiello 1995.

Chapter 10

1. Adapted from Hannon 1994 in Wallis 2004.

2. The Ontario Superior Court struck down certain sections of the prostitution laws in September 2010, though the attorneys general for Canada and for Ontario appealed the 2010 decision to the Court of Appeal for Ontario. In 2012, the Court of Appeal for Ontario agreed with two-thirds of the earlier ruling, arguing that laws against living off the avails of prostitution and keeping bawdy-houses are unconstitutional.

3. Please compare my sample with Minichiello et al. 2008.

4. I am indebted to Jeffrey and MacDonald (2006) for this argument.

5. The work of Duncombe and Marsden (1996) is also important for offering a broad understanding of "sex work" that emphasizes the many ways that paid and consensual sex can overlap.

6. On Foucault and interactionist sociology, see Denis and Martin 2005, Hacking 2004, Castellani 1999, and Cahill 1998.

Appendix

1. On narrative-based interview techniques, see Rosenthal 2003.

2. Life history refers to "the account of a person's life 'as told to' another, the researcher" (Angrosino 1989:3). Whereas life history provides narratives pertaining to particular encounters, life stories are attempts to cover the span of one's existence. I am dealing with the former.

3. Another way of putting this is that "life stories are joint actions assembled through social contexts into texts by authors and readers" (Plummer 2001:399). This interactionist approach emphasizes the role of the researcher in creating the "self" of the research participant as presented in writings. In this sense, "analysis creates the human it sets out to explore" (Bersani 1995:145).

4. Nor is there anything innovative about dealing with narrative per se. Minichiello and colleagues (2000) use diaries to collect narratives pertaining to male sex workers' practices for the purpose of categorizing and intervening in their lives vis-à-vis public health agencies.

5. See Doucet and Mauthner 2008a, Doucet 2006, as well as Mauthner and Doucet 1998 for a more in-depth discussion of the listening guide and data analysis.

6. With an "I Poem," one should not read the use of "I" in the same way as Mead separates "I" from "me." For Mead (1967/1934), the "me" takes the role of the other. The "me" is therefore "a conventional, habitual individual" (p. 197). But the "I" "reacts to the self which arises through the taking of the attitudes of others" (p. 174). Whereas the "me" is oriented toward doing a duty, fulfilling a habit, the "I" is an "action over against that social situation within his own conduct." With an "I Poem," the personal pronoun could refer to either "I" or "me" in Mead's approach—this tension needs to be sorted out through conducting analysis and replaying and making another study of the audio recording.

7. Here the respondent is referring to books like Itiel's 1998 guide to male hustlers and hustling. Itiel's consumer guide is geared toward purchasers and is a story of his many encounters with escorts. The respondent is also likely referring to the numerous memoirs and reflections of men who sell sex to men, especially Lawrence 1999, which was one of the first memoirs after computers and the Internet contributed to a big change in escort labor process; also see Jones 2007.

References

Adam, B. 2007. "Relationship Innovation in Male Couples." In *The Sexual Self: The Construction of Sexual Scripts*, ed. M. Kimmel. Nashville: Vanderbilt University Press.

Aggleton, P., ed. 1999. *Men Who Sell Sex: International Perspectives on Male Prostitution and HIV/ AIDS*. London: UCL Press.

Ahmed, S. 2004. *The Cultural Politics of Emotion*. London: Routledge.

Aléx, L., and A. Hammarström. 2008. "Shifts in Power during an Interview Situation: Methodological Reflections Inspired by Foucault and Bourdieu." *Nursing Inquiry* 15(1): 169–76.

Allman, D. 1999. *M Is for Mutual, A Is for Acts: Male Sex Work and AIDS in Canada*. Ottawa: Health Canada.

Althusser, L. 2006. *Philosophy of the Encounter: Later Writings, 1978–1987*. New York: Verso Press.

Altork, K. 1995. "Walking the Fire Line: The Erotic Dimension of the Fieldwork Experience." In *Taboo: Sex, Identity, and Erotic Subjectivity in Anthropological Fieldwork*, ed. D. Kulick and M. Willson. London: Routledge.

Angrosino, M. 1989. *Documents of Interaction: Biography, Autobiography, and Life History in Social Science Perspective*. Gainesville: University of Florida.

Ashford, C. 2006. "Only Gay in the Village: Sexuality and the Net." *Information and Communications Technology Law* 15(3): 275–90.

Atkinson, P., and S. Delamont. 2006. "Rescuing Narrative from Qualitative Research." *Narrative Inquiry* 16(1): 164–72.

Atkinson, P., and William Housley. 2003. *Interactionism: An Essay in Sociological Amnesia*. London: Sage.

Ball, C. 2003. *The Morality of Gay Rights*. London: Routledge.

Barker-Benfield, B. 1972. "The Spermatic Economy: A Nineteenth-Century View of Sexuality." *Feminist Studies* 1(1): 45–74.

Barnard, M. 1993. "Violence and Vulnerability." *Sociology of Health and Illness* 15(1): 5–14.

Barthes, R. 1975. *The Pleasure of the Text*. New York: Hill and Wang.

Bastalich, W. 2009. "Reading Foucault: Genealogy and Social Science Research Methodology and Ethics." *Sociological Research Online* 14(2–3).

Baugh, K. 1990. *The Methodology of Herbert Blumer: Critical Interpretation and Repair*. Cambridge: Cambridge University Press.

Bauman, Z. 2003. *Liquid Love: On the Frailty of Human Bonds*. Cambridge: Polity.

———. 1998a. *Work, Consumerism, and the New Poor*. Buckingham: Open University Press.

———. 1998b. "On Postmodern Uses of Sex." *Theory, Culture, and Society* 15(3): 19–33.

Bell, S., ed. 1995. *Whore Carnival*. Brooklyn: Autonomedia.

Benoit, C., and F. Shaver. 2006. "Critical Issues and New Directions in Sex Work Research." *Canadian Review of Sociology and Anthropology* 43(3): 244–52.

Benoit, C., and A. Millar. 2001. *Dispelling Myths and Understanding Realities: Working Conditions, Health Status, and Exiting Experiences of Sex Workers*. Victoria: Prostitutes Empowerment, Education, and Resource Society.

Berlant, L. 2009. "Neither Monstrous nor Pastoral, but Scary and Sweet: Some Thoughts on Sex and Emotional Performance in Intimacies and What Do Gay Men Want?" *Women and Performance: A Journal of Feminist Theory* 19(2): 261–73.

———. 2000. "Intimacy: A Special Issue." In *Intimacy*, ed. L. Berlant. Chicago: University of Chicago Press.

Berlant, L., and M. Warner. 1998. "Sex in Public." *Critical Inquiry* 24(2): 547–66.

Bernstein, E. 2007a. *Temporarily Yours: Intimacy, Authenticity, and the Commerce of Sex*. Chicago: University of Chicago Press.

———. 2007b. "Sex Work for the Middle Classes." *Sexualities* 10(4): 473–88.

———. 2001. "The Meaning of the Purchase: Desire, Demand, and the Commerce of Sex." *Ethnography* 2(4): 389–420.

Bersani, L. 2001. "Genital Chastity." In *Homosexuality and Psychoanalysis*, ed. T. Dean and C. Lane. Chicago: University of Chicago Press.

———. 1995. *Homos*. Cambridge: Harvard University Press.

Bimbi, D. 2007. "Male Prostitution: Pathology, Paradigms, and Progress in Research." In *Male Sex Work: A Pleasure Doing Business*, ed. T. Morrison and B. Whitehead. New York: Haworth Press.

Blackman, L. 2009. "The Re-Making of Sexual Kinds: Queer Subjects and the Limits of Representation." *Journal of Lesbian Studies* 13(2): 122–35.

Blumer, H. 2004. *George Herbert Mead and Human Conduct*. Berkeley: University of California Press.

———. 1972. "Action vs. Interaction: Review of Goffman." *Society* 9: 50–53.

———. 1969. *Symbolic Interactionism: Perspective and Method*. Berkeley: University of California Press.

Blumstein, P., and P. Schwartz. 1977. "Bisexuality: Some Psychological Issues." *Journal of Social Issues* 33(2): 30–45.

Boles, J., and K. Elifson. 1994. "Sexual Identity and HIV: The Male Prostitute." *Journal of Sex Research* 31(1): 39–46.

Boles, J., and A. Garbin. 1974. "The Strip Club and Stripper-Customer Patterns of Interaction." *Sociology and Social Research* 58(2): 136–44.

Bolton, R. 1995. "Tricks, Friends and Lovers: Erotic Encounters in the Field." In *Taboo: Sex, Identity, and Erotic Subjectivity in Anthropological Fieldwork*, ed. D. Kulick and M. Willson. London: Routledge.

Bolton, S., and C. Boyd. 2003. "Trolley Dolly or Skilled Emotion Manager? Moving on from Hochschild's Managed Heart." *Work, Employment, and Society* 17(2): 289–308.

Boswell, J. 1980. *Christianity, Social Tolerance, and Homosexuality: Gay People in Western Europe from the Beginning of the Christian Era to the Fourteenth Century.* Chicago: University of Chicago Press.

Boyer, D. 1989. "Male Prostitution and Homosexual Identity." *Journal of Homosexuality* 17(1/2): 151–83.

Braverman, H. 1974. *Labor and Monopoly Capital: The Degradation of Work in the Twentieth Century.* New York: Monthly Review Press.

Brewis, J. 2005. "Signing My Life Away? Researching Sex and Organization." *Organization* 12(4): 493–510.

Brewis, J., and S. Linstead. 2000. "'The Worst Thing Is the Screwing': Consumption and the Management of Identity in Sex Work (1)." *Gender, Work, and Organization* 7(2): 84–97.

Brickell, C. 2009. "Sexuality and the Dimensions of Power." *Sexuality and Culture* 13(2): 57–74.

———. 2006. "The Sociological Construction of Gender and Sexuality." *Sociological Review* 54(1): 87–113.

Brock, D. 1998. *Making Work, Making Trouble: Prostitution as a Social Problem.* Toronto: University of Toronto Press.

Brooks, C. 2006. *Every Inch a Woman: Phallic Possession, Femininity, and the Text.* Vancouver: University of British Columbia Press.

Browne, J., and V. Minichiello. 1995. "The Social Meanings behind Male Sex Work: Implications for Sexual Interaction." *British Journal of Sociology* 46(4): 598–622.

Bruckert, C. 2002. *Taking It Off, Putting It On: Women in the Strip Trade.* Toronto: Women's Press.

Bruckert, C., and C. Parent. 2006. "The In-Call Sex Industry: Classed and Gendered Labour on the Margins." In *Criminalizing Women: Gender and (In)Justice in Neo-liberal Times,* ed. G. Balfour and E. Comack. Halifax: Fernwood.

Bruckert, C., C. Parent, and P. Robitaille. 2003. "Erotic Service/Erotic Dance Establishments: Two Types of Marginalized Labour." Ottawa: Law Commission of Canada.

Burawoy, M. 1979. *Manufacturing Consent: Changes in the Labor Process under Monopoly Capitalism.* Chicago: University of Chicago Press.

Butler, J. 2004a. *Undoing Gender.* London: Routledge.

———. 2004b. "Bodies and Power Revisited." In *Feminism and the Final Foucault,* ed. D. Taylor and K. Vintges. Chicago: University of Illinois Press.

———. 1997. "Against Proper Objects." In *Feminism Meets Queer Theory,* ed. N. Schor and E. Weed. Bloomington: Indiana University Press.

———. 1993. *Bodies That Matter: On the Discursive Limits of "Sex."* London: Routledge.

———. 1990. *Gender Trouble: Feminism and the Subversion of Identity.* London: Routledge.

Cahill, S. 1998. "Toward a Sociology of the Person." *Sociological Theory* 16(2): 131–48.

Calasanti, T., and N. King. 2005. "Firming the Floppy Penis: Age, Class, and Gender Relations in the Lives of Old Men." *Men and Masculinities* 8(1): 3–23.

Calhoun, T., and G. Weaver. 2000. "Male Prostitution." In *Extraordinary Behavior: A Case Study*

Approach to Understanding Social Problems, ed. D. Peck and N. Dolch. Westport, CT.: Greenwood Publishing Group.

Campbell, J. 2007. "Virtual Citizens or Dream Consumers: Looking for Civic Community on Gay.com." In *Queer Online: Media, Technology, and Sexuality*, ed. K. O'Riordan and D. Phillips. New York: Peter Lang.

Carrier, J. 1999. "Reflections on Ethical Problems Encountered in Field Research on Mexican Male Homosexuality, 1968 to Present." *Culture, Health, and Sexuality* 1(3): 207–21.

Castellani, B. 1999. "Michel Foucault and Symbolic Interactionism: The Making of a New Theory of Interaction." *Studies in Symbolic Interaction* 22: 247–72.

Castle, T., and J. Lee. 2008. "Ordering Sex in Cyberspace: A Content Analysis of Escort Websites." *International Journal of Cultural Studies* 11(1): 107–21.

Chapkis, W. 1997. *Live Sex Acts: Women Performing Erotic Labor*. New York: Routledge.

Chauncey, G. 1994. *Gay New York: Gender, Urban Culture, and the Making of the Gay Male World, 1890–1940*. New York: Basic Books.

Coffey, A. 1999. *The Ethnographic Self: Fieldwork and the Representation of Identity*. London: Sage.

Collier, R. 1998. *Masculinities, Crime, and Criminology*. London: Sage.

Collins, R. 1986. "The Passing of Intellectual Generations: Reflections on the Death of Erving Goffman." *Sociological Theory* 4(1): 106–13.

Connell, R. W. 2002. "Understanding Men: Gender Sociology and the New International Research on Masculinities." *Social Thought and Research* 24(1/2): 13–31.

———. 2001. "Studying Men and Masculinities." *Resources for Feminist Research* 29(1–2): 43–56.

———. 1987. *Gender and Power: Society, the Person, and Sexual Politics*. Cambridge: Polity Press.

Connell, R. W., and J. Messerschmitt. 2005. "Hegemonic Masculinity: Rethinking the Concept." *Gender and Society* 19(6): 829–59.

Cooley, C. 2008/1902. *Human Nature and the Social Order*. London: Transaction Publishers.

Cover, R. 2004a. "Bodies, Movements and Desires: Lesbian/Gay Subjectivity and the Stereotype." *Continuum: Journal of Media and Cultural Studies* 18(1): 81–97.

———. 2004b. "Material/Queer Theory: Performativity, Subjectivity, and Affinity-Based Struggles in the Culture of Late Capitalism." *Rethinking Marxism* 16(3): 293–310.

———. 2003. "The Naked Subject: Nudity, Context, and Sexualization in Contemporary Culture." *Body and Society* 9(3): 53–72.

Crichlow, W. 2004. *Buller Men and Batty Bwoys: Hidden Men in Toronto and Halifax Black Communities*. Toronto: University of Toronto Press.

Crossley, M. 2004. "Making Sense of 'Barebacking': Gay Men's Narratives, Unsafe Sex and the 'Resistance Habitus.'" *British Journal of Social Psychology* 43(2): 225–44.

———. 2002. "The Perils of Health Promotion and the 'Barebacking' Backlash." *Health: An Interdisciplinary Journal for the Social Study of Health, Illness, and Medicine* 6(1): 47–68.

Crossley, N. 2007. "Researching Embodiment by Way of Body Techniques." In *Embodying Sociology: Retrospect, Progress, and Prospects*, ed. C. Shilling. London: Blackwell.

———. 2006a. "The Networked Body and the Question of Reflexivity." In *Body/Embodiment:*

Symbolic Interaction and the Sociology of the Body, ed. D. Waskul and P. Vannini. Aldershot: Ashgate.

———. 2006b. *Reflexive Embodiment in Contemporary Society*. Maidenhead: Open University Press.

———. 2005. "Mapping Reflexive Body Techniques: On Body Modification and Maintenance." *Body and Society* 11(1): 1–35.

Davies, P., and R. Feldman. 1999. "Selling Sex in Cardiff and London." In *Men Who Sell Sex: International Perspectives on Male Prostitution and HIV/AIDS*, ed. P. Aggleton. Philadelphia: Temple University Press.

De Lauretis, T. 1993. "Freud, Sexuality, and Perversion." In *Politics, Theory, and Contemporary Culture*, ed. M. Poster. New York: Columbia University Press.

Dean, T. 2009. *Unlimited Intimacy: Reflections on the Subculture of Barebacking*. Chicago: University of Chicago Press.

———. 2001. "Homosexuality and the Problem of Otherness." In *Homosexuality and Psychoanalysis*, ed. T. Dean and C. Lane. Chicago: University of Chicago Press.

———. 2000. *Beyond Sexuality*. Chicago: University of Chicago Press.

Dean, T., and C. Lane. 2001. "Homosexuality and Psychoanalysis: An Introduction." In *Homosexuality and Psychoanalysis*, ed. T. Dean and C. Lane. Chicago: University of Chicago Press.

Delacoste, F., and P. Alexander, eds. 1987. *Sex Work: Writings by Women in the Sex Industry*. Pittsburgh: Cleis Press.

Deleuze, G. 2006/1967. *Masochism: Coldness and Cruelty*. New York: Zone Books.

———. 1998. *Foucault*, trans. S. Hand. Minneapolis: University of Minnesota Press.

Deleuze, G., and F. Guattari. 2003/1980. *A Thousand Plateaus*, vol. 2 of *Capitalism and Schizophrenia*. London: Continuum.

———. 1983. *Anti-Oedipus*, vol. 1 of *Capitalism and Schizophrenia*. Minneapolis: University of Minnesota Press.

Denis, A., and P. Martin. 2005. "Symbolic Interactionism and the Concept of Power." *British Journal of Sociology* 56(2): 191–213.

Denzin, N. 2001. *Interpretive Interactionism*. London: Sage.

Diaz, R., G. Ayala, and E. Bein. 2004. "Sexual Risk as an Outcome of Social Oppression: Data from a Probability Sample of Latino Gay Men in Three U.S. Cities." *Cultural Diversity and Ethnic Minority Psychology* 10(3): 255–67.

Diprose, R. 2002. *Corporeal Generosity: On Giving with Nietzsche, Merleau-Ponty, and Levinas*. Albany: State University of New York Press.

Doherty, M. 2009. "When the Working Day Is Through: The End of Work as Identity?" *Work, Employment, and Society* 23(1): 84–101.

Dollimore, J. 2001. "Sexual Disgust." In *Homosexuality and Psychoanalysis*, ed. T. Dean and C. Lane. Chicago: University of Chicago Press.

———. 1997. "Desire and Difference: Homosexuality, Race, Masculinity." In *Race and the Subject of Masculinities*, ed. H. Stecopoulos and M. Uebel. London: Duke University Press.

Dorais, M. 2005. *Rent Boys: The World of Male Sex Workers*. Montréal: McGill-Queens University Press.

Doucet, A. 2008. "On the Other Side of 'Her' Gossamer Wall: Reflexivity and Relational Knowing." *Qualitative Sociology* 31(1): 73–87.

———. 2006. *Do Men Mother? Fathering, Care, and Domestic Responsibility*. Toronto: University of Toronto Press.

Doucet, A., and N. Mauthner 2008a. "What Can Be Known and How? Narrated Subjects and the Listening Guide." *Qualitative Research* 8(3): 399–409.

———. 2008b. "Qualitative Interviewing and Feminist Research." In *The Sage Handbook of Social Research Methods*, ed. P. Alasuutari, L. Bickman, and J. Brannen. London: Sage.

Dowsett, G. 2000. "Bodyplay: Corporeality in a Discursive Silence." In *Framing the Sexual Subject: The Politics of Gender, Sexuality, and Power*, ed. R. Parkem, R. Barbosa, and P. Aggleton. Berkeley: University of California Press.

———. 1996. *Practicing Desire: Homosexual Sex in the Era of AIDS*. Stanford: Stanford University Press.

Dowsett, G., H. Williams, A. Ventuneac, and A. Carballo-Dieguez. 2008. "Taking It Like a Man: Masculinity and Barebacking Online." *Sexualities* 11(1–2): 121–41.

Drummond, M. 2005. "Men's Bodies: Listening to the Voices of Young Gay Men." *Men and Masculinities* 7(3): 270–90.

Duncombe, J., and D. Marsden. 1996. "Whose Orgasm Is This Anyway? 'Sex Work' in Long-term Heterosexual Couple Relationships." In *Sexual Cultures: Communities, Values, and Intimacy*, ed. J. Weeks and J. Holland. Houndsmills: Macmillan Press.

Dunn, R. 1997. "Self, Identity, and Difference: Mead and the Poststructuralists." *Sociological Quarterly* 38(4): 687–705.

Dworkin, A. 1987. *Intercourse*. New York: Free Press.

Edwards, S. 1993. "Selling the Body, Keeping the Soul: Sexuality, Power, the Theories and Realities of Prostitution." In *Body Matters: Essays on the Sociology of the Body*, ed. S. Scott and D. Morgan. London: Falmer Press.

Elifson, K., J. Boles, M. Sweat, W. Darrow, W. Elsea, and R. Green. 1991. "Seroprevalence of Human Immunodeficiency Virus among Male Prostitutes." *New England Journal of Medicine* 321: 832–33.

Ellis, H. 1910. *Sex in Relation to Society*. Philadelphia: Davis Company.

———. 1897. *Sexual Inversion*. New York: Arno.

Epps, B. 2001. "The Fetish of Fluidity." In *Homosexuality and Psychoanalysis*, ed. T. Dean and C. Lane. Chicago: University of Chicago Press.

Eribon, D. 2001. "Michel Foucault's Histories of Sexuality," trans. M. Lucey. *GLQ: A Journal of Gay and Lesbian Studies* 7(1): 31–86.

Escoffier, J. 2007. "Porn Star/Stripper/Escort: Economic and Sexual Dynamics in a Sex Work Career." In *Male Sex Work: A Pleasure Doing Business*, ed. T. Morrison and B. Whitehead. New York: Haworth Press.

Fitzgerald, T. 1999. "Identity in Ethnography: Limits to Reflective Subjectivity." In *Sex, Sexuality, and the Anthropologist*, ed. F. Markowitz and M. Ashkenazi. Urbana: University of Illinois Press.

Foucault, M. 1997a. "Friendship as a Way of Life." *Ethics: Subjectivity and Truth*, ed. P. Rabinow. London: Blackwell.

———. 1997b. "Sexual Choice, Sexual Act." *Ethics: Subjectivity and Truth*, ed. P. Rabinow. London: Blackwell.

———. 1997c. "Sex, Power, and the Politics of Identity." *Ethics: Subjectivity and Truth*, ed. P. Rabinow. London: Blackwell.

———. 1997d. "Sexuality and Solitude." *Ethics: Subjectivity and Truth*, ed. P. Rabinow. London: Blackwell.

———. 1990a. "The Minimalist Self." In *Michel Foucault: Politics, Philosophy, Culture—Interviews and Other Writing, 1977–1984*, ed. L. Kritzman. New York: Routledge.

———. 1990b. "Power and Sex." In *Michel Foucault: Politics, Philosophy, Culture—Interviews and Other Writing, 1977–1984*, ed. L. Kritzman. New York: Routledge.

———. 1988. "Technologies of the Self." In *Technologies of the Self: A Seminar with Michel Foucault*, ed. L. H. Martin, H. Gutman, and P. H. Hutton. Amherst: University of Massachusetts Press.

———. 1983. "The Subject and Power." In *Michel Foucault: Beyond Structuralism and Hermeneutics*, ed. H. Dreyfus and P. Rabinow. Chicago: University of Chicago Press.

———. 1980. "The Confession of the Flesh." In *Power/Knowledge: Selected Interviews and Other Writings, 1972–1977*, ed. C. Gordon. New York: Pantheon.

———. 1978a. *The History of Sexuality*, vol. 1. New York: Pantheon Books.

———. 1978b. *Herculine Barbin: Being the Recently Discovered Memoirs of a Nineteenth-Century French Hermaphrodite*. New York: Pantheon.

———. 1977. *Discipline and Punish: The Birth of the Prison*. New York: Vintage Books.

———. 1972a. "The Discourse on Language." *The Archaeology of Knowledge*. New York: Pantheon.

Fox, R. 2007. "Gays Grow Up: An Interpretive Study on Aging Metaphors and Queer Identity." *Journal of Homosexuality* 52(3–4): 33–59.

Frank, K. 2002. *G-Strings and Sympathy: Strip Club Regulars and Male Desire*. Durham: Duke University Press.

Freud, S. 1962/1905. *Three Essays on the Theory of Sexuality*. New York: Avon.

Freyhan, F. 1947. "Homosexual Prostitution—A Case Report." *Delaware State Medical Journal* 19: 92–94.

Friedman, M. 2003. *Strapped for Cash: A History of American Hustler Culture*. Los Angeles: Alyson Books.

Gagnon, J. 2004a. "Sexual Conduct Revisited." In *An Interpretation of Desire: Essays in the Study of Sexuality*. Chicago: University of Chicago Press.

———. 2004b. "The Explicit and Implicit Use of the Scripting Perspective in Sex Research." In *An Interpretation of Desire: Essays in the Study of Sexuality*. Chicago: University of Chicago Press.

Gagnon, J., and W. Simon. 1974. *Sexual Conduct: The Social Sources of Human Sexuality*. Chicago: Aldine.

Gall, G. 2006. *Sex Worker Union Organizing: An International Study*. Basingstoke: Palgrave Macmillan.

Gammon, M., and K. Isgro. 2006. "Troubling the Canon: Bisexuality and Queer Theory." *Journal of Homosexuality* 52(1–2): 159–84.

Gamson, J. 2000. "Sexualities, Queer Theory, and Qualitative Research." In *Handbook of Qualitative Research*, ed. N. Denzin and Y. Lincoln. London: Sage.

Gamson, J., and D. Moon. 2004. "The Sociology of Sexualities: Queer and Beyond." *Annual Review of Sociology* 30(1): 47–64.

Garlick, S. 2003. "What Is a Man? Heterosexuality and the Technology of Masculinity." *Men and Masculinities* 6(2): 156–72.

———. 2002. "The Beauty of Friendship: Foucault, Masculinity, and the Work of Art." *Philosophy and Social Criticism* 28(5): 558–77.

Gastaldo, D., D. Holmes, A. Lombardo, and P. O'Byrne. 2009. "Unprotected Sex among Men Who Have Sex with Men in Canada: Exploring Rationalities and Expanding HIV Prevention." *Critical Public Health* 19(3–4): 399–416.

Gemme, R., and N. Payment. 1992. "Criminalization of Adult Street Prostitution in Montréal, Canada: Evaluation of the Law in 1987 and 1991." *Canadian Journal of Human Sexuality* 1(4): 217–20.

Giddens, A. 1992. *Modernity and Self-Identity: Self and Society in the Late Modern Age.* Stanford: Stanford University Press.

Gill, R., K. Henwood, and C. Mclean. 2005. "Body Projects and the Regulation of Normative Masculinity." *Body and Society* 11(1): 37–62.

Gilleard, C., and P. Higgs. 2000. *Cultures of Ageing: Self, Citizen, and the Body.* Harlow: Pearson.

Gilligan, C., R. Spencer, K. Weinberg, and T. Bertsch. 2005. "On the Listening Guide: A Voice-Centered Relational Method." In *Emergent Methods in Social Research*, ed. S. Hesse-Biber and P. Leavy. Thousand Oaks, CA: Sage.

Gimlin, D. 2007. "What Is 'Body Work'? A Review of the Literature." *Sociology Compass* 1(1): 353–70.

Glick, E. 2000. "Sex Positive: Feminism, Queer Theory, and the Politics of Transgression." *Feminist Review* 64: 19–45.

Goffman, E. 1967. *Interaction Ritual: Essays on Face-to-Face Behavior.* New York: Pantheon Books.

———. 1961. *Encounters: Two Studies in the Sociology of Interaction.* New York: Bobbs-Merrill.

———. 1959. *The Presentation of Self in Everyday Life.* New York: Anchor Books.

González, C. 2007. "Age-Graded Sexualities: The Struggles of Our Ageing Body." *Sexuality and Culture* 11(1): 31–47.

Goode, E. 2002. "Sexual Involvement and Social Research in a Fat Civil Rights Organization." *Qualitative Sociology* 25(4): 501–34.

Gove, B. 2000. *Cruising Culture: Promiscuity, Desire, and American Gay Literature.* Edinburgh: University of Edinburgh Press.

Green, A. 2008. "Erotic Habitus: Toward a Sociology of Desire." *Theory and Society* 37: 597–626.

———. 2007a. "Queer Theory and Sociology: Locating the Subject and the Self in Sexuality Studies." *Sociological Theory* 25(1): 26–45.

———. 2007b. "On the Horns of a Dilemma: Institutional Dimensions of the Sexual Career in a Sample of Middle-Class, Urban, Black, Gay." *Journal of Black Studies* 37(5): 753–74.

———. 2005. "'The Kind That All White Men Want': Race and the Role of Subtle Status Characteristics in an Urban Gay Setting." *Social Theory and Health* 3(2): 206–27.

———. 2002. "Gay but Not Queer: Toward a Post-Queer Study of Sexuality." *Theory and Society* 31(4): 521–45.

Green, A., M. Follert, K. Osterlund, and J. Paquin. 2010. "Space, Place, and Sexual Sociality: Towards an Atmospheric Analysis." *Gender, Work, and Organization* 17(1): 7–27.

Grenz, S. 2005. "Intersections of Sex and Power in Research on Prostitution: A Female Researcher Interviewing Male Heterosexual Clients." *Signs* 30(4): 2091–2113.

Grosz, E. 1994. *Volatile Bodies: Towards a Corporeal Feminism*. Bloomington: University of Indiana Press.

Hacking, I. 2004. "Between Michel Foucault and Erving Goffman: Between Discourse in the Abstract and Face-to-Face Interaction." *Economy and Society* 33(3): 277–302.

Hall, T. 2007. "Rent-Boys, Barflies, and Kept Men: Men Involved in Sex with Men for Compensation in Prague." *Sexualities* 10(4): 457–72.

Halperin, D. 1995. *Saint Foucault: Towards a Gay Hagiography*. New York: Oxford University Press.

Hammersley, M. 1989. *The Dilemma of Qualitative Method: Herbert Blumer and the Chicago Tradition*. London: Routledge.

Hart, G., and M. Boulton. 1995. "Sexual Behavior in Gay Men: Towards a Sociology of Risk." In *AIDS: Individual, Cultural, and Policy Dimensions*, ed. P. Aggleton, P. Davies, and G. Hart. London: Falmer Press.

Healey, D. 2001. "Masculine Purity and 'Gentlemen's Mischief': Sexual Exchange and Prostitution between Russian Men, 1861–1941." *Slavic Review* 60(2): 233–65.

Heaphy, B. 2007. "Sexualities, Gender and Ageing: Resources and Social Change." *Current Sociology* 55(2): 193–210.

———. 1996. "Medicalisation and Identity Formation: Identity and Strategy in the Context of AIDS and HIV." In *Sexual Cultures: Communities, Values, and Intimacy*, ed. J. Weeks and J. Holland. Houndsmills: Macmillan Press.

Hennen, P. 2008. *Faeries, Bears, and Leathermen: Men in the Community Queering the Masculine*. Chicago: University of Chicago Press.

Hennessy, R. 1995. "Queer Visibility in Commodity Culture." In *Social Postmodernism: Beyond Identity Politics*, ed. L. Nicholson and S. Seidman. Cambridge: Cambridge University Press.

Hickson, F., P. Weatherburn, J. Hows, and P. Davies. 1991. "Selling Safer Sex: Male Masseurs and Escorts in the UK." In *Aids: Foundations for the Future*, ed. P. Aggleton, P. Davies, and G. Hart. London: Taylor and Francis.

Hochschild, A. 2003/1983. *The Managed Heart: Commercialization of Human Feeling*. Los Angeles: University of California Press.

Høigård, C., and L. Finstad. 1992. *Prostitution, Money, and Love*. Cambridge: Polity Press.

Hoffman, E. 2007. "Open-Ended Interviews, Power, and Emotional Labor." *Journal of Contemporary Ethnography* 36(3): 318–46.

Holmes, D., and D. Warner. 2005. "The Anatomy of a Forbidden Desire: Men, Penetration, and Semen Exchange." *Nursing Inquiry* 12(1): 10–20.

REFERENCES

Holstein, J., and J. Gubrium. 1995. *The Active Interview*. Thousand Oaks, CA: Sage.

Honan, E., M. Knobel, C. Baker, and B. Davies. 2000. "Producing Possible Hannahs: Theory and the Subject of Research." *Qualitative Inquiry* 6(1): 9–32.

Irvine, J. 2003. "'The Sociologist as Voyeur': Social Theory and Sexuality Research, 1910–1978." *Qualitative Sociology* 26(4): 429–56.

Irwin, K. 2006. "Into the Dark Heart of Ethnography: The Lived Ethics and Inequality of Intimate Field Relationships." *Qualitative Sociology* 29(2): 155–75.

Itiel, J. 1998. *A Consumer's Guide to Male Hustlers*. New York: Haworth Press.

Jackson, S. 1999. *Heterosexuality in Question*. London: Sage.

Jackson, S., and S. Scott. 2010. *Theorizing Sexuality*. Berkshire: Open University Press.

———. 2007. "Faking Like a Woman? Towards an Interpretive Theorization of Sexual Pleasure." *Body and Society* 13(2): 95–116.

———. 2004. "Sexual Antimonies of Late Modernity." *Sexualities* 7(2): 233–48.

———. 2001. "Putting the Body's Feet on the Ground: Towards a Sociological Reconceptualization of Gendered and Sexual Embodiment." In *Constructing Gendered Bodies*, ed. K. Backett-Milburn and L. McKie. Basingstoke: Palgrave.

Jagose, A. 2009. "Feminism's Queer Theory." *Feminsim and Psychology* 19(2): 157–74.

———. 1996. *Queer Theory*. New York: New York University Press.

Järvinen, M. 2001. "Accounting for Trouble: Identity Negotiations in Qualitative Interviews with Alcoholics." *Symbolic Interaction* 24(3): 263–84.

Jefferson, T. 2002. "Subordinating Hegemonic Masculinity." *Theoretical Criminology* 6(1): 63–88.

Jeffrey, L., and G. MacDonald. 2006. *Sex Workers in the Maritimes Talk Back*. Vancouver: University of British Columbia Press.

Jones, C., and A. Spicer. 2005. "The Sublime Object of Entrepreneurship." *Organization* 12(2): 223–46.

Jones, J., and S. Pugh. 2005. "Ageing Gay Men: Lessons from the Sociology of Embodiment." *Men and Masculinities* 7(3): 248–60.

Jones, M. 2007. *I Had to Say Something: The Art of Ted Haggard's Fall*. New York: Seven Stories Press.

Jones, R. 2005. "'You Show Me Yours, I'll Show You Mine': The Negotiation of Shifts from Textual to Visual Modes in Computer-Mediated Interaction among Gay Men." *Visual Communication* 4(1): 69–92.

Kang, M. 2003. "The Managed Hand: The Commercialization of Bodies and Emotions in Korean Immigrant–Owned Nail Salons." *Gender and Society* 17(6): 820–39.

Katz, J. 2004. "On the Rhetoric and Politics of Ethnographic Methodology." *Annals of the American Academy of Political and Social Science* 595: 280–308.

Katz, S., and B. Marshall. 2003. "New Sex for Old: Lifestyle, Consumerism, and the Ethics of Aging Well." *Journal of Aging Studies* 17(1): 3–16.

Kaye, K. 2007. "Sex and the Unspoken in Male Street Prostitution." In *Male Sex Work: A Pleasure Doing Business*, ed. T. Morrison and B. Whitehead. New York: Haworth Press.

———. 2003. "Male Prostitution in the Twentieth Century: Pseudohomosexuals, Hoodlum Homosexuals, and Exploited Teens." *Journal of Homosexuality* 46(1/2): 1–77.

Kilmer-Purcell, J. 2008. "Career Tips for Future Whores." *Out* 16(7): 66–67.

Kilvington, J., S. Day, and H. Ward. 2001. "Prostitution Policy in Europe: A Time of Change?" *Feminist Review* 67: 78–93.

Kippax, S., and G. Smith. 2001. "Anal Intercourse and Power in Sex between Men." *Sexualities* 4(4): 413–34.

Kirsch. M. 2001. *Queer Theory and Social Change*. London: Routledge.

Koken, J., J. Parsons, J. Severino, and D. Bimbi. 2005. "Exploring Commercial Sex Encounters in an Urban Community Sample of Gay and Bisexual Men." In *Contemporary Research on Sex Work*, ed. J. Parsons. New York: Haworth Press.

Krafft-Ebing, R. 1886. *Psychopathia Sexualis*. New York: Bell Publishing.

La Pastina, C. 2006. "The Implications of an Ethnographer's Sexuality." *Qualitative Inquiry* 12(4): 724–35.

Lambevski, S. 1999. "Suck My Nation—Masculinity, Ethnicity, and the Politics of (Homo)sex." *Sexualities* 2(4): 397–419.

Lane, F. 2000. *Obscene Profits: The Entrepreneurs of Pornography in the Cyber Age*. London: Routledge.

Laumann, E., and J. Gagnon. 1995. "A Sociological Perspective on Sexual Action." In *Conceiving Sexuality: Approaches to Sex Research in a Postmodern World*, ed. G. Parker and J. Gagnon. New York: Routledge.

Lawrence, A. 1999. *Suburban Hustler: Stories of a Hi-Tech Callboy*. Warren: Late Night Press.

Lee-Gonyea, J., T. Castle, and N. Gonyea. 2009. "Laid to Order: Male Escorts Advertising on the Internet." *Deviant Behavior* 30(4): 321–48.

Leigh, C. 1997. "Inventing Sex Work." In *Whores and Other Feminists*, ed. J. Nagle. London: Routledge.

Lloyd, M. 1999. "Performativity, Parody, Politics." *Theory, Culture, and Society* 16(2): 195–213.

Logan, T. 2010. "Personal Characteristics, Sexual Behaviors, and Male Sex Work: A Quantitative Approach." *American Sociological Review* 75(5): 679–704.

Lopes, A. 2006. "Sex Workers in the Labour Movement." In *Sex Work Now*, ed. R. Campbell and M. O'Neill. Cullompton: Willan.

Lowman, J. 1992. "Street Prostitution Control: Some Canadian Reflections on the Finsbury Park Experience." *British Journal of Criminology* 32(1): 1–17.

———. 1990. "Notions of Formal Equality before the Law: The Experience of Street Prostitutes and Their Customers." *Journal of Human Justice* 1(1): 55–76.

Luckenbill, D. 1986. "Deviant Career Mobility: The Case of Male Prostitutes." *Social Problems* 33(4): 283–96.

———. 1985. "Entering Male Prostitution." *Urban Life* 14(2): 131–53.

Lupton, B. 2000. "Maintaining Masculinity: Men Who Do Women's Work." *British Journal of Management* 11: S33–48.

Lupton, D. 1995. "The Embodied Computer/User." *Body and Society* 1(3–4): 97–112.

Lupton, D., S. McCarthy, and S. Chapman. 1995a. "'Doing the Right Thing': The Symbolic Meanings and Experiences of Having an HIV Antibody Test." *Social Science and Medicine* 41(2): 173–80.

———. 1995b. "'Panic Bodies': Discourses on Risk and HIV Antibody Testing." *Sociology of Health and Illness* 17(1): 89–108.

MacInnes, J. 1998. *The End of Masculinity*. Buckingham: Open University Press.

Mallon, G. 2001. "Oh, Canada: The Experience of Working-Class Gay Men in Toronto." *Journal of Gay and Lesbian Social Services* 12(3): 103–17.

Manning, E. 2007. *Politics of Touch: Sense, Movement, Sovereignty.* Minneapolis: University of Minnesota Press.

Manning, P. 2005. "Reinvigorating the Tradition of Symbolic Interactionism." *Symbolic Interaction* 28(2): 167–73.

Marcus, S. 2005. "Queer Theory for Everyone." *Signs* 31(1): 191–218.

Markle, G. 2008. "'Can Women Have Sex Like a Man?': Sexual Scripts and Sex in the City." *Sexuality and Culture* 12(1): 45–57.

Marlowe, J. 1997. "It's Different for Boys." In *Whores and Other Feminists*, ed. J. Nagle. London: Routledge.

Marshall, B., and S. Katz. 2002. "Forever Functional: Sexual Fitness and the Ageing Male Body." *Body and Society* 8(4): 43–70.

Martin, B. 1997. "Extraordinary Homosexuals and the Fear of Being Ordinary." In *Feminism Meets Queer Theory*, ed. N. Schor and E. Weed. Bloomington: Indiana University Press.

Martin, J. 2006. "Transcendence among Gay Men: Implications for HIV Prevention." *Sexualities* 9(2): 214–35.

Marx, K. 1976. *Capital*, vol. 1. London: Penguin.

Mattley, C. 2002. "The Temporality of Emotion: Constructing Past Emotions." *Symbolic Interaction* 25(3): 363–78.

Mauthner, N., and A. Doucet. 2003. "Reflexive Accounts and Accounts of Reflexivity in Qualitative Data Analysis." *Sociology* 37(3): 413–31.

———. 1998. "Reflections on a Voice Centered Relational Method of Data Analysis: Analyzing Maternal and Domestic Voices." In *Feminist Dilemmas in Qualitative Research: Private Lives and Public Texts*, ed. J. Ribbens and R. Edwards. London: Sage Publications.

Mazzei, J., and E. O'Brien. 2009. "You Got It, so When Do You Flaunt It? Building Rapport, Intersectionality, and the Strategic Deployment of Gender in the Field." *Journal of Contemporary Ethnography* 38(3): 358–83.

McIntosh, M. 1968. "The Homosexual Role." *Social Problems* 16(2): 182–92.

McKeganey, N., M. Barnard, and M. Bloor. 1990. "A Comparison of HIV-related Risk Behavior and Risk Reduction between Female Street Working Prostitutes and Male Rent Boys in Glasgow." *Sociology of Health and Illness* 12(3): 247–92.

McLaren, M. 1997. "Foucault and the Subject of Feminism." *Social Theory and Practice* 23(2): 109–28.

McNamara, R. 1994. *The Times Square Hustler: Male Prostitution in New York City*. Westport: Praeger.

McNay, L. 2004. "Situated Intersubjectivity." In *Engendering the Social: Feminist Encounters with Sociological Theory*, ed. B. Marshall and A. Witz. Maidenhead: Open University Press.

———. 1999. "Gender, Habitus, and the Field: Pierre Bourdieu and the Limits of Reflexivity." *Theory, Culture and Society* 16(1): 95–117.

McPhail, C., and C. Rexroat. 1979. "Mead vs. Blumer: The Divergent Methodological Perspectives of Social Behaviorism and Symbolic Interactionism." *American Sociological Review* 44(3): 449–67.

Mead, G. 2008/1902. "Foreword to Cooley's *Human Nature and the Social Order*." London: Transaction Publishers.

———. 1967/1934. *Mind, Self, and Society: From the Standpoint of a Social Behaviorist*. Chicago: University of Chicago Press.

Mello, R. 2002. "Collocation Analysis: Method for Conceptualizing and Understanding Narrative Data." *Qualitative Research* 2(2): 231–43.

Merleau-Ponty, M. 2008/1945. *Phenomenology of Perception*, trans. C. Smith. London: Routledge.

Minichiello, V., P. Harvey, and R. Marino. 2008. "The Sexual Intentions of Male Sex Workers: International Study of Escorts Who Advertise on the Web." In *Sex as Crime?* ed. G. Letherby, K. Williams, P. Birch, and M. Cain. Cullumpton: Willan.

Minichiello, V., R. Marino, J. Browne, M. Jamieson, K. Peterson, B. Reuter, and K. Robinson. 2000. "Commercial Sex between Men: A Prospective Diary-Based Study." *Journal of Sex Research* 37(2): 151–60.

Monaghan, L. 2005. "Big Handsome Men, Bears, and Others: Virtual Constructions of 'Fat Male Embodiment.'" *Body and Society* 11(2): 81–111.

Moon, D. 2008. "Culture and the Sociology of Sexuality: It's Only Natural?" *Annals of the American Academy of Political and Social Science*, 619: 183–205.

Moore, L. 2007. *Sperm Counts: Overcome by Man's Most Precious Fluid*. New York: New York University Press.

Morgan, D. 1993. "You Too Can Have a Body Like Mine: Reflections on the Male Body and Masculinities." In *Body Matters: Essays on the Sociology of the Body*, ed. S. Scott and D. Morgan. London: Falmer Press.

Morse, E., P. Simon, and P. Balson. 1992. "Sexual Behavior Patterns of Customers of Male Street Prostitutes." *Archives of Sexual Behavior* 21(4): 347–57.

Morse, E., P. Simon, H. Osofsky, and P. Balson. 1991. "The Male Street Prostitute: A Vector for Transmission of HIV Infection into the Heterosexual World." *Social Science and Medicine* 32(5): 535–39.

Morton, D. 1995. "Birth of the Cyberqueer." *PMLA* 110(3): 369–81.

Muehlberger, U. 2007. "Hierarchical Forms of Outsourcing and the Creation of Dependency." *Organization Studies* 28(5): 709–27.

Munro, V. 2003. "On Power and Domination: Feminism and the Final Foucault." *European Journal of Political Theory* 2(1): 77–99.

Mutchler, M. 2000. "Young Gay Men's Stories in the States: Scripts, Sex, and Safety in the Time of AIDS." *Sexualities* 3(1): 31–54.

Nakamura, L. 2002. *Cybertypes: Race, Ethnicity, and Identity on the Internet*. New York: Routledge.

Nardi, P. 2007. "Friendship, Sex, and Masculinity." In *The Sexual Self: The Construction of Sexual Scripts*, ed. M. Kimmel. Nashville: Vanderbilt University Press.

Newton, E. 1993. "My Best Informant's Dress: The Erotic Equation in Fieldwork." *Cultural Anthropology* 8(1): 3–33.

Noble, J. B. 2006. *Sons of the Movement: FtMs Risking Incoherence on a Post-Queer Cultural Landscape*. Toronto: Women's Press.

O'Byrne, P., and D. Holmes. 2009. "Public Health STI/HIV Surveillance: Exploring the Society of Control." *Surveillance and Society* 7(1): 58–70.

O'Byrne, P., D. Holmes, and K. Woodend. 2008. "Understanding Human Sexual Networks: A Critique of the Promiscuity Paradigm." *Critical Public Health* 18(3): 333–45.

O'Connell Davidson, J. 1995. "The Anatomy of 'Free Choice' Prostitution." *Gender, Work, and Organization* 2(1): 1–10.

O'Connor, D. 2004. *Mediated Associations: Cinematic Dimensions of Social Theory*. Kingston: McGill-Queen's University Press.

O'Doherty, D., and H. Willmott. 2009. "The Decline of Labor Process and the Future Sociology of Work." *Sociology* 43(5): 931–51.

———. 2001. "Debating Labor Process Theory: The Issue of Subjectivity and the Relevance of Poststructuralism." *Sociology* 35(2): 457–76.

O'Driscoll, S. 1996. "Outlaw Readings: Beyond Queer Theory." *Signs* 22(1): 30–51.

Oerton, S., and J. Phoenix. 2001. "Sex/Bodywork: Discourses and Practices." *Sexualities* 4(4): 387–412.

Oksala, J. 2005. *Foucault on Freedom*. Cambridge: Cambridge University Press.

Oliffe, J., and L. Mróz. 2005. "Men Interviewing Men about Health and Illness: Ten Lessons Learned." *Journal of Men's Health and Gender* 2(2): 257–60.

Padilla, M. 2007. *Caribbean Pleasure Industry: Tourism, Sexuality, and AIDS in the Dominican Republic*. Chicago: University of Chicago Press.

Parker, R. 2009. "Sexuality, Culture, and Society: Shifting Paradigms in Sexuality Research." *Culture, Health and Sexuality* 11(3): 251–66.

Parsons, J., D. Bimbi, and P. Haltkins. 2001. "Sexual Compulsivity among Gay/Bisexual Male Escorts Who Advertise on the Internet." *Sexual Addiction and Compulsivity* 8(1): 101–12.

Parsons, J., J. Koken, and D. Bimbi. 2007. "Looking beyond HIV: Eliciting Individual and Community Needs of Male Internet Escorts." In *Male Sex Work: A Pleasure Doing Business*, ed. T. Morrison and B. Whitehead. New York: Haworth Press.

Pateman, C. 1988. *The Sexual Contract*. Stanford: Stanford University Press.

Phoenix, J. 1999. *Making Sense of Prostitution*. London: Macmillan.

Phua, V., and A. Caras. 2008. "Personal Brands in Online Advertisements: Comparing White American and Brazilian Rent Boys." *Sociological Focus* 41(3): 238–55.

Phua, V., D. Ciambrone, and O. Vazquez. 2009. "Advertising Health Status in Male Sex Workers' Online Ads." *Journal of Men's Studies* 17(3): 251–58.

Plummer, K. 2007. "Queers, Bodies, and Postmodern Sexualities: A Note on Revisiting the 'Sexual' in Symbolic Interactionism." In *The Sexual Self: The Construction of Sexual Scripts*, ed. M. Kimmel. Nashville: Vanderbilt University Press.

———. 2001. "The Call of Life Stories in Ethnographic Research." In *Handbook of Ethnography*, ed. P. Atkinson, A. Coffey, S. Delamont, J. Lofland, and L. Lofland. London: Sage.

———. 1995. *Telling Sexual Stories: Power, Change, and Social Worlds*. London: Routledge.

———. 1982. "Symbolic Interactionism and Sexual Conduct: An Emergent Perspective." In *Human Sexual Relations*, ed. M. Brake. New York: Pantheon Books.

———. 1975. *Sexual Stigma: An Interactionist Account*. London: Routledge.

Poel, S. 1992. "Professional Male Prostitution: A Neglected Phenomenon." *Crime, Law, and Social Change* 18(2): 259–75.

Polkinghorne, D. 1988. *Narrative Knowing and the Human Sciences*. Albany: State of New York University Press.

Potts, A. 2004. "Deleuze on Viagra (Or, What Can a 'Viagra-Body' Do?)" *Body and Society* 10(1): 17–36.

Potts, A., V. Grace, T. Vares, and N. Gavey. 2006. "Sex for Life? Men's Counter-stories on 'Erectile Dysfunction,' Male Sexuality and Ageing." *Sociology of Health and Illness* 28(3): 306–29.

Povinelli, E., and G. Chauncey. 1999. "Thinking Sexuality Transnationally: An Introduction." *GLQ: A Journal of Gay and Lesbian Studies* 5(4): 439–50.

Prasad, M. 1999. "The Morality of Market Exchange: Love, Money, and Contractual Justice." *Sociological Perspectives* 42(2): 181–215.

Presser, L. 2005. "Negotiating Power and Narrative in Research: Implications for Feminist Methodology." *Signs* 30(4): 2067–90.

Pringle, R. 1989. *Secretaries Talk: Sexuality, Power, and Work*. London: Verso.

Probyn, E. 1993. *Sexing the Self: Gendered Positions in Cultural Studies*. London: Routledge.

Pruitt, M. 2008. "Deviant Research: Deception, Male Internet Escorts, and Response Rates." *Deviant Behavior* 29(1): 70–82.

———. 2005. "On-line Boys: Male-for-Male Internet Escorts." *Sociological Focus* 38(3): 189–203.

Prus, R. 1999. *Beyond the Power Mystique: Power as an Intersubjective Accomplishment*. Albany: State University of New York Press.

Prus, R., and S. Irini. 1980. *Hookers, Rounders, and Desk Clerks: The Social Organization of the Hotel Community*. Salem, WI: Sheffield Publishing Company.

Queen, C. 1997. "Sex Radical Politics, Sex-Positive Feminist Thought, and Whore Stigma." In *Whores and Other Feminists*, ed. J. Nagle. London: Routledge.

Radley, A. 1997. "The Triumph of Narrative: A Reply to Arthur Frank." *Body and Society* 3(3): 93–101.

Reay, B. 2010. *New York Hustlers: Masculinity and Sex in Modern America*. Manchester, UK: Manchester University Press.

Rechy, J. 1963. *City of Night*. New York: Grove Press.

Reiss, A. 1961. "The Social Integration of Queers and Peers." *Social Problems* 9(2): 102–19.

Rhodes, C. 2000. "Ghostwriting Research: Positioning the Researcher in the Interview Text." *Qualitative Inquiry* 6(4): 511–25.

Riach, K. 2009. "Exploring Participant-Centered Reflexivity in the Research Interview." *Sociology* 43(2): 356–70.

Ricco, J. 2005. "Name No One Man." *Parallax* 11(2): 93–103.

———. 2002. *The Logic of the Lure*. Chicago: University of Chicago Press.

Rickard, W. 2001. "'Been There, Seen it, Done it, I've Got the T-shirt': British Sex Workers Reflect on Jobs, Hopes, the Future, and Retirement." *Feminist Review* 67(1): 111–32.

Ridge, D. 2004. "'It Was an Incredible Thrill': The Social Meanings and Dynamics of Younger Gay Men's Experiences of Barebacking in Melbourne." *Sexualities* 7(3): 259–79.

Rooke, A. 2009. "Queer in the Field: On Emotions, Temporality, and Performativity in Ethnography." *Journal of Lesbian Studies* 13(2): 149–60.

Rosenthal, G. 2003. "The Healing Effects of Storytelling: On the Conditions of Curative Storytelling in the Context of Research and Counseling." *Qualitative Inquiry* 9(6): 915–33.

REFERENCES

Rosenthal, S., and P. Bourgeois. 1991. *Mead and Merleau-Ponty: Toward a Common Vision*. Albany: State University of New York Press.

Rubin, G. 1993. "Thinking Sex: Notes for a Radical Theory of the Politics of Sexuality." In *The Lesbian and Gay Studies Reader*, ed. H. Abelove, M. Barale, and D. Halperin. New York: Routledge.

Rye, B., and G. Meaney. 2007. "The Pursuit of Sexual Pleasure." *Sexuality and Culture* 11(1): 28–51.

Salamon, E. 1989. "The Homosexual Escort Agency: Deviance Disavowal." *British Journal of Sociology* 40(1): 1–21.

Sanders, T. 2008a. *Paying for Pleasure: Men Who Buy Sex*. Cullumpton: Willan.

———. 2008b. "Male Sexual Scripts: Intimacy, Sexuality, and Pleasure in the Purchase of Commercial Sex." *Sociology* 42(3): 400–417.

———. 2005. "'It's Just Acting: Sex Workers' Strategies for Capitalizing on Sexuality." *Gender, Work, and Organization* 12(4): 319–42.

———. 2004. "A Continuum of Risk? The Management of Health, Physical, and Emotional Risks by Female Sex Workers." *Sociology of Health and Illness* 26(5): 557–74.

Sawicki, J. 2004. "Foucault's Pleasures: Desexualizing Queer Politics." In *Feminism and the Final Foucault*, ed. D. Taylor and K. Vintges. Chicago: University of Illinois Press.

Sayce, S., P. Ackers, and A. M. Greene 2007. "Work Restructuring and Changing Craft Identity: The Tale of Disaffected Weavers." *Work, Employment, and Society* 21(1): 85–101.

Scambler, G., and A. Scambler, eds. 1997. *Rethinking Prostitution: Purchasing Sex in the 1990s*. London: Routledge.

Schubert, H. 2006. "The Foundation of Pragmatic Sociology: Charles Horton Cooley and George Herbert Mead." *Journal of Classical Sociology* 6(1): 51–74.

Schwalbe, M., and M. Wolkomir. 2001. "The Masculine Self as Problem and Resource in Interview Studies of Men." *Men and Masculinities* 4(1): 90–103.

Scott, J. 2003. "A Prostitute's Discourse: Male Prostitution in Everyday Life." *Social Semiotics* 13(2): 179–99.

Sedgwick, E. 2003. *Touching Feeling: Affect, Pedagogy, Performativity*. Durham, NC: Duke University Press.

Seidman, S. 2002. *Beyond the Closet: The Transformation of Gay and Lesbian Life*. New York: Routledge.

———. 1995. "Deconstructing Queer Theory, or the Under-Theorization of the Social and the Ethical." In *Social Postmodernism: Beyond Identity Politics*, ed. L. Nicholson and S. Seidman. Cambridge: Cambridge University Press.

———. 1993. "Identity and Politics in a 'Postmodern' Gay Culture: Some Historical and Conceptual Notes." In *Fear of a Queer Planet: Queer Politics and Social Theory*, ed. M. Warner. Minneapolis: University of Minnesota Press.

Seizer, S. 1995. "Paradoxes of Visibility in the Field: Rites of Queer Passage in Anthropology." *Public Culture* 8(1): 73–100.

Sender, K. 2004. *Business, Not Politics: The Making of the Gay Market*. New York: Columbia University Press.

———. 2003. "Sex Sells: Sex, Class, and Taste in Commercial Gay and Lesbian Media." *GLQ: A Journal of Gay and Lesbian Studies* 9(3): 331–65.

Seymour, W. 2007. "Exhuming the Body: Revisiting the Role of the Visible Body in Ethnographic Research." *Qualitative Health Research* 17(9): 1188–97.

Shaver, F. 1996. "The Regulation of Prostitution: Setting the Morality Trap." In *Social Control in Canada: Issues in the Social Construction of Deviance*, ed. B. Schissel and L. Mahood. Toronto: Oxford University Press.

Simon, P., E. Morse, P. Balson, H. Osofsky, and H. Gaumer. 1994. "Barriers to Human Immunodeficiency Virus Related Reduction among Male Street Prostitutes." *Journal of Adolescence* 17(2): 320–42.

Simon, W., and J. Gagnon. 1986. "Sexual Scripts: Permanence and Change." *Archives of Sexual Behavior* 15(2): 97–120.

Simpson, R. 2004. "Masculinity at Work: The Experiences of Men in Female-Dominated Occupations." *Work, Employment, and Society* 18(2): 349–68.

Slavin, S. 2009. "'Instinctively, I'm Not Just a Sexual Beast': The Complexity of Intimacy among Australian Gay Men." *Sexualities* 12(1): 79–96.

Smith, A. 1997. "The Good Homosexual and the Dangerous Queer: Resisting the New Homophobia." In *New Sexual Agendas*, ed. L. Segal. London: Macmillan.

Smith, D. E. 2005. *Institutional Ethnography: A Sociology for People*. Walnut Creek, CA: Alta Mira Press.

Smith, M., C. Grov, and D. Seal. 2008. "Agency-Based Male Sex Work: A Descriptive Focus on Physical, Personal, and Social Space." *Journal of Men's Studies* 16(2): 193–210.

Smith, M., and D. Seal. 2008. "Motivational Influences on the Safer Sex Behavior of Agency-based Male Sex Workers." *Archives of Sexual Behavior* 37:845–53.

Somers, M. 1994. "The Narrative Constitution of Identity: A Relational and Network Approach." *Theory and Society* 23(5): 605–49.

Squire, C. 2008. "Experience-Centered and Culturally-Oriented Approaches to Narrative." In *Doing Narrative Research*, ed. M. Andrews, C. Squire, and M. Tamboukou. London: Sage.

Stacey, J. 2005. "The Families of Man: Gay Male Intimacy and Kinship in a Global Metropolis." *Signs* 30(3): 1911–35.

Stein, A. 1989. "Three Models of Sexuality: Drives, Identities, and Practices." *Sociological Theory* 7(1): 1–13.

Stein, A., and K. Plummer. 1996. "'I Can't Even Think Straight': 'Queer' Theory and the Missing Sexual Revolution in Sociology." In *Queer Theory/Sociology*, ed. S. Seidman. Oxford: Blackwell.

Stephens, E. 2007. "The Spectacularized Penis: Contemporary Representations of the Phallic Male Body." *Men and Masculinities* 10(1): 85–98.

———. 2004. "Disseminating Phallic Masculinity: Seminal Fluidity in Genet's Fiction." *Paragraph* 27(2): 85–97.

———. 1999. "Hall of Mirrors: Phallocentrism in the Fiction of Jean Genet." *Colloquy: Text, Theory, Critique* 3: 1–19.

Streeck, W. 1987. "The Uncertainties of Management in the Management of Uncertainty: Employers' Labor Relations and Industrial Adjustment in the 1980's." *Work, Employment, and Society* 1(3): 281–308.

Suarez, T., and J. Miller. 2001. "Negotiating Risks in Context: A Perspective on Unprotected

Anal Intercourse and Barebacking among Men Who Have Sex with Men—Where Do We Go from Here?" *Archives of Sexual Research* 30(3): 287–300.

Takoland, M. 2005. "Faking It for Real." *English Studies in Canada* 31(2–3): 307–25.

Talburt, S., and M. Rasmussen. 2010. "'After-Queer' Tendencies in Queer Research." *International Journal of Qualitative Studies in Education* 23(1): 1–14.

Tamboukou, M. 2008. "A Foucauldian Approach to Narratives." In *Doing Narrative Research*, ed. M. Andrews, C. Squire, and M. Tamboukou. London: Sage.

Tanggaard, L. 2009. "The Research Interview as a Dialogical Context for the Production of Social Life and Personal Narratives." *Qualitative Inquiry* 15(9): 1498–1515.

Terkel, S. 1972. *Working: People Talk about What They Do All Day and How They Feel about What They Do*. New York: Pantheon.

Theodosius, C. 2008. *Emotional Labour in Health Care: The Unmanaged Heart of Nursing*. Oxford: Routledge.

Thompson, C. 2007. "A Carnivalesque Approach to the Politics of Consumption (or) Grotesque Realism and the Analytics of Excretory Economy." *Annals of the American Academy of Political and Social Science* 611: 112–23.

———. 1989. *The Nature of Work: An Introduction to Debates on the Labour Process*, 2nd ed. London: Macmillan.

Thompson, P., and C. Smith. 2009. "Labor Power and the Labor Process: Contesting the Marginality of the Sociology of Work." *Sociology* 43(5): 913–30.

Thompson, P., and K. Newsome. 2004. "Labor Process Theory, Work, and the Employment Relation." In *Theoretical Perspectives on the Work and Employment Relationship*, ed. B. Kaufman. Champaign: Industrial Relations Research Association.

Tomso, G. 2009. "Risky Subjects: Public Health, Personal Narrative, and the Stakes of Qualitative Research." *Sexualities* 12(1): 61–78.

Tulle, E. 2008. "The Ageing Body and the Ontology of Ageing: Athletic Competence in Later Life." *Body and Society* 14(3): 1–19.

Valenzuela, T. 2000. "A Complicated Business." In *Tricks and Treats: Sex Workers Write about Their Clients*, ed. M. Sycamore. New York: Haworth Press.

Valocchi, S. 2005. "Not Yet Queer Enough: The Lessons of Queer Theory for the Sociology of Gender and Sexuality." *Gender and Society* 19(6): 750–70.

Valverde, M. 2004. "Experience and Truth-Telling in a Post-Humanist World: A Foucauldian Contribution to Feminist Ethical Reflections." In *Feminism and the Final Foucault*, ed. D. Taylor and K. Vintges. Chicago: University of Illinois Press.

———. 1989. "Beyond Gender Dangers and Private Pleasures: Theory and Ethics in the Sex Debates." *Feminist Studies* 15(2): 237–54.

———. 1985. *Sex, Power, and Pleasure*. Toronto: Women's Press.

Valverde, M., and K. White-Mair. 1999. "'One Day at a Time' and Other Slogans for Everyday Life: The Ethical Practices of Alcoholics Anonymous." *Sociology* 33(2): 393–410.

Van Doorn, N., S. Wyatt, and L. van Zoonen. 2008. "A Body of Text: Revisiting Textual Performances of Gender and Sexuality on the Internet." *Feminist Media Studies* 8(4): 357–74.

Vares, T. 2009. "Reading the 'Sexy Oldie': Gender, Age(ing) and Embodiment." *Sexualities* 12(4): 503–24.

Visano, L. 1987. *This Idle Trade: The Occupational Patterns of Male Prostitution*. Concord: Vita-Sana Books.

Wacquant, L. 2004. *Body and Soul: Notebooks of an Apprentice Boxer*. Oxford: Oxford University Press.

———. 1995. "Pugs at Work: Bodily Capital and Bodily Labour among Professional Boxers." *Body and Society* 1(1): 65–93.

Walby, K. 2007. "On the Social Relations of Research: A Critical Assessment of Institutional Ethnography." *Qualitative Inquiry* 13(7): 1008–30.

Walkowitz, J. 1992. *City of Dreadful Delight: Narratives of Sexual Danger in Late-Victorian London*. Chicago: University of Chicago Press.

Wallis, D. 2004. *Killed: Great Journalism Too Hot to Print*. New York: Nation Books.

Ward, J. 2008. *Sexualities, Work, and Organizations: Stories by Gay Men and Women in the Workplace at the Beginning of the Twenty-First Century*. London: Routledge.

———. 2000. "Queer Sexism: Rethinking Gay Men and Masculinities." In *Gay Masculinities*, ed. P. Nardi. London: Sage.

Wardell, M. 1999. "Labor Processes: Moving beyond Braverman and the Deskilling Debate." In *Rethinking the Labor Process*, ed. M. Wardell, T. Steiger, and P. Meiksins. Albany: State University of New York Press.

Warhurst, C., and D. Nickson. 2009. "'Who's Got the Look?': Emotional, Aesthetic, and Sexualized Labor in Interactive Services." *Gender, Work, and Organization* 16(3): 385–404.

———. 2007. "Employee Experience of Aesthetic Labor in Retail and Hospitality." *Work, Employment, and Society* 21(1): 103–20.

Warner, M. 1999. *The Trouble with Normal: Sex, Politics, and the Ethics of Queer Life*. New York: Free Press.

———. 1993. "Introduction." In *Fear of a Queer Planet: Queer Politics and Social Theory*, ed. M. Warner. Minneapolis: University of Minnesota Press.

Warren, C., and P. Rasmussen. 1977. "Sex and Gender in Field Research." *Urban Life* 6(3): 349–67.

Watson, T. 2003. *Sociology, Work, and Industry*, 4th ed. London: Routledge.

Weeks, K. 1998. *Constituting Feminist Subjects*. Ithaca: Cornell University Press.

Weinberg, M., F. Shaver, and C. Williams. 1999. "Gendered Sex Work in the San Francisco Tenderloin." *Archives of Sexual Behavior* 28(6): 503–22.

Weiss, R., and D. Riesman 1961. "Some Issues in the Future of Leisure." *Social Problems* 9(1): 78–86.

Weitzer, R. 2007. "Prostitution as a Form of Work." *Sociology Compass* 1(1): 1–13.

———. 2000. "Why We Need More Research on Sex Work." In *Sex for Sale: Prostitution, Pornography, and the Sex Industry*, ed. R. Weitzer. New York: Routledge.

———. 1999. "Prostitution Control in America: Rethinking Public Policy." *Crime, Law, and Social Change* 32(1): 83–102.

West, C., and D. Zimmerman. 1987. "Doing Gender." *Gender and Society* 1(2): 125–51.

West, D. 1992. *Male Prostitution: Gay Sex Services in London*. London: Gerald Duckworth.

West, J., and T. Austrin. 2002. "From Work as Sex to Sex as Work: Networks, 'Others,' and Occupations in the Analysis of Work." *Gender, Work, and Organization* 9(5): 482–503.

Whitaker, R. 1999. *Assuming the Position: A Memoir of Hustling*. New York: Four Walls Eight Windows.

Whowell, M. 2010. "Male Sex Work: Exploring Regulation in England and Wales." *Journal of Law and Society* 37(1): 125–44.

Wiederman, M. 2005. "The Gendered Nature of Sexual Scripts." *Family Journal* 13(4): 496–502.

Wilcox, A., and K. Christmann. 2008. "'Getting Paid for Sex Is My Kick': A Qualitative Study of Male Sex Workers." In *Sex as Crime?* ed. G. Letherby, K. Williams, P. Birch, and M. Cain. Cullumpton: Willan.

Wilkerson, W. 2007. *Ambiguity and Sexuality: A Theory of Sexual Identity*. New York: Palgrave.

Wilson, E. 2010. "Underbelly." *Differences* 21(1): 194–208.

Wise, S. 2001. "Redefining Black Masculinity and Manhood: Successful Black Gay Men Speak Out." *Journal of African American Men* 5(4): 3–22.

Wolkowitz, C. 2006. *Bodies at Work*. London: Sage.

———. 2002. "The Social Relations of Body Work." *Work, Employment, and Society* 16(3): 497–510.

Zatz, N. 1997. "Sex Work/Sex Act: Law, Labor and Desire in the Construction of Prostitution." *Signs* 22(2): 277–308.

Index

Note: Excursuses are numbered (in brackets) based on their order of appearance in the text.